Edward J. Rielly, PhD
Editor

Baseball
and American Culture

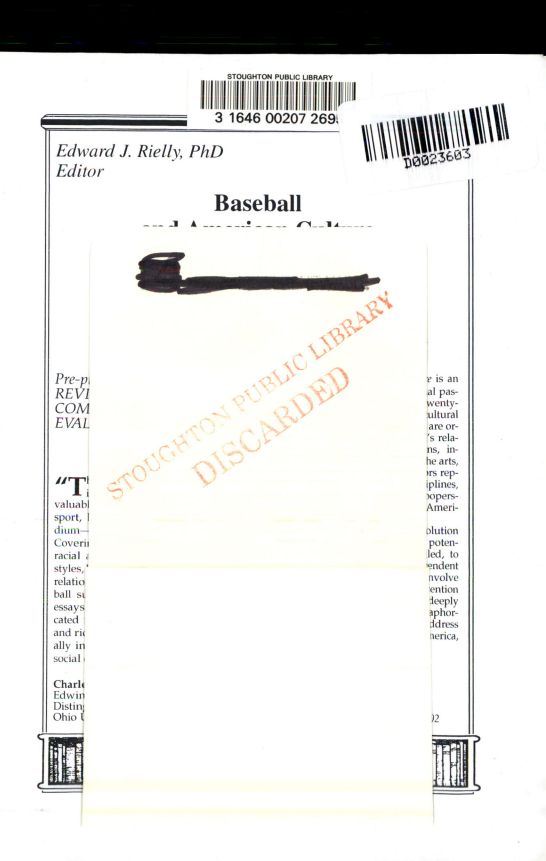

Pre-p
REVI
COM
EVAL

...e is an
...al pas-
...wenty-
...ultural
...are or-
...'s rela-
...ns, in-
...he arts,
...rs rep-
...iplines,
...oopers-
...Ameri-

"T
valuabl
sport,
dium—
Coverin
racial a
styles,"
relatio
ball su
essays
cated
and ri
ally in
social

...olution
...poten-
...led, to
...endent
...nvolve
...ention
...deeply
...aphor-
...ddress
...nerica,

Charle
Edwin
Disting
Ohio U   02

Baseball
and American Culture
Across the Diamond

THE HAWORTH PRESS
Contemporary Sports Issues
Frank Hoffmann, PhD, MLS
Martin Manning
Senior Editors

Minor League Baseball: Community Building Through Hometown Sports by Rebecca S. Kraus

Baseball and American Culture: Across the Diamond edited by Edward J. Rielly

Dictionary of Toys and Games in American Popular Culture by Frederick J. Augustyn Jr.

Baseball
and American Culture
Across the Diamond

Edward J. Rielly, PhD
Editor

The Haworth Press®
New York • London • Oxford

The Haworth Press, Inc., 10 Alice Street, Binghamton, NY 13904-1580.

Cover design by Lora Wiggins.

Library of Congress Cataloging-in-Publication Data

Baseball and American culture : across the diamond / Edward J. Rielly, editor.
    p. cm.
    Includes bibliographical references and index.
    ISBN: 0-7890-1484-X (alk. paper)—ISBN 0-7890-1485-8 (pbk. : alk. paper)
   1. Baseball—Social aspects—United States. 2. Baseball—United States—History. I. Rielly,
Edward J.
    GV867.64 .B36 2003
    796.357'0973—dc21

                                                  2002015134

This book is dedicated to the people who first talked
or played baseball with me: my father, Harold Rielly,
and my brother Lawrence. They set me on the right path.

CONTENTS

ABOUT THE EDITOR

Edward J. Rielly, PhD, chairs the English Department at St. Joseph's College in Standish, Maine, where he teaches, among other courses, "The Modern Novel, Baseball and Society." His publications include *Baseball: An Encyclopedia of Popular Culture,* eight books of poetry, a book on Jonathan Swift, and many short stories, articles, and book reviews. His baseball writings have also appeared in *Spitball, Fan,* and *Elysian Fields Quarterly.*

CONTRIBUTORS

Thomas L. Altherr is a professor of History and American Studies at Metropolitan State College of Denver. He has taught an American baseball history course since 1991, as well as an occasional class on the history of American humor. He has published several other baseball history essays, especially on pre-1839 baseball, and he has co-authored *Safe by a Mile,* Charlie Metro's autobiography. Joining vocation with avocation, Tom Altherr also plays on Denver-area over-forty and over-fifty men's baseball teams.

E. Michael Brady is a professor of Adult Education at the University of Southern Maine, where he teaches graduate courses in adult education theory, action research, facilitation, and gerontology. He was recently appointed Senior Research Fellow at the university's new Osher Lifelong Learning Institute. One week each summer he teaches a travel-based undergraduate course titled Baseball and American Society: A Journey. He reads widely on the subject of baseball and occasionally writes about it, having recently published three sandlot memoirs in *The Maine Scholar.* Mike would still rather play a game of catch with his son Ryan than do almost anything else.

Brian Carroll is a Park PhD Fellow at the University of North Carolina at Chapel Hill's School of Journalism and Mass Communication. His dissertation topic is the role of the black press in achieving baseball's integration, including spring training and the minor leagues. Carroll is e-business editor for Cahners Business Information, where he has reported on the furniture industry since 1992. Carroll was for ten years a sportswriter for the Greensboro (NC) *News and Record,* at which time he also was chaplain to the Greensboro Bats, the Single A affiliate of the New York Yankees.

Derek Catsam is a PhD candidate at Ohio University's Contemporary History Institute. His dissertation undertakes the first full-fledged exploration of the Freedom Rides. In his work he examines United States and South African history, with an emphasis on race, politics, and social movements. He does this when he is not fever-ishly following Boston sports teams and especially his beloved Red Sox. He insists that this is the year that the Sox win it all. Seriously.

Loren Coleman grew up in a baseball family in Decatur, Illinois, where his father and grandfather worked for the local Commodores minor league team. A Little League coach, he also teaches at the University of Southern Maine, serves as a consultant in suicide-prevention programs, and is a cryptozoologist. His seventeen published books include *Suicide Clusters* and *Mothman and Other Curious Encounters*. His research on the suicides of baseball players has been covered in *Sports Illustrated, The New York Times, The Sporting News,* and on ESPN.

Theresa M. Danna has a bachelor's degree in journalism from Rowan University (Glassboro, New Jersey) and a master's degree in professional writing from the University of Southern California. She says that many of her life's lessons have revolved around baseball. She dedicates her essay about backyard baseball diamonds in memory of her late brother-in-law, Jimmy Bassano, from whom she learned all the baseball basics, including the art of watching one game on TV while listening to another on the radio.

Rob Edelman is the author of *Great Baseball Films* (Citadel Press) and *Baseball on the Web* (MIS: Press), which Amazon.com cited as one of the top ten Internet books of 1998. He has lectured on the manner in which baseball films reflect America in the Speakers in the Humanities program sponsored by the New York Council for the Humanities. With his wife, Audrey Kupferberg, he has authored *Meet the Mertzes* (Renaissance Books), a double biography of Vivian Vance and fabled baseball fan William Frawley. Their latest book is *Matthau: A Life* (Cooper Square Press), a biography of Walter Matthau.

George Grella is a professor of English and Film Studies at the University of Rochester, where he teaches American literature, modern British literature, and film. In addition to many publications on baseball, he writes about detective fiction and related forms, popular literature and culture, and film. He is the film critic for *City Newspaper,* an alternative weekly newspaper, as well as the film critic for WXXI-FM, the public broadcasting affiliate in Rochester.

Kevin J. Grzymala is a father and husband, teacher and writer, living in Northern California. His interests include researching America's many pasts, espying changes in popular culture, and following baseball, all of which conflated harmoniously in the accompanying essay. At present, Mr. Grzymala is completing a book on the interface of sports and ethnicity during the nineteenth century, much of the object being to understand the choices made by immigrants and their children as they rooted themselves in churches, factories, taverns, and neighborhoods. Partaking of sports was an integral part of their new world planting.

Frank Hoffmann is a professor of Library Science at Sam Houston State University. He received his BA in History and MLS from Indiana University and PhD from the University of Pittsburgh. He is presently co-editor for Haworth Press's Contemporary Sports Issues series and has written over thirty books on various popular culture and information resources topics. His *Popular American Recording Pioneers* (co-authored by Tim Gracyk) won the ARSC Award for Excellence in Historical Recorded Sound Research from the Association for Recorded Sound Collection as Best Research in the Field of Recorded General Popular Music.

Connie Ann Kirk is a writer and scholar of American literature who lives in the Finger Lakes region of upstate New York. She is completing a scholarly monograph about writers and houses called *Writing the American Dream: Authors, Houses, and Meaning in American Literature*. She writes frequently on topics in American literature, history, and culture. Her books include *First Peoples: The Mohawks of North America* (Lerner) and *Encyclopedia of American Children's Literature* (forthcoming from Greenwood).

Karen Shallcross Koziara is a professor of Human Resources Administration at Temple University. She teaches courses in labor relations and labor law. She has written on labor relations, public policy, and labor market issues in such journals as *Industrial and Labor Relations Review, The Yale Journal of Regulation,* and *Employee Relations Law Journal,* among others. Her chapter on "Baseball Labor Relations: Lessons Learned About Collective Bargaining" appeared in *Diamond Mines: Baseball and Labor,* edited by Paul Staudohar.

Gary Land is a professor of history and chairperson of the Department of History and Political Science at Andrews University, Berrien Springs, Michigan. He has edited *Adventism in America: A History* and co-authored *Seeker After Light: A. F. Ballenger, Adventism, and American Christianity,* among other publications. A member of the Society for American Baseball Research, he is currently editing a volume of memoirs titled *Growing Up with Baseball: How We Loved and Played the Game.*

Alar Lipping received his doctorate in the area of sport history at The Ohio State University. Teaching responsibilities include courses in sport sociology, sport history, and baseball history. He has presented papers at such conferences as the North American Society for Sport History, Popular Culture Association, American Culture Association, and Southwest Texas Popular Culture Association. His publications include contributions to the *Journal of Sport History* and the *Canadian Journal of History of Sport.* He served as chair of the Sport History Academy of the American Alliance for Health, Physical Education, Recreation, and Dance.

Martin Manning is a librarian in the Office of International Programs, Bureau of Public Diplomacy, U.S. Department of State (formerly the United States Information Agency). He also is co-chair of the World's Fair Section of the Popular Culture Association, and an acquisitions editor (with Frank Hoffmann) for Haworth Press's Contemporary Sports Issues series. For Haworth, he and Frank Hoffmann are working on a book that explores the globalization of American popular culture. One of its chapters will include baseball.

Larry Moffi is author of *This Side of Cooperstown: An Oral History of Major League Baseball in the 1950s* and (with Jonathan Kronstadt) *Crossing the Line: Black Major Leaguers, 1947-1959.* His book *The Conscience of the Game* will be published by Brassey's in 2003.

Roberta Newman is a professor of Humanities in the General Studies Program at New York University, where she teaches, among other things, a course on the social history of baseball. Currently she is also working as a cultural history consultant at the Yogi Berra Museum and Study Center in Montclair, New Jersey. A Brooklyn native, she received her doctorate in Comparative Literature from NYU as well as her BFA in Illustration from Parsons School of Design. Though never a Dodgers fan, she still resides in the Borough of Churches.

David C. Ogden is an assistant professor in the Department of Communication at the University of Nebraska at Omaha. He received his PhD from the University of Nebraska–Lincoln. His dissertation focused on the application of gender-based learning theories to spectators' self-perceived experiences at minor league baseball games. He taught at Wayne State College, Wayne, Nebraska, for eleven years and has presented his research at the Cooperstown Symposium on Baseball and American Culture and at the Spring Training Conference sponsored by *Nine: A Journal of Baseball History and Culture.*

Carol J. Pierman is the author of two books of poems, *The Age of Krypton* and *The Naturalized Citizen.* She has also published essays and poetry in *Carolina Quarterly, Chicago Review,* and *Iowa Review,* among others. A 2000-2001 recipient of an Artists Fellowship from the Alabama State Council on the Arts, she is Chair of the Department of Women's Studies at the University of Alabama. Her current project is a critical study of the All-American Girls Professional Baseball League.

Richard J. Puerzer is an assistant professor of Industrial Engineering at Hofstra University in Hempstead, New York. His baseball writings have been previously published in *Fan Magazine* and in the Proceedings of the Cooperstown Symposium on Baseball and American Culture.

Seth Whidden is an assistant professor of French at the University of Missouri–Columbia. He taught English as a second language, both in France and the United States, from 1991 to 2001, and "Baseball as a Second Language" was an integral part of his curriculum. He has published articles on the works of Arthur Rimbaud, Paul Verlaine, and Marie Krysinska, among other publications. His critical edition of Krysinska's *Rythmes pittoresques* (1890) will be published by the University of Exeter Press.

William W. Wright is an associate professor of English and Director of the Writing Center at Mesa State College in Grand Junction, Colorado. He has published on baseball, nineteenth-century rhetoric, and composition instruction. Most recently, he is a Fulbright lecturer in American Studies at the University of Tromsø in Norway.

Dan Zamudio recently completed a Masters Degree in Library and Information Sciences at Dominican University in River Forest, Illinois. A member of SABR, he also is the author of *Diamond Dogs— Baseball Poems for Teens,* which is forthcoming from McFarland.

Preface

Baseball has long been known as America's national pastime. It deserves that designation for two primary reasons: the long history of the sport in America and its status as a sociological touchstone for understanding our country.

Baseball historians usually identify the first modern baseball game as a contest between two New York clubs, the Knickerbocker Base Ball Club and the New York Base Ball Club, on June 19, 1846, in Hoboken, New Jersey. The players performed on a grassy field graced with the mythic name of Elysian Fields. Baseball's antecedents, though, go much farther back, to the varieties of townball played in the United States during the eighteenth and nineteenth centuries, and, across the ocean, to the British sports of cricket (popular in England in the eighteenth century and in the United States in the nineteenth) and rounders (played in England as far back as the sixteenth century).

Of the major U.S. sports teams, baseball has the longest heritage. It also numbers among its fans such diverse people as the poet Walt Whitman, who bemoaned development of the curveball as dishonorable trickery; and Abraham Lincoln, who enjoyed baseball as both a participant and spectator. In the latter role, during his years as president, he could conveniently observe games being played on a lot behind the White House.

Baseball deserves its special status, though, even more because of its close involvement in virtually every important social development in the United States, both past and present. It is baseball from this multifaceted perspective that this book especially addresses. The essays that follow explore a multitude of ways in which baseball both reflects American society and has helped to shape that society. If baseball is a mirror held up before the collective face of America, it also is a mirror with the power to change the face that peers into it.

Because the world of baseball is the world of the United States in microcosm, it is neither all good nor all bad, but an amalgam of our better and worse selves. The game calls us to community, promotes a democracy based on merit, fosters closeness with our parents and our children, and preaches a vibrant patriotism. Organized baseball also excluded African-American athletes for much of its history, still unfurls on major league diamonds an invisible no admittance sign for women, and subjects fans to interminable economic squabbles between management and labor.

Both the good and the bad of baseball appear in these essays. Yet however one may find fault with aspects of the game, fans remain fans. Relatively few desert permanently the game they came to love. So the first section of this book is titled *The American Fan.* The essays in this section testify to ways in which Americans exhibit their love affair with baseball, a love that is sometimes inconstant, and certainly not painless, but which continues to bind, even drawing back those who stray, once they profess their attachment to the game.

The second section, *Baseball Inclusivity,* a term borrowed from the title of one of the essays, relates the ideal of baseball community against the reality that it often gave very grudging admittance to certain groups. Nonetheless, the game has grown and spread, its appeal searching out the most distant corners of the earth, until we must speak, as one of the essays does, of the globalization of baseball.

Three major dimensions of baseball are explored in the third section, *Money, Managing, and Myth.* Baseball is big business, and its long association with advertising is just one manifestation of this business. As with all businesses, managing personnel and the product sold to consumers is a vital part of that enterprise. Yet this is also a game of myth, the game transcending factual history, mountains of money, and the many divisive moments in its development to grasp at realities beyond mere mortal reach.

Baseball has made its way into almost every realm of American society, and the arts are vivid proof of this phenomenon. The essays in the section *Baseball and the Arts* recall such modes of artistic expression as film, poetry, humor, fiction, and even language arts. One might argue that baseball itself is an art form combining spectacle and beauty, grace and daring, music and drama, even tragedy, and certainly comedy, so it is entirely appropriate that other arts also align themselves with America's national pastime.

Finally, the section *Baseball and Resolution of Conflict* takes a serious, often sobering, look at ways in which the game seems more than ever to transcend sport. There is the continuous conflict between owners and players, and the role of the commissioner within that conflict, attempting, in the best of times, to bring about a fair and reasonable resolution. There is the personal, intimate struggle to find the divine within the daily competition and conflicts of the game. Dimensions of the game relate in important metaphoric ways (often signifying deeply felt truths, as good metaphors should do) to matters literally of life and death. Sometimes those deaths, as the final essay points out, are by hands that once swung a bat or threw a fastball or scooped a low throw out of the dirt.

So this is what baseball is about—virtually everything that one finds in American society—and if these essays do not cover everything, it is because finally a book must come to a conclusion, and the number of essays must fit within a modest number of pages. This book is about baseball; it is about America.

Acknowledgments

I am especially indebted for assistance with this book to Haworth series editors, Martin Manning and Frank Hoffmann, who were consistently gracious and supportive. In addition to helping me from start to finish, they also contributed with chapters of their own. Eric Tremblay and other members of the Information Systems Department at Saint Joseph's College kept me functioning technologically while solving a variety of problems for me during my work on this book. I am grateful to all of the contributors to this book, who responded with great generosity to my requests relating to both content and deadlines. Last, but certainly not least, I appreciate the continuing support of my wife, Jeanne.

SECTION I:
THE AMERICAN FAN

A Distinct Sense of Belonging

E. Michael Brady

I am a baseball fan and at the age of fifty-two, I am more interested in and passionate about the game than at any other time in my life.

I am able to say this despite the insane economics in baseball today, with player contracts written in the tens and even hundreds of millions of dollars. I love baseball despite what has become the triennial or quadrennial ritual of complex labor negotiations between owners and players which often involve not only the principals but government bureaucrats, elected politicians, and in some cases the courts. I maintain this affection even with the knowledge that cities across America are being coerced into sharing the cost of building new ballparks through threats of moving long-established franchises if tax support is not forthcoming. And I am able to maintain my passion for the game in the face of seeing The New York Yankees, the team I learned to hate as a youngster, winning the World Series year after year, decade after decade, and what I fear will become century after century. Indeed, as numerous commentators have long asserted, the game of baseball is fractured.

So the logical question becomes "Why?" Why maintain loyalty to an enterprise that is so out of touch and out of balance? Why have passion for a game mired in apparent selfishness and greed? Arguably, by this time in my life I should have developed a modicum of wisdom. So why hold onto feelings about this game I had forty years ago as a boy?

As with most stories, mine has a beginning. I grew up with baseball. At the age of seven I would have responded to the question "Who are you?" in the following manner: I am a boy; I am a Catholic;

I live on Ellsworth Drive in Bloomfield (Connecticut) with my parents and younger brother and sister; I am in the second grade at Wintonbury School; my favorite meal is either shepherd's pie or roast pork and apple sauce, and my favorite dessert is chocolate cake; my favorite month is August (no school all month and my birthday!); I play baseball nearly every day with my friends; and I like the Boston Red Sox—the order of this response not necessarily indicating the priorities in my system of values.

My dad played sandlot and high school ball in Western Massachusetts in the 1920s and 1930s as a left-handed first baseman. My younger brother Steve inherited Dad's left-handedness and position on the ball field (besides pitching or the outfield, where else would a lefty play?). Although I wish I had also been the recipient of this left-handed batting and throwing legacy, I did manage to inherit Dad's love for listening to games on the radio and reading box scores in the morning newspaper. In fact, some of my earliest and most cherished memories involve these traditions, practiced many hundreds of times throughout my childhood. Although I did not have a radio in my bedroom, I would fall asleep at night listening to the Red Sox game broadcast over Hartford's WTIC. The sounds of the game came from a clock radio on a small table on my father's side of his and Mom's bed just across the wall from where my head lay. With few exceptions I seldom stayed awake past the third inning. So the next morning, waking up to the smell of my dad's cigarette smoke, the first thing I'd do (even before visiting the bathroom!) was to walk through our living room into the kitchen. There was Dad with his face buried in the sports section of *The Hartford Courant*. The first words out of my mouth would be, "How'd the Red Sox do last night?" And because the middle and late 1950s were not the best of years for New England's team, his response would usually be a variation on the following: "You mean the Red *Slobs?* They lost again. Buddin booted an easy grounder in the ninth and let the Senators score. Now we're seventeen games behind the Yankees."

In addition to the vicarious participation in baseball I gleaned from listening to radio, reading box scores, and chatting with my dad, I had a direct experience with the game on an almost daily basis starting in the middle of April and ending in early October (around the time of the World Series). On an open field directly behind our house, my brother and I were joined on a daily basis by between ten and fifteen other neighborhood boys in playing sandlot baseball. On days when we had school our games would begin at 3:00 and go until our moms called us home for supper. And throughout summer vacation we'd more or less mimic what our big league heroes would do on Sundays—play doubleheaders—only we did it five or six days each week. Two or three hours of play in the morning would be followed by lunch and our return to the sandlot field for more baseball in the afternoon.

One of the more surprising things that has happened to me in recent years is that I have found my sandlot baseball experiences to be a rich reservoir of memory and reflection. I have taken sublime pleasure from recalling and even writing about a number of those experiences which occurred forty or more years ago. Stories unfold within stories as I recollect the rituals (choosing teams prior to each ball game), the antics (having our own "Ladies Day" when each of us borrowed our sisters' clothes and dressed up as girls), the improvisation (playing "short" if not enough kids came to fill all positions), the self-direction (umpiring our own games), the bonding of boyhood friendships, and the joy of being children playing a child's game.

One specific sandlot experience I am fond of recalling was actually my first venture into community service. My brother and I had heard about the Jimmy Fund, the fund-raising arm of Boston's Dana-Farber Cancer Institute, from listening to Red Sox games on the radio. We came up with the idea to hold a special "All-Star Game," like the one that was played each season between the American and National Leagues, involving kids on the two major streets in our neighborhood—Ellsworth Drive and Daniel Boulevard. The idea was that, for this one day only, teams would be divided by where each kid lived. We charged an admission fee to parents, aunts, uncles, and grandparents and also sold food (our pre-Women's Movement moms and younger sisters pitched in by popping popcorn and baking cookies). After the event we sent the proceeds to the Jimmy Fund in order to help kids who had cancer.

I remember the exact year we held this fund-raising game—1960—only because I still have an artifact from the experience. Several weeks after my parents sent our neighborhood's modest contribution to Boston, an envelope arrived with twenty "Jimmy Fund Membership Cards" as an acknowledgment of our gift. On one side of the card was a black-and-white photograph of my childhood hero,

Ted Williams, with a facsimile autograph. On the other side were a Jimmy Fund logo, a membership number, and a place to sign our name. Each of the kids who participated in our special "All-Star Game" received one of these cards. Out of all the baseball paraphernalia that touched my hands during my childhood years—Topps trading cards, my Rawlings glove and Louisville Slugger bat, various woolen ball caps (with wonderfully supple leather sweatbands), even a score book I brought out from under my bed every year in order to score Major League All-Star and World Series games—this "Jimmy Fund Membership Card" is the only surviving artifact. For that I must thank my mother, although in the same breath I find myself saying that I wish she had also had the foresight to save my Topps baseball cards (I could be retired today!).

In addition to sandlot play I was involved in "organized baseball." I played four years on the Lions team in Bloomfield's Little League program. I don't have many recollections about my Little League days except that my dad was assistant coach, our uniforms were white with black trim, and in my career with the Lions we ended the season in last place the first two years and won the championship the final two. I was a pretty good hitting and pretty bad fielding right-handed third baseman. More than twenty years later, when I became a youth league coach myself, I learned that poorer fielders are often "hidden" at third base (their skills tend to be only slightly better than among those players who are less discretely hidden in right field). However, the adults who managed my Little League career back between 1959 and 1962 were kind enough not to tell me about this defensive strategy.

When I turned thirteen I graduated to a diamond with ninety-foot base paths and played summer ball in what we called an "Alumni League" (although I don't know for sure whether our town was an official affiliate, I expect this was part of the Babe Ruth Organization). In addition, since baseball was my main game and the only sport I actually cared about or practiced, despite my not being an especially good athlete I managed to make the school teams in junior high and high school. For some reason which might be understandable to psychologists (but isn't yet to me), I do not have the salient memories of high school or summer league baseball that I have with my chronologically earlier sandlot days. I do remember with fondness a number of the kids I played with, several remarkable games and plays during mostly sub .500 seasons, selected travel experiences on the team bus, and ways in which we would conspire to frustrate our military-minded and not-well-liked coach, such as hiding his fungo bat in one of our lockers for a full two weeks which drove him to near madness. I also recall that, while already having been accepted into a college and experiencing the common malady of "senioritis," being on the baseball team was my sole reason to go to school and attend classes during my final semester of high school.

I even went on to play two more years of baseball at the small Catholic college I attended in the late 1960s. But by this time my passion for playing had waned considerably. I was working hard to grow up, to get serious about my life and future, and the game of baseball had little to do with those matters of import. I still managed to allow a little light from the game I loved in my childhood and adolescence to break through the window of my budding adulthood. Most days I would at least glance at the box scores in the morning newspaper. During the summer months I would catch an inning here and there on the radio while spending most of my time working in a printing factory to earn money to support my "adult agenda." I did manage to maintain another personal tradition, one which began in 1958 with my father and brother, of attending at least one game a year at Fenway Park. And I unquestionably shared the excitement much of New England felt in the fall of 1967 when, in my freshman semester of college and on the last day of the season, the Red Sox won their first American League pennant since 1946.

But things had changed. In my college years and beyond, baseball was no longer a prime focal point in my life. I now had close friends who had never played baseball.

I spent more time with the front and editorial pages than the sports section. Most nights, if given the choice between attending a concert or going to a ball game, I would have selected the music. Through my twenties and into my thirties, baseball was mostly a quaint memory of youth, a pastime long past, as neglected as the sandlot field behind our house on Ellsworth Drive which had grown dense with grass and weeds. I thought it would remain there—in a deep corner in the outfield of my consciousness—for the rest of my life.

But something happened on the way to middle adulthood. I got married, had children, and my kids became my agents for connecting their dad back to baseball. At the age of five my eldest child, a boy, joined many of his peers in our town's Saturday morning tee-ball program. I volunteered to coach. I ended up participating as one of Ryan's coaches through the developmental "Farm League," Little League, and even beyond as he eventually graduated to ninety-foot base paths and Babe Ruth League ball. Two daughters followed their older brother by playing in the town recreation (softball) league. I coached them, too, and some weeks in the spring found myself on a ball field five different nights. But there is no other place I would rather have been.

Playing a game of catch with one's father has been rhapsodized by poet Donald Hall and fiction writer W. P. Kinsella. I am not able to bring forth clear memories of playing with my dad. But my son should not have this problem. Since Ryan was four or five years old we have made it an almost daily practice—in the spring, summer, and fall—to toss a ball back and forth in the side yard or on one of the ball fields within walking distance of our house. During the long Maine winter we invented a game we could play in the basement in which we would throw a rubber ball against the concrete wall on the west side of the house and score points when the "fielder" was unable to flawlessly handle the rebound. Today my son is a college student, but he manages to bring his glove home during breaks so we can continue our tradition.

During a summer vacation in 1991, visiting my parents in the same house in which I grew up, my dad and I made a spontaneous decision to drive to Cooperstown and the National Baseball Hall of Fame and Museum. Ryan, nearly ten at the time, decided to come with us rather than join his mother and sisters for a day of swimming. For each of us—grandfather, father, and son—it was our first visit to Cooperstown. Perhaps I hyperbolize in saying that this experience was in some ways magical as we toured the various exhibits and stopped to examine artifacts. My father, who could usually go hours on end without saying as much as a word, was inspired to tell stories of his youth when he saw a uniform once worn by Jimmie Foxx and a bat used by Hank Greenberg. Then it was my turn to evoke memories and spin tales when we toured exhibits from the 1950s and 1960s, recalling episodes involving Williams, Mantle, Mays, Aaron, Koufax, and Gibson. Ryan was admittedly more interested in contemporary stars such as Ken Griffey Jr., Mark McGwire, and Barry Bonds. But he also loved sitting in one of the exhibit areas in the museum where, on a television screen which hung from the ceiling, a video of Abbott and Costello's famous "Who's on First?" skit played repeatedly throughout the day. If I'm not mistaken, he watched and belly-laughed all the way through three full performances.

Yes, perhaps hyperbole, but I believe that brief and spontaneously planned trip had a transformational role in my life. Something clicked. I felt reconnected to my own past in a strange and beautiful way. I bought several books on baseball history and a handmade vintage cap. I made a vow to myself that I would visit the National Baseball Hall of Fame and Museum again. Even more important, I vowed that I would try to read, learn, and make the game—especially its history and role in our culture—a living and generative thing for me and perhaps even for others.

Five years later, as part of my work as a professor at The University of Southern Maine, I was able, in a small way, to fulfill that promise. Thanks to the fact that I worked with a group of especially tolerant faculty colleagues and administrators, I received permission to organize an academic course which involved travel and the study of baseball. Baseball and American Society: A Journey had its inaugural run in July 1996. Forty "students," ranging in age from fourteen to eighty-six, boarded a Maine Line Company coach and departed the University of Southern Maine parking lot in Portland for destinations that included Norwich, Connecticut, Utica, Cooperstown, Scranton, Philadelphia, Baltimore, New York City (Yankee Stadium), and Pawtucket. Students who took this course for college credit were expected to read four books prior to departure and wrote reflection papers after we returned (noncredit participants were asked to read, too, in order to have everyone on the bus engaged in our discourse—but only the credit students wrote papers afterward). The bus was a rolling classroom. As we moved from city to city we had brief lectures, gave book reports, viewed videos, and managed discussions on questions ranging from "What role did baseball really play in the Civil Rights Movement?" and "Should taxpayers have to subsidize the building of major league baseball parks?" to "Will women ever play in the major leagues?" and "Is baseball still America's national pastime?"

One important goal of this course is to invite people to experience the game of baseball at different levels of play. To help meet this goal, each year we schedule visits to cities and ballparks in A-level baseball (sometimes "short season," sometimes "high A"), AA, AAA, and the major leagues. We have also examined amateur baseball through the eyes of the NCAA, the Babe Ruth Organization (when in Trenton, New Jersey), and the Little League organization (while in Williamsport, Pennsylvania). We learned about amateur baseball through the eyes of umpires when we made a stop at the National Association of Sports Officials in Racine, Wisconsin. One year we even had a seminar at the White House and learned about the tee-ball initiative George W. Bush began only months after assuming the presidency.

Along our learning journey we have been fortunate to meet with a number of knowledgeable people in the game—some famous and others not—who have shared their insights and passion. Among these have been recent Hall of Fame inductee Larry Doby (a conference on race relations), long-ago inductee Bob Feller (special focus on baseball players and World War II), Gene Benson (discussion of The Negro Leagues), Rex Barney (Jackie Robinson and the Brooklyn Dodgers in the 1940s), Dottie Collins (The All-American Girls Professional Baseball League), Ernie Harwell (experiences in a lifetime of radio and television broadcasting), and Jim Beattie (on the challenges of being the general manager of the Montreal Expos, a "small market" club). We've met with minor league owners, general managers, pitching coaches, radio play-by-play announcers, scouts, umpires, and active players. We've met with a group of Detroit Tigers players' wives to learn about the impact playing professional baseball has on family life. We've met with chamber of commerce executives and other community leaders to learn about the economic and social influences of a professional baseball team in a minor league city, and each year we confer with a baseball historian and museum curator at the National Baseball Hall of Fame and Museum in Cooperstown.

One of the most interesting aspects of this experience is the wide range of ages we attract among our participants. Some are traditional-age college students who want an intensive and travel-based course. Several who board the bus each year are younger than college-age, usually the child or grandchild of another student on the course (we set the lower age limit at fourteen). The majority of participants are adult learners—folks in their thirties, forties, and older who are part-time students trying to complete their baccalaureate degrees or who are in need of recertification credit (mostly teachers). Each year we get a handful of older travelers we call our "veterans"—people in their sixties, seventies, and even eighties. These are among the most interested and interesting members of the course and learning community. Through the voices of these elders we have heard about the St. Louis Browns before they became the Baltimore Orioles, how Hank Greenberg became a special hero to Jewish kids all across the country during his great home run hitting years, and even some of the exploits of the legendary Babe Ruth and Lou Gehrig when they played as teammates in "new" Yankee Stadium. At times the elders and the kids, who I suspect would never have met if not for this course, sit alongside each other on the bus or in the ball park stands. Stories are told and experiences shared, bringing to both generations an enhanced appreciation for this wide, deep, and subtle game.

Yes, I am a baseball fan. Indeed, I am more interested in and passionate about the game today than I've been at any other time in my life. I understand that baseball, especially at the major league level, has serious problems regarding economics and labor relations that it desperately needs to resolve. I understand that small market clubs in Montreal, Minnesota, and elsewhere will struggle in their ability to generate revenues and in their competitive strength on the playing field. But I also understand that there are myriad levels of the game—played by thousands of professionals and millions of amateurs—which stand beneath and support the high-profile major league peak of the baseball pyramid. As far as I can tell these foundational levels and leagues, several of which I played in as a youth, require little or no repair.

Being a baseball fan means that I follow the game, think and read about it, coach young people to play it, and during one week each summer plan a learning experience in which a group of students and I travel from city to city exploring baseball's history, architecture, influence on society, and the game's manifold glories. Baseball means warm days and nights, being outdoors, and sitting high in the grandstand looking down onto the splendid geometry of a brown diamond carved in a sweeping green field of grass. Baseball means memories of my father and son. And most days between early April and late September (and every so often, in a good year, into the month of October) it means paying attention to the vicissitudes of the Boston Red Sox and, with this, joining tens of thousands of New Englanders in what is more than a 100-year tradition.

Baseball is a pastime—indeed a way in which I pass my time. And because so much of my time has been lived and continues to be lived engaging baseball in some fashion, much of my personal history is there. In many ways the game has become a mirror into which I gaze to see important parts of myself. Reflected back to me are the images of relationships I have made, places I have been, events I have witnessed, and stories which have arisen from all of these experiences, themselves nestling soundly into long-term memory. When the final line score is tallied it will read that for me, being a fan of baseball has meant having a distinct sense of belonging. For that I am grateful.

2

Home Base: A Survey of Backyard Baseball Diamonds

Theresa M. Danna

A house with a yard: That was the American dream for many people when suburbs sprouted across the country after World War II. Add to that dream America's favorite pastime, a sport suited for dreamers, and the result was a patchwork of baseball diamonds in backyards of all shapes and sizes, from New England to Washington State, created by children out of their pure love of the game.

Though each of these precious backyard diamonds was unique, my research revealed that they shared charming similarities. Clothesline poles and bushes were popular choices for bases, and almost everyone had some sort of ground rule for when a ball hit the house. "Invisible runner," an imaginary player that stands in while the actual runner goes back to bat, played all around the United States and is still active today. And in one backyard diamond in northern New Jersey, he played with "invisible fielder" as well!

The Research

My survey grew out of a discussion thread on the SABR (Society for American Baseball Research) members-only e-mail list. For the most part, I was just a "lurker," someone who reads other people's messages but doesn't participate in any of the discussions. When I had joined the list, I thought it was simply a baseball discussion group. I hadn't realized that each message would be laden with statistics or other in-depth facts, often about obscure aspects of the game.

As a fan of baseball nostalgia, I soon realized that I was out of my league on the SABR list. But since my membership was now paid for a whole year, I scanned the list's daily messages anyway.

In October 2000, a thread of messages arguing whether Bob Costas was a good sports announcer caught my attention. The discussion participants—all men—seemed to be missing a point, one that came from my background in the communications industry. So I emerged from lurker silence and boldly submitted the following message to the list:

> What you guys are missing is the fact that Bob Costas is CUTE. The reason he's everywhere is because pretty faces are what the television business is all about. Sorry if this offends other women on this list, but it is a fact that some women enjoy watching baseball (or other sports) for reasons other than statistics, strategy, and competition. And network executives know that we buy from advertisers as much as, maybe even more, than serious fans do.

It spawned varied responses, including some of the male members expressing their pleasure at seeing a female contribution to the group's discussions. It also inspired some of the other women to come out of lurking to add their opinions. One of them wrote:

> Recent posts have inspired me to contribute, particularly the one from the brave female who admitted that she thinks Costas is cute. I agree, and I'm not at all offended. I certainly have had my share of baseball crushes. But that's not why I love baseball.
>
> I love the rhythms of the game—the day-in-day-out of the long season, the leisurely pace, the ordered taking of turns at bat. I love walking into a new ballpark for the first time and being joyously assaulted by the expanse and greenness of the field. I love the lore of baseball and its characters.
>
> When I was a child, we played a very simple version of the game in my backyard, where first base was the willow tree and third base the evergreen. I think we used a hula hoop for second base sometimes, though I rarely ever made it that far . . .

I responded to her message with one about my own childhood baseball memories, including a description of our family's backyard diamond. Likewise, one of the male members responded with the memories of his backyard ball field.

That's when the idea occurred to me to research backyard diamonds and write about my findings. I was curious to see how everyone's experiences compared or contrasted with my own and others. I was intrigued by the connection we seemed to have to each other, despite growing up in different regions during different decades. We seemed to share a raw—maybe even innate—passion for the game of baseball in its purest form, before our attention would be diverted by statistics, midseason strikes, and announcers' pretty faces. As with so many other basic elements of human development—education, good manners, spirituality, self-esteem—it appeared that our love of baseball begins at home.

So I then posted a message to the SABR list, as well as to all of my friends and colleagues, soliciting their response to the following questions:

1. City and state (and country if not the United States) where the backyard field was located.
2. Approximately what year(s) the field was used. (Example: mid-1960s)
3. What did you use for bases?
4. What were the ground rules?
5. Did you use "invisible" runners?
6. Briefly describe your memories of playing in this backyard diamond.

Each adult respondent to my survey recalled fond memories of their childhood baseball fields; some were proud to report that their tradition has carried on to their children and grandchildren. I myself giggled the day I laid out computer mouse pads for bases in our California yard for my three-year-old son's first field. How times have changed! When I was growing up in southern New Jersey during the 1960s, our home plate was a dirt patch in the grass left by a removed bird bath, first base was the drainage structure at the bottom of our

house's rain gutter, second base was a clothesline pole, and third was
the pussy willow bush.

Touching Base

One man whose field was in Wichita, Kansas, during the late
1950s described his bases: First base was Dad's rose bushes. "And
that is definitely the reason why it never gave him many flowers."
Second base was another bush. Third was a clothesline pole. Home
plate constantly changed, such as a piece of the white shingle siding
that broke off the house due to no backstop.

A similar scenario was being played out in Syosset, New York,
from the late 1950s to late 1960s. The woman who played in that
backyard diamond reported: First base was the willow tree. Second
base was "whatever we could find," such as a hula hoop, hose attachment, or big branch. Third was the fir tree, and home plate was simply
the area in front of the monkey bars.

A fellow New Yorker, this one a man from Troy, listed the following as his 1961 to 1963 bases: First was the doghouse. Second was the
lower end of the aluminum slide. Third base was the hydrangea bush.
Home was the dirt spot near the back wall of the house. In one Seattle,
Washington, neighborhood in the mid to late 1970s, there were no
real bases (just first base side, for example), but home plate was "a
strategically well-placed patch of earth where the grass wouldn't
grow."

Others reported that pieces of cardboard or plywood were shaped
into bases. One backyard field even incorporated a "weird, round-
shaped root" as home base. In Youngstown, Ohio, during the late
1930s to the early 1950s, wooden blocks, burlap bags filled with dirt,
and stones did the trick.

Several respondents to my survey reported that their home baseball
diamond covered two adjoining yards, their own and a neighbor's. One
such woman, whose field was in southern New Jersey during the 1970s
and early 1980s, surprised herself as she easily remembered how the
diamond looked and all the names of her neighbors who played there.
Ironically, the "dip" between the two yards was the pitcher's mound,
from which next-door neighbor Mr. Hermanson pitched to the kids.
The tree in her front yard was home base. Then the corner of the
Hermansons' brick flower garden was first base. The corner of their

sidewalk served as second base, and third was the small bush near the street. If the ball was hit into the street or onto the house, it was an automatic foul.

Unofficial League Balls and Rules

Speaking of the ball, there were about as many different types of those as there were bases in America's backyard diamonds. "We didn't use a real baseball; we used whatever kind of ball we could find," said one woman. A man from Shaker Heights, Ohio, played "pingball" in backyard driveways from 1939 to 1948. As you might be able to guess from the game's name, they used a Ping-Pong ball! Several people mentioned Wiffle balls and one even mentioned using a rolled up sock. I personally remember favoring those standard pink rubber balls because of their bouncing power off my miniature weather-beaten wooden bat.

Ground rules varied from yard to yard, state to state, from "no special ground rules" to elaborately detailed restrictions. Said one woman from New York, "We had few ground rules because we were so inept." She did recall, however, that "because the field was so small, each fielder was responsible for a base and the infield and outfield near it."

Wrigley Field magically relocated to a backyard in White Plains, New York, where a large hedge played the role of a homerun fence. Over in Troy, New York, a ball hit into the forest was a home run. In Lexington, Massachusetts, if you were lucky enough to hit the ball and score on three or four errors, that was considered a home run. In that same ball field, railroad tracks ran from left to center, but they didn't warrant any special ground rules because "they were so far away, no one could hit the ball that far anyway."

"There was my mother's flower bed to deal with in short right field," remembered one New Yorker. "It was strictly out of play—though the rule was occasionally ignored." He continued: "Once past the flower bed, the field expanded into a deep right field corner that came out parallel with the road. There's still a construction cone in the yard used for the foul pole." The neighboring yard in this ball field was home run territory, though it came with a price. "I would have to jump into the dog kennel to get the ball, carefully avoiding their yip-

ping, snapping cocker spaniels." Proudly, though, this player announced, "I broke only one window."

Nature played a role in establishing field boundaries in one New
York yard when a big tree was lost after a lightning strike. On the
other end of the spectrum, an act of man ended one boy's dream field
when his family installed an in-ground swimming pool.

Lasting Memories and Friendships

The bonding power of backyard baseball diamonds has stretched
across the decades. One woman reported that she still exchanges
Christmas cards with some of her childhood teammates. "Our games
were quite informal, but fun," she said.

One man fondly described how years later, following a memorial
service for his mother, his cousins, brother, sister, and nieces and
nephews all played at the same field, now returned to an actual lawn.
"We had a great time."

Another recalled how his father had died young in 1968, but one of
the last things they had discussed was how to create the family's third
backyard baseball diamond.

And the man reminiscing about his boyhood field in Youngstown,
Ohio, proclaimed, "We didn't fight a lot in our neighborhood. Baseball was there to help us work out our frustrations." For him, one poignant memory stands out above the rest, a memory that demonstrates
how much baseball is woven into our personal histories as well as our
country's history: "I can still remember the day we were playing and
some kid ran out to the field, yelling about President Roosevelt's
death. And how we all just stood there in shock. Then we all went
home with our tails dragging. FDR was the only president we had
ever known. The world had not ended, but the event was the nearest
thing to that."

Baseball As Teacher

All across America, for more than half a century, children have
practiced life skills, ranging from teamwork and patience to creativ-
ity and flexibility, in the comfort of their own neighborhoods, within
the confines of rudimentary baseball diamonds.

Sociologists, analysts, or even baseball researchers might never be able to measure the impact of backyard baseball on commerce and international relations. If you want your children to grow up to be successful family members, businesspersons, or diplomats, forget about MBAs and accolades. Just play with them (or cheer for them) in their backyard baseball diamond.

If they build it, the lessons will come.

3

On Fenway, Faith, and Fandom:
A Red Sox Fan Reflects

Derek Catsam

"It breaks your heart. It is designed to break your heart" (Giamatti 142). When A. Bartlett Giamatti, former Dean of Yale Law School and respected late commissioner of Major League Baseball, penned these words, he was talking about baseball and its seasonal nature. But it is no coincidence that Giamatti was also a lifelong Red Sox fan. For those words could surely be applied to being a diehard supporter of The Olde Towne Team. Year in, year out, they manage to break our heart. Some years they do it early and humanely. Other years it is painful and egregious. But ever since 1918, they have always done it. And yet being a Red Sox fan is somehow different, it is somehow special, and it is like an unrequited love affair.

What is it about certain teams that inspire what can at best be called irrational devotion? The Red Sox certainly are not alone in their faithful. Indeed all teams have their supporters for whom the team does more than play a game. There are Seattle Mariners crazies and Sacramento Kings nuts, and I am sure that out there somewhere the Nashville Predators are inspiring young boys and girls to dream of a better tomorrow through skating. But the sort of fandom I am talking about is different enough in degree to be a difference of kind. Red Sox fans are among a select group of rooters who have lived and died and avidly supported their teams through trauma, tragedy, pathos, festering boils, and swarms of locusts. Through good times and especially through bad, New Englanders, members of what area scribes call "Red Sox Nation," fixate on the Sox from April through (hopefully) October and then into the Hot Stove League season of the deep winter.

In baseball, Cubs fans know what I mean. Cardinals fans too. Star-crossed Brooklyn Dodgers fans are nodding in fateful recognition. We will not say the same for their brethren in Los Angeles. If I were feeling charitable, I would throw Yankees fans in here as well. If I were feeling charitable. I am not. Supporters of the Green Bay Packers, Cleveland Browns, and Washington Redskins can say the same about their football teams, as can Sixers and Celtics fans in basketball and anyone from an Original Six city in hockey.

What is it that causes supporters of certain teams to share this empathy? In truth, what qualifies avid supporters of most any sports team to support teams with such passion and devotion and loyalty? There are a number of characteristics. Viewing this argument from a Red Sox fan's perspective, however, two seem to overwhelm: geography and history.

For a sports fan, geography means many things. It might mean the stadium or arena in which the game is played or the field upon which it is played. Geography might mean the neighborhood where the stadium lies. It certainly means the city that hosts the team. But even this can be elusive: after all, many stadia actually lie outside of the cities the teams that play within putatively represent, in outlying suburbs that planners believed would be more accessible to a broader range of fans. Beyond the cities and suburbs, of course, is the state and region of the place where the team plays its games. And then, finally, there is the larger community of a team's fans. One need look no farther than the concept of subway alums, who root root root for the home team back at the university even after they have moved to faraway cities for their postcollege lives. In short, a sports fan's geography is not fixed terrain, but rather it shifts, and it exists in many places at once.

For the loyal fans of the Boston Red Sox, the sports geography is multifaceted. The Sox play their home games in venerable Fenway Park. Few sporting venues have inspired writers to test the purpleness of their prose as has the cramped park on the corner of Yawkey Way and Ted Williams Way (a.k.a. Landsdowne Street). John Updike perhaps most famously captured the image of Fenway Park in his famous *New Yorker* essay "Hub Fans Bid Kid Adieu." In that monumental homage to Ted Williams' last game in a Sox uniform, in which the aging, still cantankerous slugger capped his career with a home run in his last at-bat in a Sox uniform (the Sox finished that season on the road, but Williams knew a dramatic exit when he saw one, and he declined to play the remaining series), Updike wrote "Fenway Park . . . is a lyric little bandbox of a ballpark . . . offer[ing] as do most Boston artifacts, a compromise between man's Euclidean determinations and Nature's beguiling irregularities" (Updike, in Riley 53). Those irregularities are legion. Of course the most notable of these is the left field wall, The Green Monster, which juts from the stands at left field and angles out to left center, into the triangle that has provided many a slow-footed slugger with a triple that taxed his aerobic system to its limits. Indeed, the angles of Fenway are the most notable idiosyncrasy beyond the thirty-seven foot high wall and twenty-three foot high screen (recently removed) that might be the single most recognizable landmark in all of sports architecture. Corners emerge out of nowhere and disappear almost as quickly. Fenway, which is the only stadium in the major leagues without a second deck, also possesses the shortest foul territory in the big leagues. That, coupled with the Wall that coquettishly winks at right-handed batters (and not a few lefties) from just over 300 feet away at its shortest point (the actual distance has long been a point of controversy), has inevitably meant that the Red Sox have put together slugging teams capable of piling on runs while they often have had pitching staffs equally capable of keeping the other team's pile equally high. And, as we shall see, Fenway giveth, but it also taketh away.

Certainly other writers have tried to capture Fenway's sui generis aesthetic. Stephen King, Doris Kearns Goodwin, John Demos, George Will, David Halberstam, W. P. Kinsella, and every sportswriter ever to hoist a cliché (and develop new ways to describe the historic woes of the Sox) are among the many who have tried to capture the essence of Fenway. Perhaps the reason for this is that there is no definitive way to capture the essence of Fenway, which is both majestic and manageable at the same time. I know that I have tried to describe the park hundreds of times to the uninitiated, or those who have only seen it on television, and words always fail me. I usually end up returning to the same vernacular I possessed when I first emerged from the dank catacombs leading to the right field box seats on my tenth birthday. It is as if I am again seeing for the first time the inside of Fenway with its shades of green that are equal parts Irish countryside and Emerald City. "Wow!" "Awesome!" "Oh my God!" Or more likely, just mouth agape. Fenway is a lyric little bandbox of a ballpark. But it is so much more than that for baseball and Sox fans.

All of this cannot hide the fact that the Red Sox need a new ball-park. They need a larger stadium with modern amenities, including bigger seats for the expanding posteriors of well-fed Americans and their foreign guests who come to Boston, combining a trip to Fenway with visits to Fanieul Hall, Filene's Basement, and the Common. The Red Sox also need more seats with a full view of the game on the field unobstructed by a Pesky Pole in shallow right field or a column that holds up the 600 Club behind home plate. It needs sky boxes to allow the Sox to maintain their spending capacities to compete with the evil empire in the Bronx. But what many cannot agree upon is whether or not it needs The Monster. In any case, Boston politics being what they are, the odds are decent that the Sox loyal rooters will still be washing down limp Fenway Franks with tepid beer, lamenting the near misses on the field and the parking outside of it, and ruing the unfinished Big Dig well into the future.

Of course, part of the Fenway experience comes in the moments before one gets a first glimpse of the luxuriously mowed field. There is a carnival atmosphere outside Fenway on game days. There are the guys with the carts selling the hallmark sausages with peppers and onions just beyond the Wall. There are the packed walls of the Boston Beer Works and Cask and Flagon. There is the attempt to fill a five-pound bag with ten pounds of items for those foolish, stubborn, or un-aware enough to try to drive. There is the wave of humanity that car-ries fans of all shapes and sizes and ages and states of inebriation from the Green Line T Stop at Kenmore Square to the field. The neighborhood surrounding Fenway is every bit as much a part of the geography that characterizes the Red Sox as is the park itself. Cer-tainly fans of the Cubs understand the importance of the neighbor-hood in defining the game day experience. Although the Dodgers moved to Los Angeles a decade and a half before I was born, I have always surmised that the neighborhood surrounding Ebbett's Field was every bit as much a part of that experience as the Field itself.

Obviously Fenway is located within the tiny geographic entity that is the city of Boston. In a wonderful essay in an edited collection ti-titled *American Places,* historian John Demos has drawn the linkages between Fenway Park and the city of Boston. Fenway is the oldest major league stadium in use today. Boston is the American city that arguably most cherishes its many aged institutions. Boston is small and cramped. So is Fenway. Boston seems random, almost capricious, in its layout. The same can be said for Fenway Park. Boston is as intimately linked to its baseball team, and vice versa, as any sports team and its city are connected. The two are inextricably linked. The Red Sox are Boston's team. The Bruins, as with most Original Six cities, have their loyal, rabid, devoted fans. So too do the Celtics. The Patriots, who for years played some distance to the south in characterless Foxboro Stadium (until the opening of Gillette Stadium, near the Foxboro location, during the 2002 season), have always seemed the Johnny-come-latelys on the Boston sporting scene, though they too have substantial fan support. But the Red Sox are a constant love affair for Bostonians. Sometimes there is anger. Often there is frustration, but there is always unconditional love.

This unconditional love does not stop at the Boston borders. Indeed, perhaps it is because Boston itself is the smallest area-wise of any major city in the country save San Francisco (whose proximity to Oakland is a mitigating factor) that the city itself is barely differentiated from Somerville, Cambridge, Malden, Medford, Quincy, Watertown, Charlestown, Wellesley, and the dozens of other small cities that make up Greater Boston. And beyond this, in Lowell and Leominster, Worcester and Springfield, Amherst and Williamstown, the Red Sox are a source of pride and passion and palpitations. Crossing state lines, the Red Sox fans in Providence and the Manchesters (New Hampshire and Vermont) are every bit as passionate as the most loyal denizen of Beacon Hill or the Back Bay. The Red Sox are New England's team, with the exception of the curious portion of Connecticut that falls on the west side of the Connecticut River and that begins somewhere around New Haven. Residents of that odd geographical outlier often find themselves rooting for a team that wears pinstripes. But other than that grim exception, from the White Mountains of New Hampshire to the stately homes of Newport, Rhode Island; from Calais, Maine; to Pownal, Vermont; the Red Sox are more than a baseball team. They are more even than a favorite sports team. They are more like a cultural institution, something the locals take an inordinate pride in.

This odd, devoted agglomeration is Red Sox Nation. If you are stuck in an airport bar in Minneapolis, and you hear the familiar accent, or see that someone has a Sox hat on (no matter where you are, you will see men, women, and children in Red Sox hats, be it in sweltering Houston, swampy Washington, DC, or snowy Fargo), or just stumble upon a New England connection, you'll be able to talk about the Red Sox. Recently I was at a bar. We were on our way out after having some drinks. The bartender poured us each a shot of jagermeister before we left. He said, "This one's on me. It's for your hat." I was, of course, wearing a Sox hat. Certainly this is not unique to Red Sox fans. Red Sox Nation is not represented in the cartographer's art. It is not to be found in any United Nations roll call. But it is very pervasive, and very real.

Beyond regional chauvinism and provincialism, Red Sox fans are what they are because of a shared history. Despite what some shallow-thinking detractors might think, the Red Sox past century is not merely a series of unmitigated disasters, of horrible teams finishing well out of range, though there have been spans of time when that was the case. No, the Red Sox history is far more complex than that. While the wonderful fans of the Chicago Cubs have embraced their lovable loser image, Boston fans have tasted success. By and large, the Red Sox are almost always good. Some years they are very good. The Red Sox history is what it is not because of failure per se, but rather because those failures have come when the Sox so often were on the brink of success. *Romeo and Juliet* is perhaps the greatest of all tragedies because the two star-crossed lovers come oh so close to the happy ending. But instead by acting impetuously, and as the result of horrible timing, Romeo does himself in. Suffice it to say that in this analogy, the Red Sox are Romeo. But in truth, all of their fans are the star-crossed lovers.

It's hard to believe it now, but the Red Sox were the dominant team of the first two decades of professional baseball in this century. The Boston entry in the American League won (or in one case was declared winner of) the grandiloquently named World Series five times in its first seventeen years of existence. Then the bottom dropped out. The contours of the story are well known and have been well told many times before. But Sox owner Harry Frazee, wallowing in debt and not as committed to his ball club as he was to his Broadway productions, dismantled the team. Most notably, Frazee sold Babe Ruth to the New York Yankees for $100,000 and a mortgage loan on Fenway—in essence the Yankees owned the Red Sox. (Some wags would say they still do. Damn them.)

Thus followed pestilence and plague. Babe Ruth went on to become arguably the greatest player in team sports history. The Red

Sox were the bottom feeders in the American League for well more than a decade. Then in the early years of the Depression a young man named Tom Yawkey spent some of his inheritance money to buy the Red Sox. In 1934 he had Fenway renovated. He began spending money on players whom he then coddled. In 1939 a lanky, cocky, petulant San Diegan joined the Olde Towne team. Ted Williams, the Splendid Splinter, Teddy Ballgame, The Greatest Hitter Who Ever Lived. Williams would be part of a Sox resurgence. Alongside players such as Joe Cronin, Dominic DiMaggio, and Jimmie Foxx, Williams (between stints in the military serving in World War II and Korea as a decorated pilot that also took up several of his prime years) and the Red Sox became one of the greatest offensive teams the game has ever seen. But in the 1940s, the first stages of the sorts of painful losses that would haunt Sox fans emerged.

The 1946 Red Sox lost the World Series in seven games to the St. Louis Cardinals. In Ted Williams' only World Series he hit .200, and all of his hits were singles (he was injured). Johnny Pesky allegedly held the ball rather than throw out Enos Slaughter at the plate. The 1946 World Series would begin a streak of bizarre events, near misses, heartbreaking losses, and blown opportunities for the Red Sox. In 1948 the Sox lost a one-game playoff to the Indians after the two teams battled to a tie throughout the regular season. In 1949 the Red Sox again battled to the end for the American League title. Again they lost the final game of the year, this time to the Yankees. They had entered the final weekend needing only to salvage a split over two games. They lost both. From that point on through the 1950s the Red Sox would have explosive offenses capable of knocking the horsehide off the ball. But they would never have enough pitching, luck, or cohesiveness to compete with the Yankees, who established themselves as one of the most powerful dynasties in sports history in the Eisenhower era.

Longtime *Boston Globe* sportswriter Dan Shaughnessy has written one of the most popular and well-regarded histories of the snakebitten Red Sox. He is also the individual most responsible for popularizing the "Curse of the Bambino" thesis that avers that the sale of Babe Ruth to the Yankees brought a pox onto the Red Sox that lasts to this day. Whatever the merits of "The Curse" thesis, Shaughnessy hits home with his argument about the postwar Sox. In talking about the Sox' woes of these years, Shaughnessy writes:

These were the forefather sins that the Red Sox of today are still paying for—until a championship is won. The Red Sox were punished with twenty-eight years of ineptitude after Ruth was sold, but in the 1940s a new form of denial took hold, and it has proven to be a far worse strain on the fragile psyche of the New England region. The Red Sox have the best team but still manage NOT to win. "Wait 'til next year" has become "How are they NOT going to win it next year," and today's Red Sox can thank the teams of the late 1940s for this perverted legacy. (Shaughnessy 89)

After the 1949 debacle, the Red Sox settled into being a team unable to compete for some time. Indeed, by the mid-1960s the Red Sox plumbed nadirs of futility comparable in scope to some of the most wretched teams of the 1920s and 1930s. However, in 1967 the Red Sox reemerged from years of apparent somnolence to deliver to Boston fans perhaps the most magical sporting season in the city's history. New Englanders and the fellow travelers in Red Sox Nation who are of a certain age remember the 1967 "Impossible Dream" season in a wistful, sepia-toned, romantic way. It was the year that Carl Yastrzemski became an idol with arguably the most clutch season in baseball history. With a nucleus of the same team that had stunk up the American League in the season preceding it, the Red Sox engaged in a four-way battle for the American League pennant. Tough manager Dick Williams managed to handle the squad perfectly. Lefty Jim Lonborg was the staff ace. "The Boomer," George Scott, deftly handled first and jacked home runs. And Yaz almost willed victory on his own, winning baseball's last triple crown. That year's Sox team lost the World Series in seven games to the mighty Cardinals of fearsome fireballer Bob Gibson, but it was impossible for Sox fans not to feel joy about that team. Alas, future Sox teams would not be as lovable in their losses. Indeed, in the off-season immediately following the Impossible Dream, Jim Lonborg tore his knee in a skiing accident. In an age before medicine proved capable of restoring the human body in the ways it can today, the injury proved devastating. Lonborg was never again the same, and the 1968 Red Sox fell back to the middle of the pack, never really competing for the pennant. They would be good, but not great for the next handful of years.

The early 1970s marked the beginning of a Red Sox revival. As if to foreshadow future absurdities, the Red Sox lost a chance to play in the postseason because of a players' strike. After missing two weeks of the season and a handful of the early games to a strike (during which Yaz earned the scorn of many players for his opposition to the strike, which would have served mostly to help the nonstars of the era), it was agreed upon that the schedule that remained would be played, and that none of the missed games (eight in the Red Sox' case) would be made up. When the 1972 season ended, the Sox were one-half game behind the Detroit Tigers after a blunder-filled final three games in Detroit in which the Red Sox lost two of three. The Tigers finished with a record of 86-70. The Red Sox were 85-70. The Tigers went to the postseason. In 1973 the Sox again finished second in the American League East. In 1974 they won the East, but fell to the mighty Oakland A's, who had established a dynasty with a swashbuckling crew of flashy stars.

Like 1967 before it, the 1975 season was also a special one for the Red Sox and their fans. Led by arguably the greatest one-two rookie punch in baseball history, Jim Rice and Fred Lynn, and with an explosive lineup including the veteran Yaz, rugged New Hampshire native Carlton Fisk, the Boomer, and a pitching staff that included Luis Tiant, a clutch performer and a beloved Boston character, the Red Sox swept to the American League East title, vanquished the A's and their dynasty, and participated in perhaps the greatest of all World Series against the Cincinnati Reds. But, of course, it was not to be. Despite Pudge Fisk's heroics in the wee hours of Game Six, when he used his body language to will a ball to stay fair as it soared over the Green Monster, The Big Red Machine won game seven, the third such series the Red Sox had lost since World War II. As had happened after 1967, the 1976 Red Sox were a disappointment from the outset. However, the Red Sox of the late 1970s looked on the verge of establishing a dynasty of their own. They had a good mix of young stars and veterans. They had a fearsome lineup, the match of the Sox teams of the late 1940s. Indeed, if ever a team looked destined to win a World Series and end six decades of frustration, the 1978 team was the one.

Perhaps 1978 is the year the Red Sox became the Red Sox as we know them. By the middle of that summer, the Red Sox seemed unstoppable. The offense was awesome, the pitching sufficient, and by July 20 the 62-28 Sox led the Milwaukee Brewers by nine games. The

Yankees wallowed in third, a nonfactor at fourteen games back. Then in late July the Sox began a swoon that will forever haunt the hearts of Red Sox fans, at least until they win a World Series and deliver us from our tribulations. The Yankees got hot, and the Sox could not seem to put two good games together. After a ten-game road trip in which they mustered two wins, the Sox limped home only eight up on the Yankees. By September 1 the lead stood at five games. The losses began to take their toll, and internal divisions started to damage the team dynamic. Then on Thursday, September 7, the Yankees traveled to Boston for a four-game series. The Sox maintained a four-game lead. They left the series tied, after losing four straight by an aggregate score of 42-9. What many fans forget is that the Sox salvaged some nobility toward the end of the season. The Red Sox fell behind the Yanks after the Boston Massacre, but won their last eight games and eleven of their last thirteen to force a tie with New York. That led to a one-game playoff.

This is the proper interlude for a personal note. In 1978 I was seven years old. I had been a Red Sox fan for as long as I could remember, but 1978 marks my first concrete memories of Red Sox baseball. I was a huge fan of Jimmy Rice and Yaz and Lynn and Fisk, the local boy made good. (I grew up just a few miles down the road from where Carlton Fisk grew up. There is a legendary story about a home run that Fisk hit in my hometown in an American Legion game.) As did many young boys, I often pretended to be my idols, and indeed I developed fairly solid fielding skills throwing balls off my grandparents' barn, or the shed roof, or off the steeply sloped A-frame roof at Mom's. I watched the one-game playoff in the living room of the farmhouse. My grandparents owned the oldest house in Newport, New Hampshire, the beams exuding well more than two centuries of history. For me the farm, which has since been sold and stripped of much of its character, still evokes memories. But perhaps none are more entrenched than the smells and sounds and feelings of that fateful October day.

I was young, but I was well aware of the meaning of this game. Like any good Red Sox fan, I hated the Yankees. I absolutely hated them. I hated Reggie Jackson. I loathed Billy Martin, their pugnacious manager. I despised Lou Piniella. I thought Ron Guidry had gotten lucky all season. I hated the smattering of front running Yankees fans in my hometown, undoubtedly flatlanders not from around here.

My emotions probably adequately reflected those of the rest of New England that beautiful October afternoon with the possible exception of the optimism that I possessed entering the afternoon. I thought that after all of the trials and tribulations, the Red Sox had righted the ship, and would surely vanquish the Bronx Bombers. I would grow to know better as the years passed. Nonetheless, like hundreds of thousands of the citizens of Red Sox Nation, I danced around the spacious living room in the second inning when venerable warrior Yaz drove a home run that just slipped behind the Pesky Pole in right field. Yaz always played big in big games. Guidry wasn't so tough! The Sox maintained the 1-0 lead into the sixth. Between half-innings I would go out and toss a ball high into the air, pretending to make the game-winning catch. Or I would break my uncle Nick's number one law of respecting the game—I would hit rocks into the cow pasture with my pint-sized Louisville slugger. After all, chasing my bombs (game winners all) into the field might have caused me to miss a pitch.

There were two on in the seventh, two out. Mike Torrez had been effective all day. The Sox had scored in the sixth. Bucky Dent, the number nine hitter, was up. On his second pitch Dent lofted a fly ball to left. Yaz, the multiple gold glover, was in the field. The 2-0 lead would hold. Ooops. The ball kept lazily flying. Yaz stood against the Wall. The ball nestled in the net. A three-run homer. I swore and threw my glove and immediately pouted. Bucky F*&#ing Dent (the full name by which Russell Earl Dent will forever be known in New England) had just put the Yankees up 3-2. The Wall that giveth also taketh away. I've never hated a façade so much. I became a true, long-suffering Red Sox fan at that moment.

To be truthful, in my seven-year-old, cheap pop-fly addled mind, the next couple of innings were a blur of hope and prayers and entreatment and begging and disappointment. As we used to say on the playground or in the fields in our impromptu games, in what had become a 5-4 game the Sox had "last raps." They had the last at-bats of the game. After a quick out, Rick Burleson, "The Rooster," walked. Then up came Jerry Remy, our diminutive but tough-as-nails second baseman. He got a hit to right field. But in typical Red Sox karma, fate stepped in. The sun in right field was especially tough that day and especially at that time in the late afternoon. When the ball left Remy's bat, the sun blinded Lou Piniella. He did not see the ball until it dropped, but he had positioned himself well, and he stuck his hand out to prevent a multibase hit and possible Burleson score. Rice came to bat and hit a fly sufficient to send Burleson to third. It would have been sufficient to send him home had Burleson been able to advance that far on Remy's fate-damned liner. Yaz was on deck.

I was not yet born in 1967 when Yaz had his magical summer. I can barely remember snippets of the 1975 season. But I knew what it meant to have Yaz up. I knew that with two outs in a playoff game against the Yankees, with the tying run on third and the winning run at first, Yaz would find a way to get it done. On a 1-0 count, Yaz got a fastball. I will remember this moment for the rest of my life. When I am older and can't remember my grandkids' names, I'll still be able to recall the image of Yaz agonizing as his harmless fly ball settled into Graig Nettles' glove. I was numb. And my innocence was gone.

That began my full-fledged relationship with the Sox. But this long history serves not as backstory, but merely to reveal my entrée into the ongoing continuum. Because being a fan is about one's personal relationship with a team, but it is also about that team's past, and how when you become a fan, you are somehow bound with that past. I am a Red Sox fan. I can claim Ted Williams and his .406, and his MVPs, and his Triple Crowns, and because I am a fan, I take it personally if anyone dares not acknowledge Williams as the Greatest Hitter Who Ever Lived. Jimmie Foxx and Dom DiMaggio are part of my past too, even though they hung up their double knits two decades before I was born. My Red Sox won the first World Series. Cy Young, I can point out, spent eight seasons in a Red Sox uniform. The 1967 Impossible Dream? I wish I could have seen it. But I still get to savor it.

1918? That's where things get sticky.

For if the successes are mine, the failures are my inheritance as well. Those teams of the late 1940s are my legacy too. And because of the particularly, peculiarly torturous history of the Sox, perhaps the near misses and dreadful losses and bungled decisions and asphyxiated miscues in the clutch are the most substantial inheritance I take on. My friends who are Yankees fans get to claim Mantle and Maris, Gehrig and (gulp!) Ruth. Dodgers fans have their own burdens to bear, and indeed, theirs is a story that taxes my theories of geography even as they simultaneously reinforce elements of that theory.

Cubs fans, well, they inherit a legacy of lovable losers. But they do inherit that past—the past becomes part of the present even as the present inexorably becomes the future. Indeed, the present is almost never an actual thing—the moment in which you currently exist was seconds ago future, and once it happens, will forever be part of the past.

My fan's history, born of geography, is well rooted in a difficult past. But perhaps because of this tortured past, I am so well qualified to reflect on the enduring nature of being a true supporter. Maybe this is like what C. Vann Woodward had to say about the burden of Southern history—that because Southerners know defeat and failure and loss and tragedy and shame, they have much to teach the rest of the country. The history of the South can thus serve as an object lesson to the rest of a country that sees its history largely in terms of success and virtue. Perhaps Red Sox fans have something to teach the rest of the world, something that Yankees fans, with their decades of successes and victory, simply cannot understand. We have seen defeat and tragic failure. We have seen humiliation and frustration. We've been 'buked and we've been scorned. In short, in our experience as fans we have also come closest to our own fallible humanity. This may all be bunk, the art of making a virtue of necessity, but there seems to be some truth to it. Yankees fans have all of those World Series titles. We Sox fans surely want just one of them. But we'll take our Red Sox, thank you.

Almost anyone reading this knows of the Red Sox story since that October afternoon more than two decades ago. Plenty of sports fans I meet think they are the first ever to mention Bill Buckner to me. Yankees fans seem singularly unaware of the utter banality of the Bill Buckner invocation. Which isn't to say that mentioning 1986 doesn't destroy me a little bit. It does. Indeed, I watched Game Six in Mom's living room in one of the houses, the other being my grandparents' farmhouse, in which I grew up. It ranks as one of the most devastating events in my life. Game Six is as indelible to me as is the Yankee playoff. Maybe more so.

And yet hope springs eternal. Sox fans try never to admit it, but we are hopeless optimists, if you scratch the tough, cynical, jaded, pessimistic veneer. The last decade of Red Sox baseball has been a worthy, exasperating successor to the teams of the past seven decades. They have had several teams that were good, but not good enough. They have had some tough breaks go against them. They have killed themselves with untimely slumps and poor fielding. They even have played the Yankees in the American League Championship Series. They lost. Nonetheless it will happen someday. The Red Sox will win a World Series. I just know it. And so do millions of others of us in Red Sox Nation. Or in any case, we'll watch to see what they do to us next. We are fans. It's what we do.

BIBLIOGRAPHY

Demos, John. "A Fan's Homage to Fenway (Or, Why We Love It When They Always Break Our Hearts)." *American Places: Encounters with History*. Ed. William Leuchtenberg. New York: Oxford UP, 2000. 105-114.

Giamatti, A. Bartlett. "The Green Fields of the Mind." *Baseball: The National Pastime in Art and Literature*. Ed. David Colbert. New York: Time Life Books, 2001. 142-144.

Riley, Dan. *The Red Sox Reader*. Boston: Houghton Mifflin, 1991 (includes Updike's "Hub Fans Bid Kid Adieu," 53-72).

Shaughnessy, Dan. *The Curse of the Bambino*. New York: Penguin Books, 1991.

Woodward, C. Vann. *The Burden of Southern History*. New York: Vintage Books, 1960.

4

Baseball Memorabilia

Frank Hoffmann

For many collectors of baseball memorabilia, the activity is better understood as part of the broader field of collectibles. The rapid growth of the field during the last two decades of the twentieth century led to a substantial increase in the number of books, periodicals, and, in recent years, Web sites providing insights for navigating the various pitfalls—the unpredictability of supply and demand forces, unscrupulous dealers, counterfeit merchandise, etc.,—in collecting baseball souvenirs. Krause Publications, a leader in providing information for collectors, did not publish a single sports-oriented title through 1981; by 1992, however, the company had garnered 80 percent of the market for sports-collecting periodicals. At that time, founder Chester Krause noted, "Today, baseball cards are about 45 percent of our overall business. . . . Because of the popularity of baseball cards, Krause Publications surged in the '80s . . ." (Barrier 54).

The factors behind the appeal of baseball memorabilia for both the buyer and seller are as varied as American society itself. Guidebooks aimed at collectors tend to pass quickly over motivation considerations before launching into a more detailed analysis of issues such as supply and demand, care and preservation, and prognosticating future values. Dan Zachofsky's *Collecting Baseball Memorabilia* typifies such sources, noting, "Sports collectors are searching to hold onto or collect specific items from childhood memories and experiences" (4). Also in the work, he alludes to the enjoyment that can be derived from this activity, particularly in fostering a closer parent-child bond (4). In his book, *The Ultimate Insider's Guide to Baseball Cards,* Mark Stewart briefly refers to the opportunity to "make money," the "pure pleasure" of ownership, and the role of cards as a "conduit to fantasy" (1-2).

Based on the leading trade and academic publications, as well as the observations of dealers in baseball memorabilia,* people tend to collect for a combination of the following reasons:

- *Nostalgia* for the past, a time best remembered through baseball artifacts.
- *Relaxation.* A means of relieving the stress emanating from the pressures of everyday life.
- Meeting other *psychological needs,* such as
  a. *recognition;*
  b. *acceptance* by attempting to imitate and/or fulfill the expectations of one's peers, colleagues, etc.;
  c. meeting a *challenge* issued from within or without; and
  d. substituting collectibles to *fill a void* in one's life, possibly resulting from the absence of love or material possessions at some earlier time.
- The opportunity to realize a significant *profit.* Profit-seekers are apt to view collecting as an investment comparable to the buying and selling of stocks or bonds.
- A means of *promoting* one's activities, institution, or business through the display of or reference to memorabilia.
- An *aesthetic appreciation* for certain objects such as the design of a baseball card or the cut, texture, and color of a uniform. From this perspective, subjectivity in matters of taste tends to be the rule; the opinions of others are unlikely to matter to any great extent.
- The *preservation of culture or history.* Collectors in this camp see themselves as agents attempting to redress a grievous error in judgment on the part of society at large, i.e., the failure to consider certain items worth preserving.
- A strategic means by which to establish contact with certain people, whether potential friends who share an interest or the celebrities associated with the collectibles themselves.

---

*Although the author has talked with dozens of sports memorabilia retailers and dealers about the collecting phenomenon since 1989, the most comprehensive information has been obtained from a series of conversations with Michael Evangelisti, an Internet entrepreneur specializing in baseball cards who serves customers worldwide.

An entire culture has sprung up around the creation, distribution, preservation, and consumption of baseball memorabilia. Its universe is populated by teams (and related personnel), suppliers/merchandisers (manufacturers, wholesalers, retailers, etc.), and consumers—that is, the fans who have created a demand for these artifacts. John Thorn, in *The Game for All America* (1988), states that this socio-economic apparatus is not a new phenomenon:

> Baseball has been a vehicle for merchandising since at least the 1870s, when scorecard publishers sold advertising to local restaurants, sporting goods emporiums, railway companies and brewers. Today baseball sells cars, clothing, cameras, computers—anything and everything. (Light 448)

Many observers would argue that baseball memorabilia collecting today pales alongside souvenir hunting in other major professional sports, particularly basketball and football. If this is the case—due to the far-flung activities that constitute the collectibles market, any attempt at authoritatively documenting this supposition would be virtually impossible—it would simply reflect baseball's decline in popularity from its once unassailable position as our national pastime, particularly among fans growing up during the post-World War II era. *Detroit News* reporter Tom Long addressed this phenomenon in 1997, stating,

> The hockey finals are over, Detroit is victorious. The pro football season-preview magazines are on stands right now, Detroit is hopeful. But baseball is a different story. I have yet to see Detroit Tigers flags flying from anybody's window, even though the local team apparently has improved markedly. (E1)

The 1957-1960 era was significant in that it represented a transitional period in big-time American sports. The first wave of baby boomers was coming of age—i.e., developing fan loyalties—as interest in the National Football League was spurred by the legendary 23-17 overtime victory of the Baltimore Colts over the New York Giants in the 1958 championship game and the beginning of the Green Bay Packers dynasty under coach Vince Lombardi. Furthermore, the formation of the American Football League in 1960 created a healthy competitive environment with each league being heavily promoted by its own television network. The draft wars—which ultimately spawned quarterback Joe Namath's then-huge signing bonus—and events leading up to the merger of the AFL and NFL climaxing with the creation of the Super Bowl further fueled fan interest.

In the meantime, the National Basketball Association had the fabled Boston Celtics dynasty and the ongoing duels between the league's two most dominant players, prolific scorer Wilt "the Stilt" Chamberlain and defensive specialist Bill Russell. The wide-open, offensive-minded brand of play was on the verge of peaking—it was not uncommon for the winning team to score 150 or more points in a contest—an exciting style well suited to TV viewing.

Other lesser sports were also making a move toward garnering a greater market share of the American sports entertainment dollar. Hockey—while promoting appealing superstars such as Bobby Hull and Gordie Howe—was just beginning the expansion of its franchises into U.S. cities. Boxing envisioned a greater share of media coverage in the future with Cassius Clay's popular gold medal victory in the 1960 Olympics, and golf was entering a golden age that would feature the weekly showdowns among Arnold Palmer, Jack Nicklaus, and Gary Player.

The rise of satellite TV, which made possible the reception of American sports broadcasts worldwide, followed by the implementation of international marketing strategies on the part of the NFL, NBA, and other leagues have created considerable demand for memorabilia relating to sports other than baseball. Furthermore, the Internet—particularly electronic retailers and purchasing exchanges such as e-bay—has opened the collectibles field to participants (many of whom do not prefer baseball to other sports) who are often younger, less mobile, more remote (from dealers, shows, etc., where souvenirs are typically bought and sold), and less well off financially than serious collectors in the past. In short, the democratization of collecting has undoubtedly cut into baseball's share of the marketplace.

Nevertheless, baseball still comprises a substantial portion of the sports memorabilia market. According to Dan Zachofsky, the baseball collectibles hobby had reached $750 million a year by 2000 (4). Zachofsky does not make it clear exactly what activities constitute this hobby; however, it can be safely surmised that the broad field of baseball memorabilia involves considerably more money. The gross sales of authorized Major League Baseball merchandise rose from $200,000 to more than $2.4 billion in 1994 (despite the estimated loss of $280 million as a result of the baseball strike) (Light 449). The royalties paid major league players by baseball card companies alone had reached almost $100 million by 1993 (Light 448). The sport's continued appeal can be attributed to a number of factors:

- Its long, uninterrupted history; documented competition at the professional level reached back as far as the 1850s, while the major leagues dated their official origin to the formation of the National League in 1876.
- Baseball franchises have long understood the value of public relations activities that bring players and fans together. This understanding is reflected in the diversity of institutions and activities catering to baseball enthusiasts, including the Hall of Fame in Cooperstown, New York, fan balloting for the annual All-Star Game, regularly scheduled autograph sessions, and official retail outlets stocked with authorized products located both in shopping malls and the ballparks themselves.
- Although youth have always participated in the collecting phenomenon, adults—most of whom developed their sports interests at a time when baseball possessed the largest fan base—have long dominated the memorabilia marketplace, particularly the high-priced items.
- Over time, organized baseball has spawned a rich array of resources that have become desirable collectibles.

The sheer diversity of baseball memorabilia must seem mind-boggling to the nonbeliever. Mark K. Larson has created a useful typology for understanding these artifacts. His broad headings (with no particular significance attached to order) include:

- Autographs
- Uniforms
- Equipment
- Statues (including the current rage, bobbing head dolls)
- Yearbooks
- Media Guides
- Programs

- Periodicals
- Books
- Commemoratives
- Postcards
- Pins
- Ticket stubs, schedules
- Medallions
- Stamps
- Blankets, pennants, leathers, silks
- Miscellaneous: advertising/promotional materials, beer cans/pop cans, bottle caps, buttons/badges, coins, computer mouse pads, credit cards, folders, food/drink packages and accessories, Hall of Fame items, jewelry/trophies, lineup cards, magnets, marbles, matches, medals, movie memorabilia, music, newspapers, patches, personalized player souvenirs (e.g., Joe DiMaggio Fisherman's Wharf Restaurant menu), phone cards, playing cards, posters/prints/art works, stadium seats, toys (including board games), travel bags, videos/film cartridges, wire photos

Baseball cards have long been the most popular category of baseball memorabilia. Relatively inexpensive and widely available—usually as close as the neighborhood grocery, drug, or department store—they represented a rite of passage for the typical American boy. Even when the young collector outgrew them, the cards remained a fond memory to be relived time and time again. *The Great American Baseball Card Flipping, Trading, and Bubble-Gum Book* (1973) presents a typical image of such bygone days:

> They were beautiful and reassuring to behold, brand new and glistening crisply in their packages . . . stuck behind glassed partitions and stacked on counters. An indication that the world was still in order, a promise of pleasant days and easeful nights. (Light 69)

In cases where baseball cards were associated with less pleasant experiences, the former collector could often still glean some lesson of value. In *A Farewell to Heroes* (1981), Frank Graham Jr. provided an early lesson in consumer education:

But one evening my father came home from New York with the ultimate birthday present—a box of one hundred baseball cards. I unwrapped them with high expectations, only to find that twenty-eight of them were Horace Fords. Ford had departed from the majors in 1933 after a long and undistinguished career as an infielder in the National League, and the gum company apparently was trying urgently to reduce its inventory. (Light 69)

Whatever the personal impressions derived from the hobby, it is perhaps reassuring to know that the production of baseball cards—like many of the National Pastime's other artifacts—is a genuinely capitalistic phenomenon. The earliest cards to be made available in mass quantities appeared within cigarette packages (as a ploy to change the effeminate image of this new product) in the 1880s, most notably the Old Judge series manufactured by the New York-based Goodwin & Company. Cards became popular again around 1909-1910 following the appearance of the American Tobacco Company's "White Bordered Set." A significant number of candy firms (e.g., the Zeenut Candy Company, which maintained a series from 1911-1939, and Cracker Jack) and sports magazines also utilized cards as promotional items.

Following a drop-off in production during World War I, card sets were issued sporadically until a revival in the 1930s. The primary manufacturer during this period was the Goudey Gum Company, but cards virtually disappeared during World War II. The modern era for cards was introduced by the Bowman Gum Company in 1948. Bowman would be bought out by the Topps Gum Company (1950 to the present) in 1955, which was responsible for popularizing the idea of placing gums inside card packages and adding statistics to the backs of cards. Topps would dominate the field until the card craze of the 1980s.

After a court decision in 1981 ended Topps' card monopoly, new competitors entered the field, including Donruss (1981; purchased by Pinnacle in 1996), Fleer (1981; purchased by Marvel in 1992), Sportflics (1986), Score (1988; later known as Pinnacle), Upper Deck (1988), Pacific Trading Cards (1991), and Ted Williams Card Co. As a result, card revenues skyrocketed in value—five billion cards were sold in 1988—followed by an increase in licensing revenues ($2 million annually in 1981 to $70 million in 1992) to the Major League Players Association (Light 69).

In 1991, at the peak of the card craze, Los Angeles Kings hockey club owner Bruce McNall and star player Wayne Gretzky would pay $451,000 for the famed 1909 T206 Honus Wagner Sweet Caporal cigarettes card. During the 1980s—before the card industry had to retrench due to saturation of the market—the price of the most in-demand cards (e.g., Mickey Mantle's 1952 Topps rookie card) increased more than tenfold in value (Light 70).

The rapid rise in trading card valuations has not been a unique phenomenon within the baseball memorabilia field. The mass media provided exhaustive coverage of the 1998 race between Mark McGwire and Sammy Sosa to surpass the Roger Maris home run record of sixty-one; the projected value of home run ball number sixty-two— as well as each successive new record ball—was given nearly as much attention. When McGwire's seventieth home run ball was ultimately purchased for more than $3 million by comic book/film artist Todd McFarlane, the story was recounted from a seemingly endless array of perspectives, ranging from Horatio Alger rags-to-riches parables to an apocalyptic doomsday slant. Like the classic literary works, art, and music created throughout history, the exploits of baseball players—both on and off the field—are subjected to many differing interpretations. Whether seen more as god-like heroes from ancient mythologies or simply as grist for the *Entertainment Tonight* mill, baseball memorabilia enable Everyman to transcend the limits of his imagination, to project himself into our National Pastime's pastoral fantasy.

It seems logical to assume that the commercial institutions surrounding baseball memorabilia will always have their place. However, dealers, price guides, collectibles shows, and the like will always be subject to the general public's perception of the sport. Those inclined to see a continued growth of interest in baseball artifacts are apt to identify with the observation made by James Earl Jones' reclusive character in the film, *Field of Dreams:*

> The one constant through all the years has been baseball. . . . This field, this game, is a part of our past. It reminds us of all that once was good, and that could be again. (Seib 852)

This positive perspective was echoed by the former Major League Baseball commissioner, the late A. Bartlett Giamatti, who wrote that what Americans love about baseball

> is what it recalls to us about ourselves at our earliest. . . . They are memories of our best hopes. They are memories of a time when all that would be better was before us, as a hope, and the hope was fastened to a game. (Seib 852)

Although baseball has come to represent the best qualities of America, it has also reflected the nation's worst flaws. Prior to the late 1940s, "professional baseball was a striking example of American apartheid, with African-American players restricted to the Negro Leagues . . ." (Seib 848). When Jackie Robinson joined the Brooklyn Dodgers in 1947, however, the Major Leagues were instantly changed into a positive force for change, anticipating many of the social advances ensuing out of the post-World War II civil rights movement. The fact that a Robinson single-signature baseball is presently worth between $2,200 and $2,500 (in contrast, a similar autograph from fellow Hall of Famer and Dodger teammate, Pee Wee Reese, is only worth fifty to sixty dollars) would appear to indicate that sports-related events have a substantial impact upon the value of, and interest in, baseball memorabilia (Larson 26).

Whereas an upsurge of interest in baseball artifacts is often associated with positive events on the playing field (e.g., McGwire's home run record, Cal Ripken Jr.'s streak of consecutive games played), fan/collector apathy typically follows bad publicity surrounding developments outside the ballpark per se. The 1994-1995 players' strike represents a case in point. Philip Seib states:

> Even after the 1995 season finally got under way, fans' anger toward owners and players was reflected in sagging attendance. Many owners were viewed as money-grubbing villains, and some players who were labeled as pro-union activists were booed when they returned to the field. (850)

Jonathan Light noted that baseball cards, the largest sector within the memorabilia field, were directly affected by these developments:

In 1995 . . . production levels were down over prior years as much as 75 percent because of the baseball strike. In 1995 Topps had its lowest production in 30 years. . . . Donruss took a downturn when both hockey and baseball suffered labor problems. (69)

Conclusion

Countless media sources have addressed the primacy of sports in American society. In his landmark work, *Sports Spectators,* Allen Guttmann would write,

If tens of millions of ordinary Americans were not as sports-obsessed as their political representatives in Washington, manufacturers of automobiles, beer, and computers would not purchase halftime spots at $15,000 a second. Quite plainly, however, major corporations—the only ones that can afford largess on this gargantuan scale—are persuaded that these millions of dollars are well spent, and the A.C. Nielsen Company assures them that they are correct. (140)

Although baseball appears less suited to the television screen than football, it remains one of the major spectator sports in the United States. The purchase, preservation, and exchange of memorabilia—as well as the coverage of the phenomenon—represents yet another manifestation of our obsession with sports. As with so many other facets of our collective lives, whether the impetus to collect baseball artifacts can be categorized as a constructive or counterproductive activity depends upon the myriad choices made by each of us on an individual basis.

BIBLIOGRAPHY

Barrier, Michael. "Collecting the Collectors; For 40 Years, Chet Krause has published must reading for fans of coins, cars, comic books, and baseball cards." *Nation's Business* 80.10 (October 1992): 54-55.

Guttmann, Allen. *Sports Spectators.* New York: Columbia UP, 1986.

Larson, Mark K. *Complete Guide to Baseball Memorabilia.* Third Edition. Iola, WI: Krause Publications, 1996.

Light, Jonathan Fraser. *The Cultural Encyclopedia of Baseball.* Jefferson, NC: McFarland, 1997.

Long, Tom. "Chat Rooms: Is Baseball Getting Knocked Out of the Park by Hockey?" *Detroit News* 10 July 1997: E1.

Seib, Philip. "The Future of Baseball." *CQ Researcher* 8.36 (25 Sept. 1998): 848-852.

Stewart, Mark. *The Ultimate Insider's Guide to Baseball Cards.* New York: Crown, 1993.

Zachofsky, Dan. *Collecting Baseball Memorabilia.* Jefferson, NC: McFarland, 2000.

SECTION II:
BASEBALL INCLUSIVITY

5

From Jackie to Elvis, from Selma to St. Petersburg: The Desegregation of Spring Training

Brian Carroll

The swell of attention surrounding the Seattle Mariners' outfielder, Ichiro Suzuki, has earned him the nickname Elvis back home in Japan. Great play in the field, sizzle on the base paths, and leadoff hitting brilliance throughout the 2001 campaign established him as one of baseball's luminaries. Suzuki's excellence has gone a long way to legitimize the quality of Japanese baseball, and Japanese baseball as a source of major league talent. The fact that he is of another race, one that was singled out in the United States for detainment during World War II, even in Suzuki's new home, the Pacific Northwest, is rarely mentioned. It is not an issue. It was not always this way.

Elvis owes a deep and honorable bow, or at least a tip of the cap, to the black players who broke into lily-white baseball a half-century prior to his immigration in 2001, and to those who labored behind the scenes to make equal opportunity on the playing field a reality. Desegregation was not a moment in time, though Jackie Robinson's signing is often considered just that moment, and it is a process that isn't yet complete. The process has required long-suffering and a brand of patience not seen since Moses' forty-year tour through the desert. Baseball's decision, forced by such men as Branch Rickey, Jackie Robinson, Bill Veeck, and Larry Doby, preceded by seven years the Supreme Court's decision in *Brown v. Board of Education* outlawing segregation in public education. Baseball led the way for the nation. Ever since, baseball's positions on race have drawn a great deal of attention. Consider the books, articles, and essays, the major motion pictures, Broadway musicals, and art exhibits. Jackie Robinson's story has become a staple of juvenile literature and of formal social studies curricula. As the first twentieth-century black to play major league baseball, Robinson rightly has been the magnet for much of the attention. His journey from Negro League baseball to the Brooklyn Dodgers via the Montreal Royals has been analyzed from seemingly every possible angle and perspective. Historian William Simons called the Dodgers' signing of Robinson the "most widely commented-on episode in American race relations of its time" (Simons, "Jackie Robinson and the American Mind" 40).

Most popular accounts of baseball's desegregation, though, pay scant attention to the pivotal role played by the black press. Chief among these overlooked ranks was black sportswriter Wendell Smith, at the time of Robinson's signing and for ten years prior the sports editor at *The Pittsburgh Courier,* the leading black newspaper of its day (Wiggins 5). It was Smith who recommended the former UCLA standout to Dodger president and general manager Branch Rickey during a private meeting in Rickey's office in April 1945 (Smith, undated private papers, 6). It was Smith who relentlessly campaigned for Robinson's matriculation to the big leagues. It was Smith who arranged a tryout for Robinson and two other players with Boston, also in April 1945. And for more than ten years it was Smith in the pages of the *Courier* campaigning for big league baseball's re-integration (Lamb and Bleske 48).

If Smith, the first black sportswriter to enter the Baseball Hall of Fame, has been overlooked as the link between Robinson and Rickey, he has been almost completely ignored in examinations of the desegregation of baseball's six weeks of spring training, a topic that in general has received little attention in scholarship. The complex, economically driven process of integrating Florida's hotels and the reaction to Smith's crusade to bring the black players' plight into the national consciousness, particularly the reaction by the black players themselves, reveals much about the values and assumptions of the era. The drama underlines how much things have changed, and how much they remain the same.

Smith's campaign in the pages of the *Chicago American* shared much with the tactics and tenets of, among others, novelist and activist James Baldwin and civil rights champion Martin Luther King Jr., both contemporaries of Smith. As with Baldwin and King, Smith was right for his time, a mostly genteel period that ended with the increasingly violent clashes between civil rights protesters and local authorities in the early and mid-1960s. Sit-ins swept through as many as seventy Southern cities as part of a protest movement started in part by four North Carolina A&T University students protesting at the Woolworth lunch counter in Greensboro, North Carolina, in February 1960 (Chafe). As early as the fall of 1960, just prior to Smith's campaign, Martin Luther King was jailed for a sit-in protest in Georgia, one of the first of several such confrontations with police (Houk and Creamer 37). In May 1963, white and black liberals in Alabama who had loosely organized to test and force integration were attacked and beaten by white citizens in Anniston and Birmingham, where riots made national headlines (Grun 550). And the assassination of John F. Kennedy in 1963, the end of Camelot, marked for many the end of an American idealism writers such as Smith commonly evoked when calling for change, an idealism symbolized by the relentless series of marches on Selma, Alabama, in March 1965. Emblematic of the transition in the civil rights struggle, in late November 1963, Jackie Robinson found himself the subject of a series of verbal attacks by Malcolm X (Tygiel, "The Great Experiment Fifty Years Later" 262). It signaled an end to the era in which Robinson's vision of an inclusive, egalitarian America had resonance with blacks and whites, alike. Malcolm X was part of a new generation of black nationalists, militant protesters, and radicals.

As with Robinson and King, Smith was a citizen of a pre-Malcolm X era who espoused in action if not explicitly in writing what social critic Gunnar Myrdal called a shared "American Creed," a vision of a nation "older and wider than America itself" (Myrdal 25). This vision is articulated in the Declaration of Independence, Preamble of the Constitution, the Bill of Rights, and many state constitutions. It is the highest law of the land, upholding "the essential dignity of the individual human being, of the fundamental equality of all men, and of certain inalienable rights to freedom, justice, and a fair opportunity" (Myrdal 4). This understanding of American democracy led Robinson and Smith to petition for and eventually demand equal opportunity based on ability and not color. In 1956, after only a decade of integrated baseball and no more than forty black players in major league uniforms, *The Sporting News* celebrated baseball's "gradual, voluntary, and peaceful advance toward the complete fulfillment of its code that a player should not be judged on the basis of creed, connections or color, but on the basis of ability alone" (Briley 137). Complete fulfillment? Slow to eliminate quotas on the number of black players on rosters, big league clubs were glacial in moving toward racial inclusiveness within management and in the front office. Another two decades passed before baseball had a black field manager—Frank Robinson in 1975. Three decades later blacks held seventeen, or less than 2 percent, of the 880 top administrative jobs in baseball (Tygiel, "The Great Experiment Fifty Years Later" 264). It would require four more full decades before a black would occupy the office of general manager—Bob Watson with the New York Yankees.

In Smith's day, however, upholding shared concepts of equality, liberty, opportunity, and nationhood—concepts embedded in the Creed—proved an effective method of winning social change. Smith's campaign waged throughout 1961 in the *Chicago American,* resting as it did on a foundation of more than a decade of social activist writing with the *Courier,* served to hold the national pastime accountable for these shared ideals, all within the context of "working together" (Smith, "Negro Ball Players Want Rights in South" A1). His year-long effort began in the January 23, 1961, edition of the *Chicago American* with a front-page article that pierced the perception of pro baseball's racial tranquility, a perception black players, too, cooperated to encourage (Briley 138). In the article, headlined, "Spring Training Woes," Smith revealed to the nation the "growing feeling of resentment" among black players who continued to suffer "embarrassment, humiliation, and even indignities" each spring. Future Hall of Famers such as Hank Aaron, Willie Mays, and Ernie Banks were segregated from their white teammates and were forced to sleep, eat, and recreate in separate and largely inferior facilities. White players enjoyed some of south Florida's finest hotels, including St. Petersburg's Soreno (Yankees) and Vinoy Park (Cardinals), and the Sarasota Terrace in Sarasota (White Sox).

As Smith well knew, by 1961 black ball players, like a growing number of citizenry throughout the South, had had enough. Since *Brown v. Board of Education* in 1954, segregation policies were being tested throughout society. In spring training's primary home, for example, in Florida, the National Association for the Advancement of Colored People encouraged blacks to visit the state's segregated beaches in defiance of local policy (Davis 151). St. Petersburg, base camp each spring for the New York Yankees and St. Louis Cardinals, was host to a series of swim-ins at segregated swimming pools. It was in this context that Smith continued his quarter-century, career-long fight against racial discrimination by giving black players and their grievances a voice. Three years before President Lyndon Johnson signed the Civil Rights Act of 1964 to abolish legal segregation, Smith's *Chicago American* crusade called on baseball to end hypocrisy, uphold the Creed, and erase the barriers of segregation in Florida's and Arizona's baseball communities. In so doing, Smith wrote, baseball could again lead the way toward a more racially integrated, more just society. He pointed to baseball's success integrating hotels during Robinson's first few years with the Dodgers in Chicago, Philadelphia, and, finally, in 1954, in St. Louis (Smith, "Negro Ball Players Want Rights in South" 18). He reminded readers that he, too, was shut out of those same hotels along with Dodger greats Robinson, Roy Campanella, and Don Newcombe (Smith, "Negro Players Gain in Equality Bid" 16).

Writing with authority and using sophisticated, almost legal brief-style arguments, Smith blended subtle threat with paternal reassurances, much as James Baldwin successfully did during Robinson's breakthrough days (Polsgrove 178). Smith acknowledged baseball's supposed desire for fair play, thereby identifying for everyone the Creed as the goal. He paired these allowances with calls to action. In a February 6, 1961, article, Smith reported on the "many constructive steps (that) have been taken to remedy what everybody agrees is an intolerable situation" (16). The steps included mostly public assurances that team owners and baseball executives were "fighting to eliminate segregation in spring training" and statements, such as that from Commissioner Ford Frick, expressing sympathy "with the players and their problems." Later in the February 6 article, however, Smith flatly states that "much more must be accomplished before the problem is resolved satisfactorily" (16). At about the same time, Baldwin, who had just appeared on the cover of *Time,* was quoted in *Life* in an article headlined, "At a Crucial Time a Negro Talks Tough," that "there's a bill due that has to be paid" (Polsgrove 179). The climate for social change was heating up.

In 1961, only the Dodgers had desegregated their spring training facilities. To keep Robinson, Newcombe, and Campanella together with their white teammates, Brooklyn left Daytona Beach, Florida, leasing a former naval station in nearby Vero Beach and building its own training facility and living quarters (Tygiel, *Baseball's Great Experiment, Jackie Robinson and His Legacy* 317). Dodgers were the only big league players who could room together, eat together, and train together without running up against local authorities and, as Smith and Robinson discovered earlier in Sanford, Florida, facing eviction from the town (Smith, "Negro Players Gain in Equality Bid" 16). One player told the Baltimore *Afro-American* that the only segregation in Dodgertown was that based on ability—Smith's and Robinson's vision for all of America, and certainly for all of baseball.

Violent protests, militancy, and radicalism were not yet part of the civil rights struggle, so black players for the most part were not yet protesting Jim Crow practices in the South. Not surprisingly, then, big league clubs did little. As Red Barber pointed out in his memoirs, racism and segregation were so difficult to fight because they weren't explicit policies, yet "all men in baseball understood the code" (51). Many black players were content merely to be in the major leagues and, therefore, were reticent to become the resented baseball family member who raises the issue of racial dysfunction. The Giants' Monte Irvin, for example, told historian Jules Tygiel that black players "wanted to play so badly, that (segregation during spring) didn't bother us that much" (*Baseball's Great Experiment, Jackie Robinson and His Legacy* 318). Player culture discouraged disputes with management for fear of leading to expulsion from baseball. Ballplayer Chuck Harmon told Tygiel, "Anytime you dispute with the management, whether you're white or black, or indifferent, you're gone" (318). Also contributing to the silence was the fact that some southern players had grown accustomed to segregation and, therefore, didn't challenge it, at least not directly. One of the earliest and most vocal critics of spring training's Jim Crowism, Bill White, said that because most of the players on his St. Louis Cardinals team were from the South, "the hotel situation in Florida wasn't a big issue with black players in the fifties" (Aaron 153-154).

What Smith understood was the inextricable linkage between social change and economic reality. Force social change by transforming the economic reality was the approach Smith was articulating on behalf of the black players. It would prove a powerful strategy, as it proved to be for Rickey and the Dodgers twenty-five years prior.

(Soon after Robinson broke in with the Dodgers, Smith poked fun at the economic windfall Brooklyn's belated integration had generated, writing, "Jack be nimble, Jack be quick, Jackie makes the turnstiles click," in Deardorff 14). In 1959, the year Boston became the last team in the majors to integrate, Hank Aaron of the Milwaukee Braves articulated this critical linkage vis-à-vis spring training (Behn 22). Complaining to Braves management about segregated housing in Bradenton, Florida, baseball's future all-time home run king pointed to the hotel cartel as perhaps the chief barrier to progress. Segregation in the state's hotels, he said, is "the hardest thing to break down" because "they stick together," much as the big league clubs closed ranks regarding racial discrimination prior to Rickey and Robinson (Aaron 153). Hotel and resort owners knew that if one yielded, it would be very difficult for the other hotels to tow the line. Aaron's complaints were heard, but at a cost to the entire team. Rather than tolerate segregated housing in Bradenton during the spring of 1959, the entire team moved to nearby Palmetto for a "two-bit" motel with inferior food (Shoulder). The economic pressure to force change lay in the millions ball clubs spent in Florida each spring and the tourist money their presence and play attracted.

In an interview with the *Courier* re-run by *The Sporting News* and reacted to by many both inside and outside of baseball, Robinson suggested that if Miami or Miami Beach first desegregated its hotels, the others in Florida's baseball communities would soon have to follow. When racial discrimination is "broken down," Robinson told the *Courier,* "Miami will be one of the leaders in the field" (Robinson, "Jackie Tells What He Likes and Dislikes About South" 9). The entire hotel "set-up" was wrong, he said. "We are all part of a team and should be treated that way." The next year, in leading the NAACP's Freedom Fund drive, a retired Robinson told a Chicago audience that blacks had simply run out of patience. "It is time for Negroes to ask for all of the rights which are theirs," he said (Falkner 253). Robinson repeated and elaborated on his charges in his controversial 1963 book, *Baseball Has Done It,* in which he argued that baseball's dollar would speak with more force than anything else.

Emphasizing the economic linkage was one prong of Smith's strategy in the *American.* Similar to Martin Luther King's approach in his oratory, Smith's approach as a writer was one of conciliation, give-and-take, and, above all, dialogue. Smith carefully prodded baseball's owners, proposing humble first steps, such as appointing for each team a player spokesman on the issue. The black players "realize, of course, that the owners are not responsible for their plight." The players were going about their struggle "in their own quiet way" and not enlisting the aid of the NAACP "or any other such group" (Smith, "Negro Ball Players Want Rights in South" A1). This conciliatory tone was praised by the players Smith claimed to speak for, including hometown hero Ernie Banks. "We all are particularly pleased with the sane and dignified way (the black players' position) has been presented," said the Cubs' shortstop. "There has been nothing inflammatory about the stories, and for that we are especially grateful" ("Negro Players Gain in Equality Bid" 16).

Smith claimed to speak for all black players, something few writers could have credibly done. Two months into the *American* campaign, in March 1961, he was denied housing along with the White Sox players of color reporting to Sarasota, Florida, for spring training. He could document firsthand the conditions the players faced in a way only a handful of black press reporters could have. When the Sarasota Terrace Hotel refused accommodations both to the players and to Smith, hotel management cited economic reasons for refusing blacks (Smith, "Negro Stars Find Themselves Caged"). Management was afraid of losing its affluent, white clientele. So Smith and Chicago's black players together faced the lack of recreational options and restricted public eating places, bowling alleys, and taxis. Special permission was required even to visit the Sarasota Terrace, where their white teammates were housed.

From a journalistic perspective, it is worth noting that Smith relied exclusively on unattributed sources when breaking his campaign in January, presumably to avoid putting the players in jeopardy with their respective clubs. This decision implied a high level of cooperation and confidentiality with the players, an intimacy no longer possible and, perhaps, no longer desired by media practitioners. Further underlining his own unique credentials for such a journalistic campaign, Smith used firsthand experience to add credence to his calls. In particular, he referenced his successful alliance with Robinson in breaking the color barrier and the road they together traveled before and after. "I cannot forget that March day in 1945," he wrote, when the two were asked to leave Sanford "by sundown. We got out of town

. . . but neither of us has ever forgotten" ("Negro Players Gain in Equality Bid" 16).

Following the January 23 salvo, change was relatively swift. The White Sox began negotiating with the Sarasota Terrace hotel to win accommodations for its six black players. According to Smith, Sox owner Bill Veeck also moved team reservations from Miami's McAllister Hotel to the more open-minded Biscayne Terrace hotel for a pair of exhibition games in April against Baltimore. The Chicago Cubs decided to house the entire team in Mesa, Arizona, at the Maricopa Inn, and not to play exhibition games in cities where black players would be forced to sleep in separate quarters. Baltimore's general manager, Lee MacPhail, reported to Smith that he, too, was working to keep his team together at a Miami hotel. And New York Yankees president Dan Topping told Smith he wanted all Yankee players training in St. Petersburg to "live under one roof," including the club's only black player, catcher Elston Howard ("Negro Players Gain in Equality Bid" 16).

The issue of economics would prove decisive. As Smith reported, the Yankees' St. Petersburg home, the Hotel Soreno, and the Cardinals' spring home, St. Pete's Vinoy Park Hotel, had no intention of changing their policies, advising the Yanks and Cards to "look for other hotels" (Smith, "Negro Players Gain in Equality Bid" 16). The two hotels were owned by the same Kansas City-based company. The Yankees immediately took the advice and moved to Fort Lauderdale, abruptly ending thirty-six years of training in St. Petersburg and stunning both the Soreno and the greater St. Pete community. Pressure shifted to the Vinoy Park to keep the Cards in St. Pete.

In July of 1961, as Maris and Mantle were chasing the Babe, the Cardinals, Yankees, Braves, and Orioles each announced they had secured integrated spring training housing, albeit under different circumstances. Levying economic pressure, the Cardinals benefited from the Yankees' decision to vacate St. Petersburg. Neither the town nor hotel ownership wanted to lose another big league club. The Cards were given permission to keep the team together at the Vinoy Park (Smith, "Players Take Up Color Bar Issue" 15). The Braves moved their living quarters from Bradenton to nearby Palmetto in order to stay together. MacPhail's Orioles, meanwhile, came to terms with Miami's McAllister.

Smith's hometown Sox negotiated with the Sarasota Terrace for much of the season. In November, Veeck announced the team was simply buying the hotel outright "so that all of their players can live under the same roof during their training season" (Smith, "American's Campaign Succeeding in Florida" 31). By Smith's description, it was an "extreme step (and) a direct result of the campaign waged thru [sic] last season by *Chicago's American.*" In response to the hotel purchase, the city of Sarasota agreed to chip in three baseball fields and clubhouse accommodations. The tide had turned.

There still were teams with segregated spring training, including Washington (Pompano Beach, Florida), Minnesota (Orlando), Detroit (Lakeland), and Kansas City (West Palm Beach), but each team was "taking measures" to end segregation, according to Smith. Full integration throughout spring training in Florida would require just two more years (Meyer D1), far less than the dozen needed following Robinson's signing by the Dodgers to see a player on every major league roster. Upon Smith's death in 1972, the *Chicago Defender,* a leading black newspaper, wrote that the journalist had articulated

> a vision of an American society, where ability, skill and character are the sole measures of a man and not the color of his skin. He pursued that idealism . . . not with the militancy of the new breed of black spokesman, rather with the calm and patient logic of a wise man whose vision was sharp enough to see the light at the end of the tunnel. He has made his contribution. History will not pass him by. (Reisler 34)

Smith's idealism, shared by Robinson, King, Baldwin, and wide swaths of the American population, belonged to his time, and it helped bring down the formal barriers, the traditional Jim Crow strictures and structures that prevented blacks' full participation. The economic legacy of slavery and of segregation, however, is incompatible with and has outlived the shared vision. America's inner cities are evidence of the fundamental inequities in opportunity that remain. While Smith would no doubt be heartened to see Colin Powell as our Secretary of State and Clarence Thomas as a United States Supreme Court justice, the vitality of racial profiling among police departments from Los Angeles to New Jersey and the ever-widening income gaps along racial lines are harsh reminders of how much of the vision has gone unfulfilled.

Smith, who died in November 1972, just four months after the passing of Robinson, would find much to celebrate in baseball, as well. Ichiro, as he is known in Seattle, demonstrates to a large extent how color- and race-blind baseball has become, and how close to the "based purely on ability" ideal the sport has progressed. Opportunities as field managers have opened up to men of color, as well. But the executive suite still is largely off limits, the exclusive domain of upper-class, white males. Black team ownership is nonexistent. It will likely continue to be with ownership stakes increasingly held by corporations and not individuals, a trend pointed to by the economics of team and stadium ownership. A Japanese Elvis is a good thing— culturally, socially, and as a signpost to a truly egalitarian sports world. African Americans in front-office management positions and with ownership stakes, signifying as they would fundamental change in economic opportunity, would be an even better thing and a more robust fulfillment of Robinson's and Smith's vision of what America should be and could become.

BIBLIOGRAPHY

Aaron, Henry. *I Had a Hammer.* New York: HarperCollins Publishers, 1991.

Baltimore *Afro-American,* 10 April 1948: page unknown.

Barber, Red. *1947: When All Hell Broke Loose in Baseball.* Garden City, NY: Doubleday and Co., 1982.

Behn, Robert. "Branch Rickey as Public Manager Fulfilling the Eight Responsibilities of Public Management." *Journal of Public Administration Research and Theory* 7.1 (January 1997): 1-34.

Briley, Ron. "Ten Years After: The Baseball Establishment, Race, and Jackie Robinson." *The Cooperstown Symposium on Baseball and American Culture, 1997.* Ed. Peter Rutkoff. Jefferson, NC: McFarland and Co., 1997. 137-150.

Chafe, William. *Civilities and Civil Rights: Greensboro, North Carolina, and the Black Struggle for Equality.* New York: Oxford University Press, 1980.

Davis, Jack. "Baseball's Reluctant Challenge: Desegregating Major League Spring Training Sites, 1961-1964." *Journal of Sport History* 19.2 (Summer 1992): 144-162.

Deardorff, Donald L. "The Black Press Played a Key Role in Integrating Baseball." *St. Louis Journalism Review* 23.168 (July-August 1994): 12-15.

Falkner, David. *Great Time Coming: The Life of Jackie Robinson from Baseball to Birmingham.* New York: Simon and Schuster, 1995.

Gross, Milton. "Baseball's Negroes Facing Brighter Spring," *Chicago American,* 1 Dec. 1961: 23.

Grun, Bernard. *The Timetables of History,* 3rd ed. New York: Simon and Schuster, 1991.

Houk, Ralph and Robert W. Creamer. *Season of Glory.* New York: G.P. Putnam's Sons, 1988.

Lamb, Chris and Glen Bleske. "Covering the Integration of Baseball—a Look Back." *Editor and Publisher,* 27 Jan. 1996: 48-50.

Meyer, Paul. "Columnist was 'Baseball' Star." *Pittsburgh Post-Gazette,* 29 Sept. 1994: D1.

Myrdal, Gunnar with Richard Sterner and Arnold Rose. *An American Dilemma: The Negro Problem and Modern Democracy.* New York: Harper and Brothers, 1944.

Polsgrove, Carol. *Divided Minds: Intellectuals and the Civil Rights Movement.* New York: W.W. Norton and Co., 2001.

Reisler, Jim. *Black Writers/Black Baseball: An Anthology of Articles from Black Sportswriters Who Covered the Negro Leagues.* Jefferson, NC: McFarland and Co., 1994.

Robinson, Jackie. "Jackie Tells What He Likes and Dislikes About South," *The Sporting News,* 6 June 1956: 9.

———. *I Never Had It Made.* New York: G.P. Putnam's and Sons, 1972.

Shoulder, Ken. "Grand Yankee, Brooklyn-Bred Joe Torre Steers the Yankees to a World Championship, Overcoming Personal Troubles and Personal Trauma." *Cigar Aficionado.* Feb. 1997. *Cigar Aficionado.* 26 March 2001. <http://www.cigaraficionado.com/Cigar/Aficionado/people/fe597.html>.

Simons, William. "Jackie Robinson and the American Mind: Journalistic Perceptions of the Reintegration of Baseball." *Journal of Sport History* 12.1 (Spring 1985): 39-64.

———. "Jackie Robinson and American Zeitgeist." *The Cooperstown Symposium on Baseball and American Culture, 1997.* Ed. Peter Rutkoff. Jefferson, NC: McFarland and Co., 1997. 77-105.

Smith, Wendell. "American's Campaign Succeeding in Florida," *Chicago American,* 9 Nov. 1961: 33.

———. "End Spring Degradation, Negro Players Ask," *Chicago American,* 30 July 1961: 31.

———. "Houses Sox Negro Stars," *Chicago American,* 6 April 1961: page unknown.

———. "Negro Ball Players Want Rights in South," *Chicago American,* 23 Jan. 1961: A1.

———. "Negro Players Gain in Equality Bid," *Chicago American,* 6 Feb. 1961: 16.

———. "Negro Stars Find Themselves Caged," *Chicago American,* 4 April 1961: page unknown.

———. "Player Chief Backs Negro Plan," *Chicago American,* 19 June 1961: page unknown.

———. "Players Take Up Color Bar Issue," *Chicago American,* 31 July 1961: 15.

———. "A Strange Tribe," *Pittsburgh Courier,* 11 May 1938: page unknown.

_____. Undated Manuscript, Wendell Smith Papers, Cooperstown, NY: National Baseball Hall of Fame Library (MSB 1), no date.

_____. "What a Negro Ballplayer Faces Today in Training," *Chicago American,* 3 April 1961: 16.

The Sporting News, 9 Sept. 1956, quoted in: Briley, Ron. "Ten Years After: The Baseball Establishment, Race, and Jackie Robinson," 137.

Tygiel, Jules. *Baseball's Great Experiment, Jackie Robinson and His Legacy.* New York: Vintage, 1983.

Tygiel, Jules. "The Great Experiment Fifty Years Later." *The Cooperstown Symposium on Baseball and American Culture, 1997.* Ed. Peter Rutkoff. Jefferson, NC: McFarland. 257-270.

Whiteside, Larry. "Smith Helped Get the Ball Rolling: Black Sportswriter to be Honored by Hall," *The Boston Globe,* 25 July 1994: 37.

Wiggins, David. "Wendell Smith, the Pittsburgh *Courier-Journal* and the Campaign to Include Blacks in Organized Baseball," *Journal of Sport History* 10.2 (Summer 1983): 5-29.

6

Creating Home with the Ball Field: The Dynamics of Baseball and Civic Inclusivity for Germans, Irishmen, and Blacks During the Late Nineteenth Century

Kevin J. Grzymala

The Multiethnic Evolution of Baseball

Organized baseball's proponents have long boasted of the sport's heritage of inclusiveness, whereby members of various ethnic groups essentially became American folk through partaking of the "National Game" either as players or as spectators. A cursory listing of baseball luminaries—Mike Kelly and John McGraw, Napoleon Lajoie and Jean Dubuc, Babe Ruth and Lou Gehrig, Hank Greenberg and Sandy Koufax, Al Simmons and Carl Yastrzemski, Jackie Robinson and Henry Aaron—stirs romantic sentiments about the egalitarian, edifying nature of the game, painting it as a genuinely virtuous artifact of Americana ready for packaging and posting to more acrimonious peoples in need of a cultural panacea. The critical rays of close examination, however, burn off such mawkish fog and uncover a far more convoluted picture of the interfaces between the artifact and its aficionados, the game and its fans. When the sons of Irish and German immigrants embraced baseball, they did so among themselves and through their own organizations, most notably churches, political ward groups, fraternal orders, and trade unions. City streets made vibrant through tools engaged in artisans' shops, brass-band music penetrating saloon doorways, and ubiquitous parading became even more so as rival ballclubs entertained fellow ethnics and helped to create a communal atmosphere within newcomers' neighborhoods. Baseball nurtured through an exclusivity of choice, however, formed only one branch of the game's development, while a more nefarious exclusivity of imposition formed another branch, the cross of racial prejudice affixed to the staunch shoulders of African Americans. Yet there were precious moments when the era's escalating racism was challenged by African-American men who dared to become ballplayers, intimating once again that baseball was more than just another pastime.

Yet, as evidence from the nineteenth-century commercial metropolis of Buffalo, New York, suggests, Germans, Irishmen, and blacks appropriated the pastime of baseball in very different ways, the distinctiveness based as much upon their jobs, their leisure traditions, and their relationships with the surrounding native-born community as upon spoken language and skin color. By playing and watching baseball, immigrants and their children were taking part in an important civic act, one full of symbolic meaning, which in many ways conferred a brand of citizenship more legitimate than any procured through courthouse naturalization proceedings. When the all-German Union Base Ball Club challenged the all-Irish Travelers Base Ball Club to a match game in 1875 on the Parade, one anchor in the newly created city park system, something more than a baseball game was taking place. Ethnic rivals, whose predecessors once battled each other with fists and clubs at picnic grounds and on disputed city byways, found a new way to interact, so that the baseball diamond became a sort of middle ground where one's manhood could be tested and where new identities could be molded from material uniquely American. That understanding was lost on none of that contest's participants or onlookers.

African-American men, too, used their limited resources as service sector employees and neighborhood residents to build competent, well-stocked ball clubs, and because of their workplace positions in a tourist center, they were able to secure a foothold in the entertainment industry known as semipro baseball. On Independence Day of 1889, the African-American Buffalo Stars lost the opening game of a single-elimination tournament to one of their league's white rivals, the Excelsiors, the tournament's eventual champion. But that defeat meant less than the victory they had claimed simply by participating. By the late nineteenth century, baseball games on the

July 4th holiday had become a national tradition, grand civic events, and participating in them, not just as observers but as fielders, pitchers, and hitters, elevated one's status in the eyes of onlookers. African Americans craved moments like these, ones which allowed them to demonstrate their abilities, their manhood, which the larger culture did its best to deny. The ball fields of western New York became some of the proving grounds for African-American acceptance into the broader society, venues where black men demanded to be recognized as Americans by donning the uniform of America's game.

Indeed, the evolution of baseball in nineteenth-century Buffalo was a multiethnic phenomenon. Native-born men of Yankee descent introduced bat-and-ball games to the Niagara Frontier and nurtured them into the organized club sports of townball and baseball. Men of Scottish descent arranged for the settling of the often-disputed city championship at their annual Caledonian athletic games of the 1870s. The Irish from the First and Eighth Wards were instrumental in the formation of the city's first baseball leagues, products of their eviction from the city parks for causing excessive turf damage while playing baseball during prolonged periods of unemployment and bluntly informing park officials what they could do with their remonstrances. German speakers and their children played ball at summergardens amid the bombast of brass instruments, the flow of lager beer, the crash of kegeling pins, and the euphony of group singing. African-American waiters, porters, and day laborers played against touring national black teams in the late 1860s, competed with their rivals from other hotels in the early 1880s, and fielded a team to participate in the multiethnic, semipro West Side League in 1889 and 1891. The tales of all these men merit telling so as to uncover that mosaic which people fashioned in the process of earning a living, raising a family, paying a mortgage, and gathering with kith and kin, the mosaic we refer to as American history. Discerning those voices requires a glimpse into the municipal crucible in which they were forged, the Queen City of the Great Lakes.

Formative Steps

Buffalo's favorable geographic location figured prominently in its growth from provincial outpost to commercial boomtown. Situated at the head of the continuously navigable portion of the Great Lakes, it was chosen as the site for the western terminus of the Erie Canal. Through this inland port passed manufactured goods and immigrants destined for settlements due westward as well as grains from the farmlands of the old northwest which were transshipped to eastern urban and European markets or stored at Buffalo in huge elevators in anticipation of higher future prices. Tens of thousands of German-speaking and Irish immigrants found the location attractive, the former for the opportunity to ply trades under assault in European villages and the cities along the Atlantic seaboard, the latter for the abundance of unskilled jobs associated with the canal trade, and both for the expanding construction industry which promised informal apprenticeships to all willing temporarily to play the "go for." With the constant influx of European newcomers, relatively homogenous ethnic neighborhoods blanketed the cityscape, the German speakers fanning out eastward from the central business district, the Irish settling to the south and along the canal. The residents of these neighborhoods, however, were not the city's first ballplayers. That honor belonged to the native-born men of Yankee descent.

Townball and baseball clubs began to form in 1857, the preeminent of the latter being the Niagara Base Ball Club, primarily an elite men's social club consisting of between sixty and seventy members who participated in the emerging creed of rational recreation by dividing themselves into "nines," or teams, and engaging in "the high-old-game of Base Ball." Social clubs like the Niagaras were composed of clerks, professionals, students, and the sons of influential businessmen, who used club membership as opportunities for joyous physical recreation away from the office and as mechanisms to meet or consort with others of similar backgrounds or social aspirations, something which became increasingly essential to material advancement in urban life. They embraced baseball instead of wrestling or boxing, two equally common activities in the neighboring countryside and canal district, because baseball held the promise of respectable recreation, something which comported well with the intellectual stimulation offered by the Young Men's Association or the spiritual edification received at St. Paul's Episcopal Church. James B. Bach and Richard Oliver, one-time members of the famed Brooklyn Excelsiors, relocated to Buffalo and urged members of the newly-formed Niagaras to adopt the rules and bylaws of the downstate club, rules that included nine players per side, bases placed ninety feet apart, infielders situated at the bases, and the use of a diamond-shaped field, so as to distinguish themselves from the growing bevy of clubs that engaged in townball, a much older bat-and-ball pastime played on a U-shaped field without distinguishing fair from foul territory; the "one-out, side-out" inning format reigned on the more congested townball fields, at least one local variety permitting fifteen men per squad. Their efforts proved so successful that soon other clubs copied their methods, and baseball and townball thrived side by side until events at Fort Sumter summoned a reconsideration of priorities.

Certainly the Irish and Germans played some type of ball games in their antebellum neighborhoods when the time, opportunity, and inclination permitted them to do so. One-time patrolman John J. Gainey from Precinct #7 reminisced about two such bat-and-ball games which were still played in the city's ethnic neighborhoods in 1866 prior to the embrace of the "New York Game," the expression used by the day's purists to distinguish baseball from the many versions of townball played in almost every locality. They were Town's Licker and Dutch Long. The former used four bases, a catcher, a pitcher, as many fielders as each team desired, and "two batsmen in," but no basemen; upon striking the ball, the hitter was safe at first unless struck with the fielded ball while en route to the base. These were the rules for townball, though the configuration of the field remains a mystery. Dutch Long was considered an "improvement" on Town's Licker, since rather than soaking the batter to obtain an out, "if a player got the ball and threw it across the line" prior to the batter reaching first base, he was declared out. Any hits caught on the fly or first hop also retired the batter. Interestingly, the term "Dutch" was a common nineteenth-century corruption of *Deutsch,* so the temptation exists to dub Dutch Long as part of the premodern cultural baggage Germans transplanted in North American soil. Unfortunately, the era's newspapers and personal narratives provide no evidence to substantiate such a conjecture. It seems more likely that the Irish dismissed the native-born baseball players as fops or an effete elite whose drudgery they performed on the docks for a pittance; fistfighting, wenching, and carousing more readily fit their working-class notion of manliness. For the Germans, political considerations superseded those of baseball, as nativism swept through northern cities as part of the larger tumult involving states rights and slavery. Their preeminent athletes were to be found in the *Turnvereine,* or German gymnastic societies, which sought to inculcate courage, strength, and agility through systematic calisthenics; to them, baseball seemed an illegitimate cousin to lectures, debates, and essay writing contests, all of which sought to nurture a critical intellectual spirit toward authoritarianism in church and government. It was, instead, wartime sacrifices that prompted the peacetime appropriation of baseball by Germans and Irishmen: by enduring homefront inflation, material shortages, chronic bivouac boredom, and battlefield carnage, these immigrants and their sons purchased an indelible place in the American fabric. The formation of all-German and all-Irish baseball clubs became a postbellum imperative.

From Schlagball to Baseball

Germans arrived in America with an appreciation of play, recreation, and exercise as part of their European folk tradition and, once here, continuously battled puritanical, teetotaling elements who held an ideological bias against this triumvirate of gaiety, perceiving such frivolities as currying the Lord's wrath and as evidence of lost control in the new urban environment. Baseball fit securely within this tradition of active recreation. During the antebellum years, Buffalo's Germans first encountered baseball while attending picnics sponsored by churches and fraternal societies at the Cold Spring, a favorite bucolic haunt of native-born ballplayers and volunteer firemen who often struck up impromptu ballgames during the usually raucous election campaigns or on the Independence Day holiday. Military service brought German men still greater familiarity with baseball, as the nearly 200,000 Teutonic soldiers who served with the Union forces witnessed the game often played during encampments to keep up soldiers' spirits and preparedness. Initially the German-language press referred to baseball as *Schlagball,* using the verb *schlagen* (to hit or strike) as the root word and essence of the game German-speaking reporters were observing, rather than the more conventional name signifying advancement from base to base; when the term "baseball" was used, it was usually placed in quotation marks, implying its relative newness to the Germans reporting the activity or else the reincarnation of a folk game with which they were familiar while residing in Europe, sort of a Germanic variation of rounders. Either way, baseball quickly found its way to the most hallowed of German institutions, the saloon.

Between 1868 and 1880, over 75 percent of the teams in which German Americans made up a majority of the players or team officers, usually ballplayers themselves, were connected in some way with breweries, saloons, and their unlicensed equivalents, the ubiquitous groceries. Only three of these clubs were connected with a *Verein,* the German version of a voluntary association, whose quarters they certainly used for socializing; therefore, lacking necessary funds to lease clubrooms of their own, the remainder resorted to saloons and groceries as their clubhouses. Alcohol establishments played equally prominent roles in the formation of the early German athletic clubs, bowling teams, and rifle-shooting matches, ensuring that King Gambrinius, the mirthful creator of beer celebrated in Teutonic folklore, reigned nobly throughout the German sporting world. Most of these baseball "clubs" were simply teams and short-lived ones at that, lasting between one and three years. Unlike the early teams of native-born Americans, the overwhelming majority of players on these initial German baseball teams were tradesmen, especially carpenters, machinists, and printers, though clerks did appear on several teams. They were organized according to street or neighborhood of residence, political affiliation, and common workplace and were stocked almost exclusively with men bearing German surnames. This embrace of baseball by German craftsmen gave them one more outlet for continuing their performed culture of rituals and physical activities, which historically included singing, parades, bowling, and gymnastics. In this sense it served the essential function of group cohesion among German workingmen, whose ranks were replenished throughout the remainder of the century by more immigrants, giving ethnic workers a new civic act to perform, a sporting corollary to the ballot box, further indicating their inclusion in American society.

It was the workingman's pastime which became the child's obsession. Published excerpts from police blotters and injury reports tell of the magnitude of ballplaying that took place on city streets contrary to the will of the Common Council, the municipality's supreme legislative body. Newspapers railed that street games were dangerous to passersby, destructive to property, and just a general nuisance, requiring more arrests to ensure compliance with the law; as years passed, Michael Roth, Georg Christ, Georg Turner, Joseph Getheger, Julius

Keppner, and Charles Schultz would be arrested for this infraction, the final duo compounding their misdemeanor by doing so on the Sabbath. Common baseball injuries, such as black eyes, "wry noses," dislocated fingers, and "internal abscesses," were endured by these fellows as badges of incipient manhood, a tremendously important issue for adolescents. Wartime reminiscences were perceived as the incessant droning of elders, reminders to the born-too-late generation of the many sacrifices endured by elders for the benefit of posterity, whose penance was to endure exaggerated rehashings of glory days; the sight of lame and maimed veterans reinforced feelings of inadequacy in adolescents. Baseball allowed them to step upon a battlefield of their own and gain the glory which a late birth had earlier denied them.

The ardor of youngsters for baseball troubled some advocates of ethnic group solidarity, leading to generational conflict or, at least, generational confusion. The Buffalo *Turnverein* sought to develop in German youth "a sound mind in a sound body," but garnered little success. The preference of German-American youth for baseball over the rigors of systematic exercise, including sets on the horizontal and parallel bars, vaulting horse, and rings, is easy to understand. Gymnastics were regimented, overseen by adults, and only the German language could be spoken on the exercise grounds, while baseball was more akin to play, organized by the players themselves, and demanded no language requirement. The language of the streets was English, and the preeminent game on those streets was baseball; for German-American males the choice was not a difficult one to make. Policymakers within the local *Turnverein* recognized this penchant among the young and incorporated baseball into their society life. The active gymnasts within the organization formed their own baseball teams in the late 1870s, and the association's gymnastics instructor took his youngest pupils to a city park where, along with some calisthenics, they enjoyed boat rides and baseball games. The national game had become part of ethnic athletics. The Irish would take the lead in selling a top-flight brand of that commodity to fellow ethnics as visual entertainment.

Emeraldites, Broadswords, and Baseball

Categorizing newcomers as hyphenated Americans is fraught with problems, but the Germans and the Irish did integrate themselves into the broader American society as groups, not as individuals. This was especially the case in regard to politics where they advanced a diverse agenda of issues, such as bilingual language instruction in the public schools, licensing transit lines to extend service into their neighborhoods, denouncing Sunday blue laws, demanding unlimited liquor licensing, and paving and lighting their streets. In Buffalo, that agenda included the use of city parks for baseball games, instead of as resplendently cultivated ornaments where the citizenry could take refreshing evening strolls. The significance of baseball as a group activity Hibernians rings out in these battles over the proper uses of public space.

Baseball fever raged within and without Buffalo's ethnic neighborhoods during the 1870s, the athletic ague acutely afflicting the Irish. These southsiders, mostly the second- and third-generation sons of canal longshoremen, earned their keep through the more modern conveyance of the railroad, in expanding foundries and myriad finishing shops, and through political patronage positions. They fielded the city's finest ball clubs during the 1870s, though municipal supremacy had been in question throughout the decade, as the team which won a challenge match proclaimed itself the city champion only to see two other clubs undertake the same process with the victor making a similar boast. The Caledonian Society, an organization of men celebrating their shared Scottish heritage, provided the opportunity to settle the confusion in 1875 and 1876 by holding a series of championship games with the final two remaining clubs playing each other at the Scots' annual sporting festival, the baseball contest enhancing an already abundant program of ethnically-inspired track-and-field events, such as tossing the caber, heavy- and light-hammer throws, and the broadsword dance. All-Irish ball clubs, the Socials and the Travelers, finished either first or second in both tournaments. The transplanted Highlanders' efforts at determining a city champion proved ephemeral, though their involvement in baseball furthered the desire for interneighborhood competition, which many players and fans soon realized could only be maintained within a league framework, the structure receiving a further boost from Irish ballplayers' battles with civil authorities.

The development of the new municipal park system, undertaken by the renowned architectural firm of Olmstead and Vaux, designers of New York City's Central Park, also occurred during the turbulent 1870s. Park planners did not prohibit baseball games in the Queen

City's new trio of parks, but only restricted them to areas bearing a "common" sign, where baseball clubs had the privilege of playing on a portion of these grounds, and the authorities did mean "privilege," for prohibitive sentiment arose with the degree of turf damage incurred from consistent baseball practice. The economic collapse which followed the financial panic of 1873 struck especially hard upon common day laborers, meaning the Irish. Unable to procure jobs in the contracted local economy, Hibernians from the First and Eighth Wards honed their ballplaying skills, practically taking over the common areas of Front Park. Hoping to eliminate the ominous specter of "large numbers of idle youth of a class utterly regardless of park regulation, and not amenable to the courteous advice or directions of the keeper in charge of the grounds," the parks commissioners outlawed baseball at city parks frequented by the south-side Irish. The bounds of the permissible had been crossed, so the Irish removed their ballgames back to the First Ward. With the financial support of community businessmen and ward politicians, they secured their own grounds at Katherine and Sandusky Streets, and entertained neighborhood residents who watched the daring diamond doings from elevated sidewalks, the bleachers of the era, as the Socials, Travelers, Independents, and OK's continued to master the game.

Comfortably situated next to the Buffalo River, Irish ballplayers proceeded to form the city's first amateur baseball league in 1879, a short-lived venture still aimed at determining an indisputable city champion. The league's collapse failed to dishearten its organizers. They recognized the attachment of the citizenry to the Buffalos of the National League, dubbed the "Bisons" by local sports writers, and remained convinced that their league could acquire a share of the baseball entertainment market geared toward workers who were inured to dawn-till-dusk work regimens with the Sabbath as their lone day of rest. Since blue laws prohibited professional Sunday games until 1919, these Irish "amateurs" saw an untapped resource available for draining. Semipro baseball was born. Their next league blossomed, and its triumph bred imitation: by 1888, at least three semipro leagues operated in western New York, one of which was the West Side League, the first league in which local white ballplayers competed against local black ballplayers. These Hibernians unwittingly created an organizational structure whereby African Americans could gain a foothold at inclusion into the broader society. That their foothold was a temporary one, should not reduce the importance of their efforts.

An African-American Experience

Playing baseball afforded black men many of the same benefits it afforded white men: improved physical health through vigorous exercise; active recreation which temporarily eased the calluses of work; building bonds of friendship which could be parlayed into employment, courtship, or lodging opportunities; engaging in the national phenomenon of athleticism sweeping into the daily lives of men; and demonstrating one's maturity, one's manhood. It was essential to African-American men for still another reason: they could use baseball as an exercise in identity construction, in trying to demonstrate to others around them that they, too, were Americans, ones whose ancestors arrived here involuntarily, bound to labor for the benefit of their owners rather than for themselves and their families, but Americans all the same. Taking to the diamond was one way they asserted that claim.

Persistent racial prejudice usually limited African Americans to games in which they competed against one another, the marquee contests involving a local team against a more talented touring ballclub. In advertising a contest between "a colored club from Washington, DC" named the Mutuals and a local nine of African-American waiters, porters, and cooks, a white reporter quipped that the locals had been "slinging hash balls at Johnny Macs and the Tifft House lately, more than they have baseball," though he hoped the locals might give the visitors more than they could handle. They didn't: the Mutuals drubbed their hosts in this 1870 exhibition, 69-11. Earlier this same local club had fallen to another touring black team, the Fearless of Utica, New York, 88-18. Such lopsided scores indicate the newness of baseball as a recreational activity within the African-American community. Getting thrashed by competitors was not unique to the city's first black teams, as the first teams from Buffalo's German neighborhoods suffered similar blowouts in contests against their native-born opponents, 74-16, 64-17, and 62-14. However, these defeats never prompted ethnically based criticisms in the English-language press. One-sided contests were then, and remain still, an inevitable part of learning about baseball. Moreover, blowouts forged bonds of loyalty for the game, as the vanquished cherished some future moment when they would be the victor.

The size of the African-American community was relatively small in Buffalo, as it was in all cities bordering the Great Lakes, labor demand already being effectively met by European immigrants and their progeny. Those residing blacks had the choice of working in the service sector or battling the Irish for unskilled positions on the waterfront or with the railroads. They usually chose the former, not simply because it promised less bloodshed, but because blacks had already established a foothold in the city's hotels and restaurants. Summertime tourist demand for Lake Erie's cool breezes made the Queen City a mecca for wealthy tourists from the Atlantic seaboard, thereby helping to stimulate the construction of numerous hotels which African-American employees staffed. Their narrow occupational niche, working as butlers, cooks, barbers, porters, drivers, waiters, and day laborers, meant their baseball teams would originate from the same occupations, often from the same establishments. While vacationing in Buffalo, it was customary for visitors to frequent harness racing tracks, to go boating on the lake and Niagara River, or even to attend illegal, surreptitious prize fights held a brief ferry ride across the lake on Canadian soil; therefore, as black ball playing proficiency increased, the possibility of these athletes demonstrating those talents to entertainment-hungry spectators also increased, since hotel owners would seek to market the superiority of their venue's amenities over those of their competitors. The uniqueness of skillful black baseball games, if the enterprise proved to be a successful magnet for tourist interests, promised imitation by rival establishments and still more opportunities for blacks to become involved in the national game. Acceptance on the diamond seemed just a matter of time.

That time appeared to have come in 1889 when the all-black Buffalo Stars joined the semipro West Side League. The affiliated teams (the Excelsiors, Cold Springs, Diamond Kings, Richmonds, and Buffalo Stars) played on grounds adjacent to the Cross-Cut Junction House, a new sporting resort in north Buffalo co-owned by a laundry magnate and a saloon-owning boxer. Alternately they held boxing and wrestling matches, cycling contests, roller skating exhibitions, track and field events, and baseball games, the last of which averaged 2,000 to 3,000 beer-drinking, sandwich-eating fans per game. The press failed to provide box scores for league games, printing only occasional, brief summaries of a contest's high and low points. The Stars generally received favorable press, being referred to as "our well-known colored team," "the noted colored team," and "the colored champions," though newspapers are silent on just which other black teams they played to gain championship status. Nor was their playing venue restricted to Cross-Cut Junction, where the league had scheduled one contest each Sunday from May to November, all clubs being assured of two contests every three weeks. The Stars were free to play wherever they were invited, and they were invited to many places inside and outside of the city limits. Some of these invitations stemmed, no doubt, from the novelty of playing against a black ball club, but to reduce the matter to mere novelty distorts the far broader importance of baseball, where it functioned as entertainment, as civic icon, and as exercise in manly responsibility. Spectators craved top-flight contests, and African Americans joined in meeting that need.

The checkered league performance of the Stars matters far less than the manner in which they sought complete inclusion in American society, specifically by meeting the needs of others, nurturing local black baseball talent, and keeping their own league afloat. In response to the devastating Johnstown flood of 1889, officials of the West Side League organized an all-star benefit game against the powerful Casinos, the all-German club which had won the semipro Champion League the previous year, total gate receipts destined for the ravaged iron-and-steel city. The Stars' battery of pitcher Ed Thompson and catcher Lincoln Strong proved "very effective" in the five-inning, rain-shortened affair, as Thompson struck out seven Casinos en route to an 8-7 victory on their opponent's home field. In helping to raise disaster relief funds, African Americans exercised their civic responsibility, while the west-siders' victory heightened their prestige in the eyes of their more established, east-side rivals and also demonstrated to players and spectators alike that black ballplayers could excel when teamed with white ballplayers. To continue the process, however, they needed to improve the quality of their on-field performance, a requirement met structurally by developing their own junior amateur clubs from which to draw new talent. The Stars replenished their roster with players from the Eries and Black Diamonds, two all-black junior clubs composed of teenagers. Indeed, five of the Black Diamonds also played for the Stars, which indicates the relative youth of the Stars themselves and, by inference, the dearth of older, skillful black players residing in western New York. Improvement came gradually, so that by midseason of 1891, victorious forays to nearby townships coupled with fewer embarrassing losses in league play lifted the men's spirits, especially those of manager J. W. Mitchell.

No club member wore more hats than Mitchell. He corresponded with potential nonleague opponents, represented the Stars on the league's judiciary committee, and served as the president of the West Side League, the only time during the nineteenth century that an African American held that position in local baseball's administrative hierarchy. Along with his primary duty of communicating with Cross-Cut's owners about gate count and teams' shares of revenue, as league president he had to accomplish the difficult tasks of creating a peaceful environment during the usually raucous league contests, ensuring teams arrived for their scheduled contests so as not to alienate themselves from their customers, and, as an African American, tackling instances of institutional racial prejudice. Oftentimes the three issues overlapped, making effective action essential for the survival of the league and the continuation of integrated ballfields. The agenda's demands would have taxed the talents and patience of the most skillful administrator.

Neither the West Side League nor the Stars resurfaced in 1892. In fact, the only news of blacks' involvement with Buffalo baseball during the remaining years of the century was of contests between touring professional black teams and local white semipros. This dearth of documentation on local black ballplayers contrasts sharply with that of local ballplayers of German and Irish descent, whose names resound in published semipro box scores, lists of elected baseball club officers, and formal challenges to any taker within a designated cohort. All-ethnic teams continued to represent their home turf, but beginning in the late 1880s, team compositions became more ethnically varied, instigated by the determination to get the best available ballplayers so as to augment team strength and, at least for semipro ball, lure more paying customers to their grounds than to those of a rival league. German and Irish Americans experienced few restrictions based on ethnic background in regard to access to baseball facilities at all levels of the sport's hierarchy. For them, baseball's heritage of inclusiveness was genuine. For African Americans, however, the banjo strummed a more melancholy tune.

BIBLIOGRAPHY

The Society for American Baseball Research (SABR) maintains a large collection of essays on the relationship between race and ethnicity. These essays are more plentiful for the twentieth century than they are for the nineteenth century because the professional Negro Leagues generated a tremendous amount of interest in black America and, therefore, received considerable coverage in the African-American press. Furthermore, the aged voices of ex-Negro Leaguers have been recorded by passionate historians plying their trade at oral history. Such organizational aids are far fewer in number for the nineteenth century; consequently, newspapers on microfilm, records of city parks commissioners, and annual city directories remain the factual mines for uncovering the attachment of hyphenated Americans to the national game.

Any examination of African-Americans' attachment to baseball must begin with Sol White's *Official Base Ball Guide: History of Colored Base Ball and Robert Peterson's Only the Ball Was White: A History of the Legendary Black Players and All-Black Professional Teams*. In laying the foundation for the black professional game, they discuss the marquee clubs of the late-nineteenth century and the travails borne by black ballplayers and touring teams. The final section of Harold Seymour's *Baseball: The People's Game* also tackles the evolution of black baseball. David W. Zhang's *Fleet Walker's Divided Heart* addresses the pathos of the first black player in major league baseball.

The relationship between ethnicity and baseball is demonstrated in Peter Levine's *Ellis Island to Ebbets Field: Sport and the American Jewish Experience*, though the nineteenth century receives marginal coverage due to the relatively late arrival of immigrants from Eastern Europe. Melvin Adelman's *A Sporting Time: New York City and the Rise of Modern Athletics, 1820-70* and Steven A. Riess's *City Games: The Evolution of American Urban Society and the Rise of Sports* add baseball to the broader grouping of urban sports, addressing the consequences of ethnics' give-and-take with athletics. John Bodnar's *The Transplanted: A History of Immigrants in Urban America* suggests how sports were used by immigrant elites, particularly heads of fraternal orders, churches, and politicians, in securing the loyalty of second- and third-generation youths as well as of recent newcomers.

The significance of nineteenth-century sports in identity construction is developed in Ronald Story's "The Country of the Young: The Meaning of Baseball in Early American Culture," included in the *Cooperstown Symposium on Baseball and American Culture, 1989;* in Elliott Gorn's *The Manly Art: Bare-Knuckle Prize Fighting in America;* and in two books edited by J. A. Mangan, *Manliness and Morality: Middle-Class Masculinity in Britain and America, 1800-1940,* and *From 'Fair Sex' to Feminism: Sport and the Socialization of Women in the Industrial and Post-Industrial Eras.*

7

The Internet and the Popularization
of the Negro Leagues

Alar Lipping

The 1990s included a number of events that fueled a heightened popularization of baseball's past. The public was entertained with visual and oral accounts of baseball's historical development by Ken Burns's eighteen and one-half-hour documentary on baseball in 1994. The physical landscape of baseball took on a nostalgic complexion as new stadium openings ushered in the age of "retro ballparks," for example, Comiskey Park (April 18, 1991), Camden Yards (April 6, 1992), Jacobs Field (April 4, 1994), and Coors Field (April 26, 1995). In addition to retro fitted stadiums, the 1990s included several weeks of scheduled games that were conducted with players wearing uniforms of baseball's previous decades.

A major popular focus of baseball's past in the 1990s was the inclusion of the Negro Leagues. Ken Burns's baseball series included the developments of African Americans in baseball with the attendant social forces of racism. Popular exposure of the Negro Leagues was further advanced in 1997 during the year-long celebration of the fiftieth anniversary of Major League Baseball's integration. Events that portrayed visualization of the Negro Leagues during 1997 included the inauguration of the "Wall of Fame" at County Stadium, the previous home of the Milwaukee Brewers. The Wall of Fame was established to dedicate the achievements of Negro League baseball players by displaying their names within the confines of the stadium. In 1997 eight Negro League stars were honored. Sam Jethroe, Buck Leonard, Cowan Hyde, Ted Radcliffe, Verdell "Lefty" Mathis, Josh Johnson, Monte Irvin, and William "Bobbie" Robinson were the first inductees to have their achievements exposed at County Stadium. Included in baseball's retro uniform games of the 1990s were several games depicting regalia of the Negro Leagues; for example, the Kansas City Royals were outfitted in Monarchs' uniforms on several occasions.

Mass media played a significant role in exposing the awareness of the Negro Leagues in the 1990s. Television and newspapers provided the traditional means to engage popular interest in the Negro Leagues, but another form of mass media emerged in the 1990s to help popularize baseball. In 1993, the Internet came of age for mass consumption when Marc Andressen and his team at the National Center for Supercomputing Applications at the University of Illinois at Urbana-Champaign developed the first graphical browser, Mosaic. Later Andressen became the driving force behind Netscape.

By the mid-1990s baseball Web sites on the Internet had mushroomed. To provide a catalog of these Web sites, Rob Edelman published *Baseball on the Web* in 1998. Edelman's text provides a useful reference to baseball-related sources on the Internet, and the sites are categorized in twenty-five groups including baseball history of players and teams, baseball in literature and the arts, museums and halls of fame, minor and independent leagues, amateur baseball, baseball humor, baseball fantasy, newsgroups, and the Negro Leagues. The Internet sites dealing with the history of baseball disproportionately focus on promoting nostalgia in the form of brief biographies of teams and players, collections of photographs and artifacts, statistical data, and chronological timelines of baseball events without interpreting the historical context of these events in regard to social, political, and economic forces in society at large. However, careful selection of sites and organization of these sites can provide a convenient means to gain knowledge about the Negro Leagues. In addition, the utilization of online photographs, artifacts, and audio interviews can provide an effective backdrop to the historical analysis of baseball history.

In locating sources on the Internet one is always confronted with searching, evaluating, and selecting useful sites. This is indeed the case when locating sites dealing with the historical accounts of the Negro Leagues. A search on this topic will bring up a number of sites that primarily focus on marketing Negro League memorabilia or sites that provide very brief nostalgic descriptions of Negro League players or teams. Another problem with using Internet sites is that of mortality. Many sites, particularly non-institutional sites, are short lived. For instance, among the seventeen history of Negro League related sites documented in Edelman's text, seven were no longer active as of three years after publication of his text. Even with existing sites there is the occasional problem of maintaining the site. Some sites are left unattended and as a result many of the links have become inactive, which can become a frustrating experience for the user. The purpose of this paper is to present Internet sites that make some meaningful contribution to learning about the history of the Negro Leagues; that are periodically updated; and that have exhibited longevity of at least two years. Hopefully, the following sources, some of which were developed after the publication of Edelman's text, can serve as useful resources for purposes of research, teaching, or self-enlightenment regarding the Negro Leagues.

Journal of Sport History Online
www.aafla.org

The online version of the *Journal of Sport History* is maintained by the Amateur Athletic Foundation of Los Angeles. Select "virtual archive" and then select "Journal of Sport History." This site includes full text articles, book reviews, and film reviews published in the *Journal of Sport History* as well as conference proceedings of the North American Society for Sport History. All files on this site are in Portable Document Format (pdf) and can be downloaded with Acrobat Reader. This is an extremely useful site to gather in-depth articles on the historical analysis of sport written by professional sport historians. For a critical examination of the conduct of historical research on baseball, see Larry R. Gerlach, "Not Quite Ready for Prime Time: Baseball History, 1983-1993." Gerlach provides a section on historical research on the professional Negro Leagues (121-126). For studies examining the social context of race relations and the integration of baseball, see David K. Wiggins, "Wendell Smith, the Pittsburgh Courier-Journal and the Campaign to Include Blacks in Organized Baseball, 1933-1945"; William Simons, "Jackie Robinson and the American Mind: Journalistic Perceptions of the Reintegration of Baseball"; Chris Lamb, "'I Never Want to Take Another Trip Like This One': Jackie Robinson's Journey to Integrate Baseball"; Richard I. Kimball, "'Beyond the Great Experiment': Integrated Baseball Comes to Indianapolis"; and Larry R. Gerlach, "Baseball's Other 'Great Experiment': Eddie Kelp and the Integration of the Negro Leagues." Aaron Baker's "Sports Films, History, and Identity" provides an in-depth examination of two popular films depicting the integration of major league baseball: *The Jackie Robinson Story* (1950) and *Soul of the Game* (1996). For a review of two documentary films dealing with the Negro Leagues, see William J. Baker, "Kings and Diamonds: Negro League Baseball in Film." For critical commentary on Ken Burns's *Baseball* documentary, see Steven A. Riess, "The Early Innings"; Larry R. Gerlach's documentation of over 100 mistakes in the film, *The Final Three Innings;* and Jules Tygiel's review of some of the historical inaccuracies regarding Burns's coverage of Jackie Robinson and the integration of baseball, "Ken Burns Meets Jackie Robinson."

The Library of Congress
http://www.loc.gov

Select "American Memory" on the Library of Congress home page; then select "collection finder," "Recreation and Sports," and finally "Baseball and Jackie Robinson." This site, developed in October 1998, includes highlights of baseball and the topic of African-American involvement in baseball. This site is organized according to the time periods 1860s-1890s, 1900s-1930s, 1940-1946, 1947-1956, and 1957-1972. This site includes text, photos, and artifacts. Among the artifacts from the Library of Congress Collection are a transcript of the speech made by Branch Rickey for the "One Hundred Percent Wrong Club" banquet, Atlanta, Georgia, January 20, 1956, in which Rickey describes the problems he faced in the 1940s when he decided to integrate major league baseball; a letter from Jackie Robinson to Branch Rickey, July 13, 1946, in which Robinson informed Rickey of his agreement to play for the Kansas City Monarchs; and a multipage program guide between the Indianapolis Clowns and Kansas City Monarchs, July 21, 1954, with photos of Buck O'Neil, the Monarchs in action, and female stars of the Negro Leagues. This site also includes an annotated bibliography with Library of Congress call numbers and ISBNs of various sources dealing with the Negro Leagues.

The National Baseball Hall of Fame and Museum
http://baseballhalloffame.org

This site includes brief biographies of Hall of Fame inductees, among them eighteen Negro leaguers (Negro League stars were first inducted in 1971). The Research Library includes three useful sources: (1) the Abner Library Catalog has eighty-two entries of books dealing with the Negro Leagues (call numbers are provided); (2) under Selective Bibliographies there are forty-four book titles and 147 journal articles dealing with Jackie Robinson; and (3) Archival Finding Aids and Inventories, Wendell Smith Papers. Wendell Smith played a significant role in the desegregation of professional baseball. Beginning in 1937, he accepted a position at the *Pittsburgh Courier.* After a year, Smith was appointed sports editor. Smith campaigned for the integration of major league baseball, and in 1945 he arranged a meeting with Branch Rickey to discuss the integration of baseball. Although this site does not include a digitized collection of his papers it does provide a biographical sketch of Wendell Smith and description of the papers. The collection itself is housed in one archival box; although not comprehensive, the papers do contain correspondence from 1945 to 1949, including letters among Smith, Branch Rickey, and Jackie Robinson. In addition, there are newspaper clippings from 1943 through 1961.

The Jackie Robinson Society
http://www.utexas.edu/students/jackie/index.html

This site was developed in February 1997 by a student organization at the University of Texas. This site includes interviews about Jackie Robinson with Carl Erskine, former Brooklyn Dodger pitcher, and Branch Rickey III, grandson of Branch Rickey. Also available is President Clinton's speech delivered on April 15, 1997, during a Mets-Dodgers game as part of the celebration of the fiftieth anniversary of the integration of baseball. This site includes an image gallery of Jackie Robinson.

Negro Baseball Leagues
http://www.blackbaseball.com

This site is intended to be the most informational and entertaining resource on the Internet for information pertaining to the Negro Baseball Leagues. Baseball content is provided by James A. Riley, Director of Research at the Negro Leagues Baseball Museum. This site includes brief biographies of players, team histories, and articles about the Negro Leagues. Included are monthly items from the Negro Leagues Committee of the Society for Baseball Research (SABR).

Negro League Baseball Dot Com
http://www.negroleaguebaseball.com

This site provides a list of articles devoted to Negro League players and teams. A discussion forum is provided to exchange information on the Negro Leagues.

The Sporting News
http://www.sportingnews.com/archives/jackie.html

Includes story files: selected articles from the *Sporting News* during Jackie Robinson's career (total of sixteen articles). Also there are photo files: twenty-three photos of Jackie Robinson; a Negro Leaguers photo gallery: photos and story lines of Negro League players who were alive in 1997 when this collection was compiled; and a World Series file including an archive of Jackie Robinson in the World Series (1947, 1949, 1952, 1953, 1955, 1956), a description of his accomplishments and a review of his stats for each World Series.

CBS Sportsline
http://www.cbs.sportsline.com

This site calls for a little navigation: at the home page select "MLB," then "History/Records." Scroll to "Destinations" and select "Online Library." At the library there is a link to "Negro Leaguers." This site provides biographies of ninety-three Negro League players.

Negro Leagues Baseball Museum
http://www.nlbm.com

The Negro Leagues Baseball Museum opened in Kansas City, Missouri, in January 1991. The exhibits in the museum occupy 10,000 square feet. This site provides information about the exhibits as well as a museum store. Under "General History and Research" is a listing of the leagues and a listing of teams by region.

David Marasco's Diamond Angle
http://www.thediamondangle.com/marasco

This site is maintained by one of the staff writers of *Diamond Angle,* an "eclectic baseball journal" published in Hawaii. This site includes twenty-four articles published by Marasco. These articles deal with various aspects of Negro League baseball. In addition to Negro League baseball, this site has resources dealing with Caribbean baseball and Asian-American baseball.

National Archives and Records Administration
http://www.archives.gov

This site provides educational sources relating Jackie Robinson to the Civil Rights movement. It includes links to the Civil Rights movement and nine original letters sent by Jackie Robinson to the White House.

Jackie Robinson: A Baseball Celebration
http://www.nytimes.com/specials/baseball/robinson-index.html

This site includes *New York Times* articles about Robinson that appeared in 1997 during the fiftieth anniversary of Robinson breaking baseball's color line. Included are archival photos of Robinson from *The New York Times* collection and brief audios from Duke Snider, Rachel Robinson, Hank Aaron, and James Baldwin.

BIBLIOGRAPHY

Baker, Aaron. "Sports Films, History, and Identity." *Journal of Sport History* 25 (1998): 217-233. 5 April 2001,<http://www.aafla.org>.

Baker, William J. "Kings and Diamonds: Negro League Baseball in Film." *Journal of Sport History* 25 (1998): 303-308. 2 March 2001, <http://www.aafla.org>.

Edelman, Rob. *Baseball on the Web*. New York: MIS Press, 1998.

Gerlach, Larry R. "Not Quite Ready for Prime Time: Baseball History, 1983-1993." *Journal of Sport History* 21 (1994): 103-137, <http://www.aafla.org>.

Gerlach, Larry R. "Baseball's Other 'Great Experiment': Eddie Kelp and the Integration of the Negro Leagues." *Journal of Sport History* 25 (1998): 453-481. 3 April 2001, <http://www.aafla.org>.

Kimball, Richard I. " 'Beyond the Great Experiment': Integrated Baseball Comes to Indianapolis." *Journal of Sport History* 26.1 (1999): 142-162.

Lamb, Chris. " 'I Never Want to Take Another Trip Like This One': Jackie Robinson's Journey to Integrate Baseball." *Journal of Sport History* 24 (1997): 177-191. 3 March 2001, <http://www.aafla.org>.

Riess, Steven A. "The Early Innings." *Journal of Sport History* 23.1 (1996): 63-68.

Simons, William. "Jackie Robinson and the American Mind: Journalistic Perceptions of the Reintegration of Baseball." *Journal of Sport History* 12 (1985): 39-64. 3 March 2001, <http://www.aafla.org>.

Wiggins, David K. "Wendell Smith, the Pittsburgh Courier-Journal and the Campaign to Include Blacks in Organized Baseball, 1933-1945." *Journal of Sport History* 10 (1983): 5-29. 14 February 2001, <http://www.aafla.org>.

8

Baseball and Blacks: A Loss of Affinity, a Loss of Community

David C. Ogden

Introduction

Buxton, Iowa, has disappeared from the map. The once vibrant town of 9,000 in the south central part of the Hawkeye State was built around the mines of the Consolidation Coal Company. At its height between 1905 and 1920, Buxton touted a YMCA, men's lodges, numerous civic organizations, and at least eight churches. One of the town's greatest points of pride, however, was its all-black baseball team, the Buxton Wonders (Beran 90-92).

Half of Buxton's population was African American. Although black and white coal miners worked side by side and there was little racial strife, unlike other areas of the state and nation, African Americans carved out a distinct ethnic community. The Wonders were an important part of that community's identity and played teams throughout the Midwest. "The Buxton Wonders were considered the terror of the diamond and had a tremendous following. The skill and playing style resulted in large crowds at hometown games. They regularly played on weekend afternoons and evenings" (Beran 90). But the Wonders and Buxton lasted only as long as the coal vein. By 1925 the coal supply dwindled and the Consolidation Coal Company moved its operations elsewhere. The town's population moved with it, and the prairie reclaimed the Wonder's baseball diamond.

Today, diamonds in other African-American communities are also silent. Just as Buxton and its Wonders have faded from maps and memories, baseball has seemed to fade from today's African-American communities throughout the Midwest. Research has shown that even in cities such as Omaha, Nebraska, and Kansas City, Kansas, which have large African-American communities, few black youths are playing baseball at its highest levels of competition (Ogden, "African Americans and Pick-Up Ball" 201-204). Baseball's role for African-American communities in the 1920s, 1930s, and 1940s was a far cry from the role the sport serves today in those communities.

Baseball and African-American Communities

Buxton was a microcosm of the relationship between black baseball teams and their communities. Buxton was not the only town where "the viewing stand would be packed" on game days. "Black teams were points of enormous pride in black communities all over segregated America" (Ward and Burns 244). Former Kansas City Monarch player Sammie Haynes remembered the affection and support Kansas City had for his team. "You'd walk right by the stands and everybody knew your name and you'd talk to them before the game and after the game. And the fans looked at the guys in our league as heroes" (Ward and Burns 244).

The roots of black professional baseball can be traced to the 1880s, to one of the first notable teams, the Cuban Giants. That team was formed in 1885 in Long Island (Peterson 34-35). Over the next few decades baseball became the primary spectator sport for blacks (Early 28). It wasn't just professional baseball that drew crowds and captured the imagination of black communities. Games pitting St. Louis' two black high schools, Vashon and Sumner, were considered among the major sporting events in that area during the 1930s. "Even players from the St. Louis Stars, the black professional team in the area, came out to watch" (Early 48).

In Chicago in the late 1930s and 1940s, the Negro League's East-West All-Star Game drew 50,000 spectators. As with the crowds at Buxton Wonders games, spectators at the All-Star Game wore "their Sunday best. . . . It was the place to see and be seen" (Skluzacek 269). In 1942, Negro League games drew an estimated two million spectators (Rader 145). By the end of World War II, the Negro Leagues were grossing two million dollars annually and had become one of the nation's largest black-owned industries (Chalberg 90).

Almost sixty years later, African-Americans' support of and interest in baseball have substantially declined. Evidence of that decline can be found in who watches the game and who plays the game. An examination of attendance at major league games, percentage of major leaguers and college players who are African American, and youth participation in "select" baseball indicates a lost affinity for baseball by African Americans.

Watching the Game

According to *Ebony* magazine, approximately 6 percent of those who passed through the turnstiles of Major League games in the early 1990s were African American (Leavy 37). By 1997, that attendance dropped to 5 percent (Melcher 8). For the Kansas City Royals, African-American spectators are scarcer. Surveys in 1997 and 1998 showed that blacks comprised less than 3 percent of the attendance at Kauffman Stadium (Flanagan C2). Such figures have baseball marketing executives, such as the Royals' Mike Levy, stymied. "For whatever reason," he said, "baseball is not getting that minority in the stands on a frequent basis" (Flanagan C2).

Some speculate that African Americans no longer attend games because they feel baseball lacks action, compared with such sports as basketball, and that attending a baseball game no longer evokes a sense of community. Bob Kendrick, director of marketing for the Negro Leagues Baseball Museum, carries such explanations a step farther. He said black attendance declined with the Negro Leagues and their players. "The Negro Leagues officially ended in 1960," he noted.

> And there was a carryover effect after that of blacks going to major league games to follow those players from the Negro Leagues. But when those players from the Negro Leagues finished their careers, the number of black fans began to taper off. (Flanagan C2)

Kendrick observed that a decreasing number of black players has translated to a decreasing number of black spectators; that trend is likely to continue, based on the number of African Americans playing the game.

Playing the Game

The pipeline for African Americans in baseball is constricting, a phenomenon evidenced by the percentage of African Americans at various levels of play, from youth baseball to the major leagues. The percentage of players in Major League Baseball has continued to drop through the 1990s. In 1998, 15 percent of major league players were black, the lowest such percentage in the 1990s (Lapchick 7). That percentage was down from a decade-high of 19 percent in 1995 and the all-time high of 25 percent in 1974 (Johnson 2). Only one African American could be found on the 1999 opening day roster of the Kansas City Royals, and the same held true for the New York Yankees (Gomez A1).

At the college level the percentage of African Americans in the NCAA Division I player ranks is even lower than at the professional level. In 1997 blacks comprised three percent of Division I players, a drop of more than one percent since 1992 (Lapchick 8). Among baseball players at the Pac-10 schools, 4 percent are African American. University of California outfielder Curtis Johnson said the lack of African-American peers makes his playing experience "frustrating. . . . It's hard to deal with when you look around and don't see any others" (Boivin A28).

The percentage of African-American players at the high school level is no better. During the summer of 2001 the rosters of American Legion varsity baseball teams in Omaha contained few blacks. Of the seven Legion varsity high school teams and the 107 players on those teams, six (or 5.6 percent) were African American, according to *Omaha World Herald* sports reporter Cliff Brunt. Overall, almost 30 percent of Omaha high school students are African American, said Brunt. It's not been determined whether similar disparities exist between high school baseball players and the general high school populations in other Midwestern cities. But in Phoenix, Arizona, South Mountain High School, where 25 percent of the students are African American, has only one black player on its baseball team. Exacerbating the situation is the elimination of baseball programs by many inner-city high schools (McKinley 48).

The prospects of increasing the percentages of black players at the high school and college levels, at least with African-American youths from the Midwest, seem slim. Research during the summers of 2000 and 2001 in the Midwest showed few African Americans entering the pipeline at the highest levels of competition in youth baseball. Those levels are primarily the domain of "select" teams. Unlike the usual "Little League" teams, where anyone gets to play regardless of skill level, select teams acquire players via tryouts and enlist only those who display the greatest skills. In some cases, players may circumvent the tryout process and be individually chosen because of ability demonstrated in another league or through personal contact. Select teams are often composed of one age group, usually between nine and fourteen years old. Some of these teams serve as incubators for nurturing talent for their local high school teams. Others are managed or coordinated by parents who hope to see their sons play in college or even at the professional levels. Such teams usually play an average of seventy to eighty games each summer, with some teams playing as many as 130.

In the Midwest, numbers of African-American youths on select teams are not commensurate with the numbers in the general population. A survey in 2000 of fifty Midwest select teams (with players twelve to fourteen years old) showed that eight of the 624 players on those teams, or 1.3 percent, were African American. In the communities from which the teams drew its players, 14 percent of the youths under eighteen years of age are African American, according to U.S. Census figures for 2000. A survey in 2001 of seventy-eight Midwest select teams with 807 players showed that seventeen, or 2.1 percent, were African American.

Such small percentages of blacks playing youth ball may not be restricted to the Midwest or to select ball. In Phoenix a "steady decline" occurred in participation by African Americans in Little League baseball (Boivin A28), and nationwide only three percent of "frequent" Little League players are black (Edmondson 37).

Said former Oakland Athletics pitcher and Toronto Blue Jays executive Dave Stewart:

> I think black kids look at baseball and ask, "Why should I invest the time and effort into a sport where the players who look like me are so few?" You look at baseball and you do not see a lot of black faces in the seats and you definitely don't see them on the field. As a black kid, why should you be encouraged to play baseball? (Gomez A1)

Why Baseball Has Left Black Communities

Dave Stewart is not alone in pointing to the lack of role models as an issue related to the low number of African-American youths playing the game. Interviews with twenty-seven youth baseball coaches and officials, including eighteen select team coaches from the Midwest, show that one of their major concerns is the diminishing number of major league players that African-American youths can emulate (Ogden, "African Americans and Pick-Up Ball" 203). Many of the coaches said there are few role models to teach African-American youths the game and to instill an interest in baseball.

Those coaches also cite other reasons for this lack of interest. Other sports, especially basketball, have captured the imagination of African-American youngsters. Basketball, wrote author Gerald Early, "is the most commonly played game that one can see in a casual tour of any black community" (32). Early noted that basketball is a game blacks have shown they can master "under the most harsh social and economic circumstances, under the most impoverished conditions" (30). Many of the sports role models for African Americans are basketball players. Almost 80 percent of the players in the National Basketball Association are African American, compared with 15 percent of Major League Baseball players. An ironic example of basketball's dominance over baseball among African Americans is the Ebbets Field Houses in Brooklyn. The high-rise apartment complex, which stands at the site of Ebbets Field and is occupied mostly by minorities, no longer has a youth softball diamond. The diamond was changed into basketball courts (McKinley 48).

Ebbets Field Houses are also an example of the scarcity of baseball-related facilities for African-American youths. Such scarcities were another reason the Midwest coaches gave for the lack of African-American youths on their teams. City administrations in metropolitan areas such as Omaha and Sioux City, Iowa, no longer coordinate youth leagues, so inner-city neighborhoods must depend on private support for such leagues and for upkeep of the leagues' ball fields. Several coaches noted the lack of such support and the poor condition of ball fields in minority neighborhoods. The best maintained and groomed ball fields, the coaches said, are usually found in the suburbs. Good facilities attract players (Ogden, "African Americans and Pick-Up Ball" 202).

Economics is another factor cited by several coaches. Registration fees for select teams often cost $200 to $300, not to mention the equipment needed by the player. Since select teams often play in tournaments in other states, parents who want to watch their sons must pay the extra expenses for food, lodging, and travel. Many minority families do not have such discretionary income, said several coaches (Ogden, "African Americans and Pick-Up Ball" 201).

Indeed, select baseball seems to have become a game based on economics and has followed the middle- and high-income families to the suburbs. By one estimate, 90 percent of little league programs are located in the suburbs or rural areas (McKinley 48). The percent of select teams in the suburbs in the Midwest may be higher, according to unpublished research conducted in the summer of 2001. Of seventy-eight Midwestern select teams surveyed during that time, none was based in the inner city. The vast majority of the players were from the suburbs of such cities as Chicago, Denver, Des Moines, Kansas City, Omaha, and St. Louis. Very few of the players on those seventy-eight teams were recruited from the inner city.

The suburbanization of select league baseball may reflect not only the economics of the game, but also other reasons cited by the Midwest coaches for the lack of blacks on the diamond. The predominantly Caucasian population of the suburbs has the discretionary time and income to maintain fields and to inculcate baseball in youngsters through the organization of leagues.

Early, however, refutes such reasons. He argues that the loss of interest in baseball among blacks goes deeper than economics and lack of community support. With few African Americans in the stands and a shrinking number on the field, baseball reminds blacks of their minority status. Blacks who attend games must sit in a "sea of beer-swilling whites," an experience he describes as "unnerving" (47). Early adds that an even more fundamental reason for the apathy toward baseball is that blacks' attraction to the game historically was "broad" but never "intense" (41). The death of the Negro Leagues, he writes, marked the end of blacks' attempts to embrace the sport culturally:

> What the end of the Negro Leagues meant was the end of the ability of the blacks to pass down the tradition of "their" game in the defective way that they did. But I do not think blacks were

ever particularly interested in what whites got from the game or in how the baseball myth worked for them. African Americans experienced the game through their flawed Americanism, imposed on them by whites, and this is why they are somewhat alienated or distanced from the game today. (41)

Although the Negro Leagues didn't dissolve until 1960, long after the integration of Major League Baseball, black baseball at the professional level remained, in Early's description, "defective" in never achieving the support and recognition that its white counterpart did. Indeed, Negro League teams depended in large part on barnstorming and their precarious existence exemplified the oppression, or "flawed Americanism," that blacks encountered in other aspects of life in the United States.

Conclusion

More than fifty years after Jackie Robinson desegregated Major League Baseball, questions linger about how much progress baseball has made in making the game inclusive of all U.S. cultures. The system of select youth baseball makes it difficult for boys from low-income families to compete against the best players of their age. Several Midwest coaches commented that blacks who play select ball as teens often didn't play as children and thus don't have the knowledge of the game or skills found in teens who were baseball players throughout childhood. Former Omaha athletic and educational administrator Don Benning said baseball may be losing a generation of African Americans as a result of the game not being taught to youngsters:

> When we start to skip individuals in generations, they have no knowledge of what we value, and there's a big void as it relates to baseball. Kids have to learn to appreciate skills that a Cone or Griffey have, and then they have to want to do it. The less exposure they have, the less chance they have to participate. (Ogden, "African Americans and Pick-Up Ball" 201)

Major League Baseball is addressing the problem through its RBI (Reviving Baseball in the Inner Cities) program. The program is designed to stir interest in baseball among youths through the formation of leagues in the urban core and in low-income neighborhoods. Major League Baseball has partnered with the Boys and Girls' Clubs of America to administer the program in the clubs' respective cities. Individual major league teams in many cities also sponsor RBI programs.

RBI has detractors who question its effectiveness in getting black youth to pursue baseball into high school (Gomez A1). According to RBI directors in Des Moines and Kansas City, most RBI teams play ten to fifteen games a year. As mentioned previously, youth select teams play an average of seventy games per season. RBI, however, has exposed baseball to thousands of black youths, who otherwise might never have played the game, and has attracted attention to the issue.

Some observers, like officials in the Rainbow/PUSH Coalition, believe more needs to be done. Coalition officials suggest educating children on the history of blacks in baseball, stressing greats such as Jackie Robinson, Willie Mays, and Hank Aaron (Kenney 3CWS). Others say such nostalgia would have a negative effect by reminding blacks of the era of Jim Crow (Melcher 8). Providing opportunities to play the game may have a lasting impact on children. Those trying to market baseball to blacks might heed the advice of Midwest coaches and RBI directors: If you want blacks to develop an interest in baseball as they grow older, give them opportunities to play the game at an early age. That advice is supported by research showing that the more years a person played ball as a child, the more likely that person was to follow a particular major league team (Ogden, "A Sports Sociological Perspective" 81-82).

Baseball may never again reach the zenith it did in African-American communities in the 1930s and 1940s. But a fading presence of African Americans at all levels of baseball means a loss of cultural representation. Baseball, at least at the major league level, has become international, as exemplified by the growing number of Hispanic and Asian players. At the same time baseball, with its thinning ranks of African-American players, is becoming culturally impoverished in representing the demographic panorama of the United States. As with the veins of coal in Buxton, the affinity for baseball has been exhausted for blacks, and they are leaving that community of sport.

BIBLIOGRAPHY

Beran, Janice A. "Diamonds in Iowa: Blacks, Buxton, and Baseball." *The Journal of Negro History* 75 (1990): 81-95.

Boivin, Paolo. "Fewer Playing the Game." *The Arizona Republic* 2 May 1999, late ed.: A28.

Chalberg, John C. *Rickey and Robinson: The Preacher, the Player, and America's Game*. Wheeling, IL: Harlan Davidson, 2000.

Early, Gerald. "Why Baseball *Was* the Black National Pastime." *Basketball Jones*. Eds. Todd Boyd and Kenneth L. Shropshire. New York: New York UP, 2000: 27-50.

Edmondson, Brad. "Baseball's Next Generation." *American Demographics* Sept. 1997: 37.

Flanagan, Jeffrey. "Baseball Continues to Ponder How to Attract Black Fans." *The Kansas City Star,* C2.

Gomez, Pedro. "Baseball Striking Out with Blacks." *The Arizona Republic* 2 May 1999, late ed.: A1.

Johnson, Jessica A. "Slam Dunks Versus Grand Slams." Unpublished research proposal, 2001.

Kenney, Colleen. "Baseball Loses to Other Sports." *Omaha World Herald* 12 June 1999, metro ed.: 1, 3CWS.

Lapchick, Richard E. Ed. *Racial and Gender Report Card.* June 1999. Northeastern.

Leavey, Walter. "50 years of Blacks in Baseball." *Ebony* June 1995: 36-37.

McKinley, Jesse. "Out of the Ball Park: For Black Americans, Baseball Loses Its Luster." *The New York Times* 10 Oct. 1999, metro ed.: 43, 48.

Melcher, Richard A. "Foul Ball for Blacks." *Business Week* 19 May 1997: 8.

Ogden, David C. "African Americans and Pick-Up Ball: The Loss of Diversity and Recreational Diversion in Midwestern Youth Baseball." *Nine: A Journal of Baseball History and Culture* 9.2 (2001): 200-207.

_____. A Sports Sociological Perspective: Gender and Sense of Community of Spectators of Professional Baseball. Diss. University of Nebraska-Lincoln, 1999.

Peterson, Robert. *Only the Ball Was White.* Englewood Cliffs, NJ: Prentice-Hall, 1970.

Racial and Gender Report Card. Ed. Richard E. Lapchick. June, 1999. Northeastern.

Rader, Benjamin G. *Baseball: A History of America's Game.* Urbana: U of Illinois P, 1994.

Skluzacek, Julianna. "Mixed Singles: The Story of Effa Manley and the Negro Leagues (A Play)." *The Cooperstown Symposium on Baseball and American Culture, 1999* (pp. 261-278). Eds. Alvin L. Hall and Peter M. Rutkoff. Jefferson, NC: McFarland and Company, Inc., 2000.

University Center for the Study of Sport in Society. 28 May 2001, <www.sport insociety.org>.

Ward, Geoffrey C., and Ken Burns. *Baseball: An Illustrated History.* New York: Alfred A. Knopf, 1994.

9

The All-American Girls Professional Baseball League: Accomplishing Great Things in a Dangerous World

Carol J. Pierman

The All-American Girls Professional Baseball League (AAGPBL), with teams in five Midwestern states, was organized in 1942. The league, which expanded steadily through the 1948 season, saw attendance peak that year and then gradually taper off, leading to the AAGPBL's disbanding in 1954. Over those twelve years, more than 600 women played in the league (which has become known through *A League of Their Own,* a 1988 documentary directed by Mary Wallace, and the 1992 feature film directed by Penny Marshall).

Recruited by major league scouts, players joined the AAGPBL from all over the United States, Canada, and even Cuba. They participated in regional tryouts and spring training (in places such as Havana, Cuba; Opa-Locka, Florida; and Pascagoula, Mississippi). Some traveled on touring teams which played exhibitions in the United States, Central America, and South America.

On average, the women of the league earned $75 per week, plus expenses, a salary that allowed players to attend college, open businesses, and travel. In other words, the AAGPBL offered its professional women players the opportunities—social mobility, improved life chances, and good incomes—that professional male athletes had. For women who would compete in a team sport, a comparable opportunity would not come again until well after the passage of Title IX in 1972.

The league chronology—of 1942 to 1954—and the postwar expansion of teams and fans contradict one popular misperception: that the All-American Girls Professional Baseball League was a World War II phenomenon exclusively. As soon as the men came home from war, everything returned to normal, or so the story goes; men resumed playing baseball, they reclaimed their jobs in the factories, and women went back to keeping house.

In fact, the story of the AAGPBL is much like the story of the rest of the nation. After World War II new opportunities in an expanding economy became available for a generation of men and women, even as they were confronted with the pressure to conform by returning to traditional social roles. Women athletes had to confront these pressures, but it was during this period that the women's professional golf tour also formed, leading to the LPGA's founding in 1950.

And yet, despite their similarities as emerging women's professional sports organizations, the LPGA developed and eventually prospered well beyond its midcentury origins, while the AAGPBL went into decline. Since its dissolution in 1954, no women's professional baseball league has persisted.

It is the purpose of this chapter to address the question of why women have failed to sustain participation in organized baseball, and further to explore the critical similarities between women's experience in baseball and their weak—and only very recent—presence in any professional team sport. The connection between women's baseball and basketball is particularly illuminating with regard to cultural beliefs about athletes and gender, and the very tenuous place for women in team sports. Thus a discussion of women's team play must return to origins, to the formation of the All-American Girls Professional Baseball League and, before that, to the nineteenth-century beginnings of two of our most popular American team games.

By the end of the 1942 baseball season, U.S. involvement in World War II had cut so deeply into professional baseball rosters that the minor leagues alone saw their numbers diminished by almost 3,000 men. As the pool of available baseball players dwindled, so did the quality of play, and finally even the crowds at games began to disappear.

Worried that national morale might be diminished with soldiers risking their lives on two fronts and those at home working overtime, President Franklin Roosevelt expressed his concern. In a letter to baseball commissioner Kenesaw Landis, he urged Major League Baseball to continue its schedule, even if it meant fielding teams of dubious strength. "I honestly believe it will be best for the country," Roosevelt wrote, "to keep baseball going" (qtd. in Macy 6). Baseball would provide a welcome distraction from war.

In fact, Philip K. Wrigley, owner of the Chicago Cubs, came up with a better plan. Why not recruit some of North America's best women players and field teams of high quality? If fans wouldn't pay to watch a men's game made up of leftover players, why not tap that pool of ballplayers who hadn't gone to war? All across the United States, Canada, and even Cuba women played fast-pitch, and they had fans. In addressing the president's concerns over morale, Wrigley reasoned that by creating a new league the market for the national game might be expanded.

National Pastime: The phrase would imply a universality that holds among Americans, a vast body of participants who derive pleasure from one game and express through its play aspects of the national character. "Baseball fulfills the promise America made to itself to cherish the individual while recognizing the overarching claims of the group," wrote Bartlett Giamatti. "It sends its players out in order to return again, allowing all the freedom to accomplish great things in a dangerous world" (103).

Contemplating the aesthetics of baseball—its *poetica*—one would assume that the game holds sway over the imagination, that something inherent in the American character would move us all to play ball and "accomplish great things in a dangerous world." The game is so unique in its aspect that it has given rise to a canon of belletristic, critical, and film literature. Giamatti, a renaissance scholar who stepped down from his position as president of Yale University to become baseball commissioner, had such a deep passion for the sport that he analogized its play to paradise. The game is, after all, timeless. It is a sport played within a complex pattern of diamonds, circles, pentagrams, and infinite lines—a geometer, as God has been called.

"From something as simple as the small red scorebook in which I inscribed the narrative of a ball game, I saw the inception of what has become my life's work as a historian," writes Doris Kearns Goodwin, one of many who have traced the ability to recollect narrative and structure plot back to the game's unique statistical method (10).

Baseball has no height, weight, or brute strength requirement. The rules preclude contact except that which is oblique. There is nothing comparable to tackling, body checking, or the scrum. Unlike Canadians' relationship to ice hockey (or Britons to football), baseball does not celebrate an extreme version of masculinity "grounded in toughness and force" (Theberge 15).

There is sliding into base and blocking the plate, but softball has that too. According to its celebrants, the sum of baseball rests in its theme—family, reunion, players having as their goal a return to home. As parent is to child, it is "the silky leather of an old mitt slipping into place around the warm hand it has come to replicate" (Angell ix).

Surely a game with so many warm and ennobling qualities would be played by the entire family for, as the *New Yorker*'s Roger Angell writes, the appeal of baseball rests in its "rustic, unviolent, and introspective" nature (351). How then did such a game come to exclude the greater percent of the American population, that percent imputed to possess an essentially nonviolent nature and all the instincts of home?

Participation in a sport flows directly from a culture's commonly held ideas, including notions of gender—ideals of manhood and womanhood. Standards of etiquette codify and set boundaries around gendered practices. As he was setting down the first standardized rules for many of our sports, A.G. Spalding wrote in *America's National Game* that baseball was "too strenuous for womankind" (11). Thus—and so easily—was the exclusion of women from this elegant, noncontact sport formalized.

Spalding would see his perspective incorporated into the rules of nearly every game of the era, making sport a reflection of late-Victorian ideals. Thus women would not play baseball, but as a bifurcated set of rules for sport evolved, they would be steered toward a game played on a small field with a larger, softer ball—one more awkward to handle—and spatial impediments would be placed on players, such as the rule precluding baserunners from taking a lead. A complete game would be seven, not nine, innings.

In the same way that restrictive sets of rules were written for every sport played by women—regulations of play that implied inherent differences between the sexes (women tired more easily, were prone to nervous excitement, were constitutionally frail)—baseball became softball for women. In some places it became slow-pitch.

And yet women do play baseball. Since its inception, women have found ways to play the national game. Baseball "ballists" were playing in Manchester, New Hampshire, in 1879, at the Squog Grounds in short skirts of red flannel and blue stockings (Leibrich n.p.). Barbara Gregorich notes that the first women's teams emerged shortly after baseball's development in the mid-nineteenth century. Vassar, Smith, and Wellesley played one another; the Resolutes were one of two teams at Vassar.

Professionally, the Blondes and Brunettes competed for pay from 1875 to 1880. Taking advantage of a clothing style that allowed women to run or bicycle without becoming tangled in yards of skirts, various Bloomer Girl teams barnstormed throughout the eastern United States from 1890 through the 1920s (Gregorich 3-5). A news item included in the scrapbook of Fort Wayne Daisies first baseman Vivian Kellogg notes, "Jackson [Michigan] has known girl and women baseball players almost as long as the game has existed" (n.p.).

At every stage, women have been involved in the national pastime, in the backyard where pitching overhand is "rapture," according to Annie Dillard (97), or they have managed, played, and umpired men's games. Often this has required subterfuge or a stunt, such as Babe Didrikson's pitching for the House of David. But merely classifying a sport "male" will not keep women from playing the game. Physically, there is nothing to prevent it.

Thus in envisioning the business potential for women's professional baseball in the early 1940s, Philip K. Wrigley was contemplating an opportunity to expand the national pastime. In fact, Wrigley concluded that once he created the league, the best women players would soon be as famous as female stars in other sports—such as tennis player Helen Wills, swimmer Gertrude Ederle, or golfer Patty Berg (Macy 7).

But shadowing the exclusion of women from baseball is a simple truth: fans were not accustomed to seeing women running the base paths. They were not accustomed to seeing women play at all if it meant they were playing hard as a group. So unnatural did it seem—and some physicians were still telling women that they would destroy their limited supply of vital energy, jeopardizing the essential tasks of reproduction if they were to exert themselves athletically (or even intellectually)—that it was considered to be in the nation's best interest to discourage girls and women from competing on teams.

Physical educators, eager to gain acceptance for themselves as well as for their profession, had implemented a regime that would impede the development of girls' and women's sport for almost the full twentieth century. In "The Ethical Value of Sports for Women," Frances Kellor states at the outset of the 1900s: "It is essential in playing games that women stand well, walk well, run well, throw well, and have a neat, attractive appearance. The habits and manners of players on the field are also a part of the aesthetic training" (306). Kellor, who took responsibility for the rule stating that aesthetic form be a requirement for being on a university team, listed those traits that would be violations—for which one would be penalized or even excluded from play: "Disagreeable expressions, uncouth language, squealing and yelling, crying, lying about the floor, eating between halves of games, masculinity, boisterousness" (306).

In an era when our modern team sports were being designed, it was (and to a degree still is) considered unnatural for a female to develop her athleticism beyond a certain point. In his "Fencing for Women," William J. Herrmann of the Institute of Physical Training urged women toward his sport, "[Fencing] gives physical elasticity, which women in particular desire above muscular development." He continued by noting that "heavy muscular development is not in keeping with the real conception of feminine grace" (112).

The certainty with which one could express such sentiments coexisted with common understandings about what physical activities females could engage in and how much exercise they could sustain at any given time. These misperceptions led directly and logically to limiting access, for even while a sport such as fencing might be conducive to a feminine appearance—"lightness of foot and all-around gracefulness as dancing" (Senac 112)—the period of time permitted for practice was restricted. Thus, the *Maitre d'Armes* of the New York Fencing Club would note in 1907 how certain hours were reserved at all the large fencing clubs for wives and daughters of members. At his club those hours were 10 a.m. to 1 p.m. three days per week (Senac 112). Hours and access at most private clubs are limited to this day.

Frances Kellor and her colleagues who determined that women's sport would be a private affair, secluded from the eyes of spectators and "not for the purpose of getting . . . championship teams" (304), would welcome Spalding's pronouncement that baseball was too strenuous for womankind. For women, sport would be private, recreational, and she would be directed toward pastimes such as golf, horseback riding, tennis, archery, fencing—all being individual sports available exclusively to the wealthy, where a female would be isolated, constrained by her surroundings, running at most a few steps at a time. Here form would count more than effort, and a lady would never try too hard to win; she would disdain any prize in the form of payment. Competition would be demonized, with team competition being the worst, especially in sports where running and "bunching" were required (Cahn 99). Stigmatized by association with the working class girl, or, worse, one who was sexually suspect, team sports were off limits for the middle- and upper-class female.

It is in the reception of women playing basketball, another non-contact sport which emerged in the nineteenth century, that we discover a template for the process by which women were directed away from certain kinds of athletic competition. Evidence comes directly from the game's inventor.

In the fall of 1891, Luther Gulick, superintendent of the Springfield Training School, charged one of his young instructors, James Naismith, to come up with a game that could be played inside in the winter months. In truth, there were no indoor games that captured either fans' or participants' interest.

In a few weeks, after several false starts, Naismith designed a game that combined aspects of soccer and lacrosse. Students took to it immediately. "Word soon got around that they were having fun in [my] gym class," wrote Naismith later, "and only a few days after the first game we began to have a gallery" (57).

The gallery was, in fact, a group of female teachers from a nearby elementary school. The women, overhearing the excitement inside the gym, stopped by on their lunch hour. After several days of observing the fun, they asked Naismith, "Why can't girls play that game?"

"I told them," Naismith wrote, "that I saw no reason why they should not, and this group organized the first girls' basketball team" (58).

In a remarkably short period of time, the game spread across the United States. Up the road at Smith College, a young physical education instructor, Senda Berenson, noted in her journal, "Group games of any kind were unheard of. . . . We no sooner tried it . . . than we liked it" (qtd. in Spears 23). Luther Gulick celebrated basketball as being "significant" for women in that for the first time they were entering public life. By playing team sports he believed they could learn the principles of teamwork and cooperation (Gulick 97).

Others thought it would be the perfect sport for women. It was played indoors on a small court, out of view, and therefore it satisfied the opinion that any sport played specifically by women must be inherently modest in its qualities. For a short time basketball had a "feminine reputation" due to its being judged "too effete for rugged male athletes" (Cahn 85). Naismith himself encouraged women to play, and through basketball he met his wife, a member of that first women's team at the Springfield school. "Throughout her life," he wrote, "she remained actively interested in the game" (163).

The first intercollegiate basketball game for women was held on November 18, 1892—just one year after the sport's invention (a testament to the breathtaking speed with which this popular game spread)—between the University of California and Miss Head's School. The game is on record as being played by that time in all regions of the nation, even in the south where a team formed at Sophie Newcomb College under Clara Baer.

And just as quickly as the game and its popularity spread were the rules rewritten, modifying Naismith's sport for women.

In later years Naismith would write of Clara Baer, who eliminated nearly all physical aspects from the game except passing: "In her effort to eliminate some of the most strenuous parts, Miss Baer modified the game so much that the only things left were the ball and the goals" (165).

What had prompted the abridgment of basketball if not the sight of women competing as a group? On seeing a game at Smith College, a reporter wrote that what he'd witnessed was "a mad game" (Cahn 85). It was noted that players' hair flew loose. Girls shouted loudly while racing downcourt. Out of breath, they panted and perspired heavily. Smith's coach, Senda Berenson, found her enthusiasm dimmed after adverse reactions from reporters. Rather than make the case for the energetic games her new sport inspired, she voiced this concern: "Rough and vicious play seems worse in women than in men" (qtd. in Hult 55).

Protesting what they were seeing as "sadly unwomanly," women's coaches drew up new rules (Paul 45). Stealing and dribbling were banned. The court was divided into small sections to which players were confined. At Newcomb, Baer went into high gear, declaring falling down, hand signals, speaking aloud—even during timeouts—violations. Emphasizing refinement, she renamed her version of the game Basquette.

Throughout the United States, intercollegiate and scholastic play were discontinued, and soon basketball, like fencing, existed mostly for the young lady to learn sportsmanship and rhythmic grace. Indeed in her *Basketball for Women,* Lou Eastwood Anderson of the University of Washington drew up a repertoire of instrumental selections appropriate for accompanying basketball drills. For running drills she suggested Schubert's *Valse Noble;* and for slow running with "slight leaps," Tchaikovsky's *Humoresque* (9).

With competition and the team play characteristic of men's sport prohibited (Anderson 120), basketball was made static, with players standing around in assigned sections, passively awaiting the ball. Because it would take almost the entire twentieth century before a women's professional basketball league of any duration came to exist, it is all the more remarkable that the All-American Girls Professional Baseball League was launched and drawing its biggest crowds before the midcentury.

In fact, to promote the league, Wrigley and his colleagues knew they would have to manage the image of the players, and sell femininity as much as skills. The strategies used to market women's baseball is a complex topic, one that requires a more detailed examination than can be given here. But a brief summary of Wrigley's marketing plan goes part way toward explaining how the league gained acceptance. The first order of business was to convince fans of the players' true womanhood, so they might be allowed to participate in the national game.

Spring training came to be focused on remodeling the mostly rural and working-class athletes, with hours each night devoted to comportment, etiquette, hygiene, and elocution lessons. Wrigley's teams would play in skirts, and chaperones would enforce strict rules of conduct.

Players were issued an eleven-page "Guide for All American Girls: How to Look Better, Feel Better, Be More Popular" along with "Your All American Girls Baseball League Beauty Kit" which specified even the color of rouge (medium) and face powder (for brunette).

After games, players were to follow a ten-point cleaning and makeup checklist.

Appeals to patriotism were incorporated into league activities, with an All-American Girls victory song and a victory march before each game. Teams organized blood drives and other charitable activities for war wives, widows, and veterans. Nothing was left to chance; the league did everything possible to present its players as "the right kind of girls."

For twelve years the strategy worked. The war, which called for sacrifices from so many, also presented unexpected opportunities for women to step into vital defense roles.

A woman who was "proud to carry the blowtorch for Uncle Sam" (as read ad copy for Kotex in 1943) might also be celebrated for her morale-building efforts on the baseball diamond. Even in 1949, four years after the war, the *Chicago Daily News* reported, "The girls have brought unity and good will to their towns far out of proportion to the money involved" (8).

Nevertheless, in the 1950s several factors led to the league's decline. Innovations in an expanding economy led to new forms of mass entertainment, new kinds of communities, and greater mobility. Even as Americans shopped, they began to abandon neighborhoods and central downtowns for malls. In light of these developments, women's baseball came to seem increasingly old-fashioned, even peculiar. (At the same time, Minor League Baseball also saw its audience disappear, as customers would drive great distances for some kinds of entertainment, but not to a downtown ballpark to watch minor league ball.)

As armament contracts diminished, companies stopped hiring women for jobs now reserved for veterans. Women were expected to return gratefully to homemaking and prefer the role of wife and mother. Media reinforced an image of femininity that was anything but athletic. Women ballplayers found themselves now "in a society that perceived them as less womanly for their athleticism" (Cahn 227). The art of persuasion, so successful in mobilizing women into the workforce during the war, now turned against those who remained in "male" jobs.

Even league structure was less than supportive of its own survival. Merrie Fidler has documented how the league operated under three ownership cycles: after the 1943 season, Philip Wrigley sold his interest in the AAGPBL to his advertising executive, Arthur Meyerhoff. From 1943 through 1950, the league expanded under a centralized management which provided a steady stream of advertising copy and promotion in exchange for fees from individual teams. But in 1950, chafing at those mandatory fees, which cut into their profits, individual team owners bought out Meyerhoff and no longer contributed to a central office which might coordinate publicity. "The promotional budget was cut drastically, and if board meeting minutes are any indication, attendance also began dropping drastically" (Fidler 602). The timing for a change in league structure couldn't have been worse—it played into the perceptions of a society that had transformed, one that now expected women to be waiting at home for husbands and children at the end of day. Despite every attempt to accommodate to changing times—Red Cross benefit drives, exhibitions at V.A. hospitals, national and international tours—nothing could save the league or its players from seeming increasingly out of step with the times.

The story of how the AAGPBL absorbed its players, refashioned and marketed them as ladies, then changed over the years until it became a true professional baseball league is a compelling one. Even more compelling is the story of the players, hundreds of whom are still alive at the start of a new century. They enriched the game of baseball and then, in turn, benefited from their experiences in the league, altering forever the lives they would lead. They left a remarkable legacy for future generations of young women who might yet return to the diamond, reclaiming the national pastime as a game in which all can accomplish great things in a dangerous world.

BIBLIOGRAPHY

Anderson, Lou Eastwood. *Basketball for Women: With Special Reference to the Training of Teachers.* New York: Macmillan, 1929.

Angell, Roger. *Once More Around the Park: A Baseball Reader.* New York: Ballantine, 1991.

Brumfield, Delores. Personal Interview. 7 February 2001.

Cahn, Susan K. *Coming on Strong: Gender and Sexuality in Twentieth-Century Women's Sport.* Cambridge: Harvard UP, 1994.

Chicago Daily News, 31 July 1949, *This Week Magazine:* 4-8.

Dillard, Annie. *An American Childhood.* New York: Harper and Row, 1987.

Draper, Andrew Sloan, ed. *Draper's Self-Culture.* Vol. 6. St. Louis: Twentieth-Century Self-Culture Association, 1907.

Fidler, Merrie. "The All-American Girls' Baseball League, 1943-1954." In *Her Story in Sport: A Historical Anthology of Women in Sports.* Ed. Reet Howell. West Point: Leisure Press, 1982, 590-607.

Giamatti, A. Bartlett. *Take Time for Paradise: Americans and Their Games.* New York: Summit Books, 1989.

Goodwin, Doris Kearns. *Wait Till Next Year: A Memoir.* New York: Simon and Schuster, 1997.

Gregorich, Barbara. *Women at Play: The Story of Women in Baseball.* San Diego: Harcourt, 1993.

Gulick, Luther Halsey. *A Philosophy of Play.* New York: Scribner's, 1920.

Herrmann, William J. "Fencing for Women." Draper 110-112.

Hult, Joan S. "The Governance of Athletics for Girls and Women: Leadership by Women Physical Educators." Hult and Trekell 3-18.

Hult, Joan S., and Marianna Trekell, eds. *A Century of Women's Basketball: From Frailty to Final Four.* Reston: American Alliance for Health, Physical Education, Recreation and Dance, 1991.

Kellogg, Vivian. Papers. National Baseball Hall of Fame Library, Cooperstown.

Kellor, Frances A. "The Ethical Value of Sports for Women." Draper 304-312.

A League of Their Own. Dir. Penny Marshall. 1992. Videocassette. Columbia, 1992.

A League of Their Own: The Documentary. Dir. Mary Wallace. 1988. Videocassette. Columbia, 1992.

Liebrich, Barbara. Papers. National Baseball Hall of Fame Library, Cooperstown.

Macy, Sue. *A Whole New Ballgame: The Story of the All-American Girls Professional Baseball League.* New York: Henry Holt, 1993.

Naismith, James. *Basketball: Its Origin and Development.* New York: Association Press, 1941.

Paul, Joan. "Clara Gregory Baer: Catalyst for Women's Basketball." Hult and Trekell 37-52.

Senac, Louis. "Fencing, The Rewards of." Draper 110-112.

Spalding, Albert G. *America's National Game.* 1911. Lincoln: U of Nebraska P, 1992.

Spears, Betty. "Senda Berenson Abbott: New Woman, New Sport." Hult and Trekell 19-36.

Theberge, Nancy. *Higher Goals: Women's Ice Hockey and the Politics of Gender.* Albany: State U of New York P, 2000.

10

Globalization of Baseball in Popular Culture

Martin Manning

Background

Mickey Mouse, Babe Ruth, screwball comedy, G.I. Joe, the blues, *The Simpsons,* Michael Jackson, the Dallas Cowboys, *Gone with the Wind,* the Dream Team, Indiana Jones, Catch-22—these names, genres, and phrases from American sports and entertainment have joined more tangible American products in traveling the globe. For better or worse, many nations now have two cultures: their indigenous one and one consisting of the sports, movies, television programs, and music whose energy and broad-based appeal are identifiably American; the sport that evokes more nostalgia among Americans than any other is baseball, a game so many played as children (or its close relative, softball) that it has become known as "the national pastime." It is also a democratic game which, unlike football and basketball, can be played well by people of average height and weight.

Baseball originated before the American Civil War (1861-1865) as rounders, a humble game played on sandlots. Early champions of the game fine-tuned it to include the kind of skills and mental judgment that made cricket respectable in England. In particular, scoring and record keeping gave baseball gravity. While the legend that a young West Point cadet, Abner Doubleday, invented baseball in 1839 at Cooperstown, New York, (the conclusion of a committee commissioned by the major league owners of 1905 to determine the origins of the sport) has permeated American thinking for most of this century, ample evidence indicates that it underwent a long period of development considerably earlier than that date. Despite the revisionist efforts of the committee, led by sporting-goods tycoon Albert Spalding, a product of the rampant nationalist fervor of the late nineteenth century, baseball's ancestors consisted of various stick-and-ball games played by generations of Englishmen and American colonists, e.g., "old cat" games, rounders, town ball. Printed references to "base ball" appeared as early as 1700 in America. Robin Carver, *Book of Sports* (1827), noted that Americans called their form of rounders "base ball" because they used bases instead of stakes as in cricket.

In 1871, the first professional baseball league was born. By the beginning of the twentieth century, most large cities in the eastern United States had a professional baseball team but baseball came of age in the 1920s, when Babe Ruth (1895-1948) led the New York Yankees to several World Series titles and became a national hero on the strength of his home runs.

David Voigt noted that grown men played baseball in rural villages of New York as early as the 1820s and that the sprightly Massachusetts game lasted until the 1840s when the rival "New York game" ascended to the dominant position, largely due to the efforts of an urbane New Yorker, Alexander Jay Cartwright, who, in 1845, persuaded his friends to play a symmetrical version of the game which he'd devised. His plan, notable for its use of a diamond-shaped infield with bases set ninety feet apart, caught on in short order. Baseball clubs sprang up in abundance throughout the urban centers of New York and nearby states such as New Jersey, Pennsylvania, Maryland, and the District of Columbia, many based upon Cartwright's rules as employed by his Knickerbocker Base Ball Club. The game's appeal, according to Mark Twain, resided in the fact that it is "the very symbol, the outward and visible expression of the drive and push and rush and struggle of the raging, tearing, booming nineteenth century." While the Civil War caused a lull in the baseball boom, the post-Civil War period kindled a new surge of nationalism, with baseball chosen as the athletic expression of this unifying force. Growing professionalism in baseball proved to be the prime force behind this new growth phase, beginning with the barnstorming success of the Cincinnati Red Stockings in 1869, and culminating with the founding of the National League in 1876. The league entered a "Golden Age" (1890s) which, along with the institution of the American League (1901) and the establishment of the World Series (1903), assured baseball's continued recognition as "the national game," an appellation which remained unchallenged until the rise of professional football during the Super Bowl era.

The Foreign Scene

The popularity of baseball abroad coincided with the rise of American imperialism at the beginning of the twentieth century. Soldiers stationed at bases in the Caribbean and in the Pacific, and, still later, in Western Europe, played a major role in teaching the game to local citizens. During the 1898 Spanish-American War, American servicemen introduced baseball in the Philippines. After World War II, the practice of barnstorming in the off-season by major league teams (particularly in the East and Latin American countries), combined with the spread of radio and television broadcasting, did much to further the popularity of baseball. By 1950, the American Baseball Congress had affiliates in Argentina, Australia, Canada, Ecuador, Guatemala, India, Israel, Japan, Korea, Mexico, Netherlands Antilles, Nicaragua, Panama, Philippines, Taiwan, and Venezuela. In the 1950s, Little League baseball had participating leagues in six continents; today it is very popular in the Far East, especially in Japan, in the Philippines and in Taiwan, and it has an estimated million plus viewing audience. Its international tournament, the Little League World Series, which began in 1947, has had winners from such far-flung locales as Mexico, the Philippines, Venezuela, and Taiwan. As a parallel to this, the World's Children's Baseball Fair was initiated (1989) by world home run kings Sadaharu Oh and Hank Aaron to diffuse and promote correct baseball throughout the world, and at the same time, to widen the circle of friendship and goodwill among the children of the world. Baseball clinics and exchange events are conducted.

Starting in the late 1940s, baseball expanded its geographical range. By the 1980s, the game's appeal was sufficiently widespread in scope to result in its adoption as a competitive sport by the International Olympic Committee. In the 1996 Olympics, it was a measure of baseball's appeal outside the United States that the contest for the gold medal came down to Japan and Cuba (Cuba won).

Since its creation, Major League Baseball has employed an increasingly larger number of foreign players. On Opening Day 2000, approximately 20 percent of the combined team rosters consisted of players from the Dominican Republic, Puerto Rico, Venezuela, Canada, Mexico, Cuba, Panama, Australia, Jamaica, Japan, Aruba, Colombia, Curacao, England, Nicaragua, South Korea, and the Virgin Islands. Fred Ferreira, the Montreal Expos' director of international operations, believes that this roster figure will increase to around 35 percent before 2008. Some baseball executives say a soccer-style World Cup and perhaps a worldwide draft is on the horizon. The national pastime is becoming more global, and many baseball officials in this country say that process is being driven by a lack of domestic talent and interest. Given the international scope of baseball, it is perhaps inevitable that geopolitics have become a factor in major league baseball policies.

Latin American Baseball

Along with Japan, Latin America has been one of the major sources of players to the American national pastime. In Cuba, where the game was introduced in the 1860s by students returning from the United States, baseball became such a favorite among Cuban youth that the Spanish colonial rulers banned it, fearing that the money collected from the traditional "passing of the hat" would be used to support opponents of the Spanish government. Today, what amounts to a postrevolution exists with the development of talent on the island, beginning with children's training schools. The search for young talent, particularly pitching, has caused teams to tender offers to leading Cuban players. Although Cuba was once a valued source of big league talent, access was terminated when Fidel Castro banned professional sports in the early 1960s. Since then, Cubans signing major league contracts have been forced to seek political asylum in the United States but, due to the sensitive nature of the defection process, the baseball commissioner's office has warned teams not to take an aggressive role in recruiting players. The importance of the sport is emphasized by the role of Castro, himself a former star baseball player in his youth, who controls baseball in his country and the effect of the U.S. embargo on Cuban-U.S. baseball relations. However, the Baltimore Orioles played a series of games with a Cuban national team in March 1999 for which Cuban exile groups criticized Orioles owner Peter Angelos as being pro-Castro, but the game in Latinoamericano Stadium in Havana was significant on a cultural level because it was seen as an attempt by the United States to reach out to the Cuban people. Cuba's national baseball team, the best in a nation of 11 million people, has regularly bested the best American players in the Pan Am games and other international competitions, although this has changed with the downward economic spiral of the post-Soviet era in Cuba. In the first thirty years since the Cuban revolution, none of the immensely talented players on the national team defected, but this changed on Independence Day 1991 when Rene Arocha missed the team plane; he was the first baseball defector. What followed was the defection of more Cuban baseball stars for the wealth and big crowds that American baseball offered, more cause for continuing hostility between the U.S. government and Castro.

Baseball was established in Puerto Rico long before the Marines landed there in the early 1900s. The American presence influenced the development and popularity of Puerto Rican baseball but, as with so much throughout the Caribbean basin, most of its impetus came from Cuba. The Puerto Rican professional leagues, bolstered by black Americans barred from the U.S. major leagues, remained strong throughout the 1930s and into the 1940s until Jackie Robinson broke the color barrier and blacks and dark-skinned Latinos were allowed to play on American teams.

It is still unclear exactly when baseball was introduced in the Dominican Republic; some sources believe it occurred in the 1870s, while others claim it happened in 1891. Either way, this small, impoverished Latin American country has become the home of intense baseball activity with rum, drums, and the mambo as part of the colorful festivities. Former United States Information Agency (USIA) Public Affairs Officer (PAO) Alfred Laun remembers his 1965 tour in the country when he was asked to assist several neighborhood youth baseball leagues in Santo Domingo. Thanks to USIA's Office of Private Cooperation, Laun was able to get donations of baseball equipment for the teams, including balls, gloves, and bats.

In Venezuela, baseball was also introduced after a group of Venezuelan students returned from study in the United States and in Europe (1895); the sport started in Caracas. The Venezuela Federation of Amateur Baseball was formed in 1927; today baseball is the country's national sport. This is not the situation in Colombia where soccer, bicycling, and tennis are all much more popular than baseball.

Japan

Baseball (yakyu) was introduced to Japan in the 1870s by American teachers during the Meiji Era drive for modernization and Westernization, but it truly became popular after American soldiers introduced it during the occupation following World War II. The game caught on fast because the Japanese perceived it as a form of martial arts. Today, about 20 million people play some form of baseball in Japan, including "rubber baseball," a youth game that is the Japanese substitute for tee-ball. Over 9 million play softball and almost 850,000 play regular amateur league ball. In the 1990s, a Japanese player, Hideo Nomo, became a star pitcher for the Los Angeles Dodgers. In Japan, youngsters played baseball in the snow in order to get in more practice, a forty-two-year-old native of Takamiya turned an abandoned rice paddy into a faithful reproduction of Kevin Costner's "Field of Dreams" ballpark, and sales of U.S. baseball paraphernalia took off following Hideo Nomo's success pitching for the Dodgers. Another international incident involved the 1997 hiring of New Yorker, Mike Di Muro, as the first foreigner to work as an umpire in Japan's professional baseball leagues. Arguing that players and fans had lost faith in their homegrown umpires, Japanese baseball officials saw the need to motivate their umpires by encouraging imitation of Di Muro. The experiment backfired when a controversial call by Di Muro in early June led to an on-field fracas in which several players and coaches shoved and struck him, prompting U.S. Major League Baseball officials to call the twenty-nine-year-old umpire home.

Australia

The Congressional Record of April 21, 1987, included Arizona Senator Dennis DeConcini's glowing description of the USA/Australia Baseball Exchange, a program designed for "young amateurs to use the platform of sports to experience a better understanding of other nations and their people." Baseball was introduced into this country by American gold miners in the 1850s and, next to the United States, it is perhaps the most sports-crazy country in the world; but it has a built-in handicap in that distances are so great to the other Oceania island countries, such as New Zealand, and within Australia itself. Huge travel costs are incurred to stage national and regional tournaments and this remains the major hindrance to increased popularity of the sport. More sponsors need to be attracted to the game. Yet Australia's interest in sports was highlighted in 1988 when that country hosted Expo 88 in Brisbane. American sports memorabilia has always been a popular attraction at the U.S. Pavilions at international expositions (world fairs) but the biggie was probably Expo 88, which had sports and recreation as its theme. The entire U.S. Pavilion was about sports. Part of the exhibition area included artifacts and memorabilia from the various U.S. sports halls of fame, including Babe Ruth's glove and Lou Gehrig's bat. A batting machine was available for visitors to practice their swings. To underscore the seriousness of drugs in athletics, a seminar on the subject that was attended by several well-known coaches and medical personnel, some from baseball. Outside the U.S. Pavilion, a sports court experienced constant activity. Since the Olympics were being held that year, Andrew Jay, the program officer, was able to attract participation by many prominent athletes going or coming from the Games. The Brisbane records, now in the National Archives, College Park, Maryland, have correspondence with the athletes or their agents, the halls of fame, and various other athletic organizations and groups that were asked to participate or to contribute funds.

America's Neighbors North and South

Canada is reported to have had its first baseball game (1838) in Beachville, Ontario, but the sport was well established there by 1872. Today, America's northern neighbor is home to two major league professional baseball teams, the Montreal Expos (National League) and the Toronto Blue Jays (American League), and eight minor league franchises, with more planned over the next decade. To the south, American railroad workers introduced baseball in Mexico in the 1880s. A Mexican semipro league was formed in the 1920s, followed in the 1930s by professional leagues, and black players contributed greatly to Mexican baseball in the 1940s before Robinson broke the color barrier in the United States. Today, baseball is popular in the northern and eastern states of the country but it is not played much in the southern and western areas. There has been very little success with professional teams. One reason may be the grueling bus rides and hot weather endured by Mexican League players and that big league clubs have to pay the Mexican League teams relatively high prices to sign players. It is said by major American league scouts that "you can sign four Dominicans for the price of one Mexican." Two successful transplants were pitchers Fernando Valenzuela and Ted Higuera.

Europe

Although baseball is based on an old English sport, it has had mixed success in Europe. In France, baseball was popular during and after each of the world wars, when occupying Americans introduced the game, then experienced a renaissance in the 1980s when baseball clubs expanded to over 270 with 12,000 players, but it has not really taken hold in this country. Italian team matches began in 1919 and an amateur baseball association was formed in 1931 which sent forty-three instructors to the United States to learn the game. After World War II, a baseball federation was formed which led to the European Baseball Federation in 1953. Italy is considered the strongest European baseball country, closely followed by the Netherlands where honkbal was introduced in 1910. However, the Dutch do not have baseball programs, or any other sports programs, in their high schools and universities. To play organized baseball or any sport, a player must join a club; today there are over 200 of these clubs.

Private club members began sponsoring baseball teams in Italy in 1919; competition between club teams started in 1945. After the formation of the Italian Baseball Federation (1950), Italy was instrumental in the creation of the European Baseball Federation (1953). Today, over 100,000 Italians play organized baseball.

Although Italy and the Netherlands have the strongest baseball teams in Europe, they are actually considered the third tier of world amateur baseball. At the top level are Cuba, the United States, Japan, Taiwan, and Puerto Rico. Below that, the group includes South Korea, Canada, Venezuela, and the Dominican Republic. Italy, The Netherlands, Nicaragua, Australia, Panama, and Mexico are at the bottom.

Baseball is not a major attraction in other Low Countries. Spain and Belgium cannot really be considered serious baseball countries. Belgium's baseball history dates back to 1923 and Spain's to 1920 but they are minor players in the sport, much like the United States in field hockey and in rugby. During World War I, Lauri Pihkala adapted parts of American baseball to the old Finnish game of King Ball and created, by 1921, the Finns' national pastime of Pesapallo. Germany is the center of much American baseball but this is due chiefly to the large amount of American servicemen stationed there who play the game. Otherwise, the country is not a baseball power.

Russia

In the former Cold War superpower, there is an axiom: "There are more Americans interested in Soviet baseball than Soviets interested in Soviet baseball." This is an interesting observation since some Russians contend that lapta, a Russian folk game with a bat and ball, was the inspiration for American baseball. This point was clarified when the Soviet state newspaper *Izvestia* (February 4, 1962), reported categorically that baseball was Russian in origin; a similar claim was made in a 1925 edition of the Russian magazine *Smena*, which called *beizbol* an imitation played in Russian villages when "the United States was not even marked on the maps."

Global Baseball League

This was an ill-fated attempt in the late 1960s by Walter J. Dilbeck of Evansville, Indiana, to place teams in Latin America, in Japan, and in the United States to encourage international friendship and understanding through athletic competition. After Japanese players were signed and other players were training in the Caribbean in 1969, the league suffered financial problems and went bankrupt. It was purchased by the Baptist Foundation, part of a complicated scheme to defraud investors. Dilbeck later pleaded guilty to tax violations.

Sports in U.S. Cultural Diplomacy

A discussion of the globalization of baseball is not really complete without mention of its role in U.S. cultural diplomacy. For the period 1954-1970, there are documents in the Bureau of Educational and Cultural (CU) Affairs History Office Collection at the University of Arkansas, Fayetteville, including tour reports and photographs of the various college teams that the U.S. Department of State sent overseas in baseball, track and field, swimming, and other summer Olympics types of activities. By 1978, just after the Bureau of Educational and Cultural Affairs was absorbed into USIA as the U.S. International Communication Agency (later changed back to USIA in 1982), there was some sports programming going on but it was not particularly active. However, much action occurred when USIA took on responsibility for U.S. participation at international expositions (world fairs) between 1986 and 1992. Vancouver (Expo 86) had sports teams as performers in the U.S. Pavilion and Seville (Expo 92) even had Arnold Schwarzenegger as Deputy Commissioner General for Sports until he withdrew to start production on a film. He gave an interview and was advertised in the U.S. Pavilion until his withdrawal canceled these plans. However, a great deal of sports activity took place. The biggie, though, is Brisbane (Expo 88).

The idea for sports exchanges came as an attempt by the United States to counter Soviet championships at the 1948 and 1952 Olympics. They officially began in 1954 when President Eisenhower received from Congress $5 million in funds to be appropriated to the president's emergency fund for international affairs for a special international program for cultural presentations, which included sports (both competitions and demonstrations). It was strengthened by the establishment of the Interagency Committee on International Athletics (ICIA) in 1963. After this, Congressional debate ensued about U.S. support for athletes in the 1964 Olympics and Johnson Administration efforts to help them along with a proposal to set up a sports foundation for this purpose. In 1971, the Harris/Ragan Management Report was undertaken to determine how the State Department could maximize the effects of the sports exchange program of the Bureau of Educational and Cultural Affairs, and the results indicated that sports had largely been ignored by the State Department.

In 1956, baseball as art became controversial when the American Federation of Art assembled an exhibition, "Sport in Art," for *Sports Illustrated* that was to tour the United States before going to Australia under USIA auspices for the Olympics. Two months before its arrival at the Dallas Museum, local anti-communists demanded the exclusion of four paintings because of the alleged subversive associations of the artists involved. One of these was Ben Shahn's drawing of a baseball game, titled *National Pastime*. Despite pressure from groups such as the Communism in Art Committee of the Dallas Patriotic Society, the exhibition went on as planned in Texas but USIA Director Theodore Streibert, fearing congressional criticism, reversed the decision to send "Sport in Art" to the Olympics.

BIBLIOGRAPHY

Material on baseball teams was sent overseas as part of the State Department's sports exchanges program in the Bureau of Educational and Cultural Affairs (CU) History Office Collection, University of Arkansas, Fayetteville. The Public Diplomacy History Collection, in the Bureau of Public Diplomacy (formerly United States Information Agency), U.S. Department of State, has files on the Brisbane exposition, including the sports programs. The rest of the records on this very popular world's fair is in Record Group 306 (USIA) at the National Archives and Records Administration, College Park, Maryland.

Clumpner, Roy A. "American Federal Government Involvement in Sport, 1888-1973" (PhD dissertation, University of Alberta, Edmonton, Canada; 1976).

Dickey, Glenn. *The History of National League Baseball: Since 1876.* New York: Stein and Day, 1982.

Engel, Margaret, and Bruce Adams. "A League of Their Own." *The Washington Post Magazine,* 11 March 2001: 20-25, 39.

Fainaru, Steve. "The Business of Building Ballplayers." *The Washington Post,* 17 June 2001: A1, A10-A11.

Fainaru, Steve, and Ray Sanchez. *The Duke of Havana: Baseball, Communism, and the Search for the American Dream.* New York: Villard, 2001.

Jamail, Milton H. *Full Count: Inside Cuban Baseball.* Carbondale: Southern Illinois, 2000.

Levine, Peter. *A.G. Spalding and the Rise of Baseball: The Promise of American Sport.* New York: Oxford UP, 1985.

Light, Jonathan F. *The Cultural Encyclopedia of Baseball.* Jefferson, NC: McFarland, 1997.

Maske, Mark. "Baseball Is Fast Becoming the International Pastime." *The Washington Post,* 30 January 1998: C1, C6.

_____. "Special Agent, Bearing Arms." *The Washington Post,* 11 February 1996: DI, D9.

Mathews, Jane D. "Art and Politics in Cold War America." *American Historical Review* 81 (October 1976): 762-787.

McNeil, William F. *Baseball's Other All-Stars: The Greatest Players from the Negro Leagues, the Japanese Leagues, the Mexican League, and the Pre-1960 Winter Leagues in Cuba, Puerto Rico, and the Dominican Republic.* New York: McFarland, 2000.

Oxford Companion to Sports and Games. Edited by John Abbott. London: Oxford UP, 1975.

Struck, Doug. "Japanese Gems on U.S. Diamonds." *The Washington Post,* 5 June 2001: A1, A15.

Sullivan, Kevin. "American Ump Shakes Japan's Major Leagues; For Many, New Yorker's Style Is Strike Against Their Culture." *The Washington Post,* 10 April 1997: Al, A30.

_____. "Strike 2—and the American Ump's Out!" *The Washington Post,* 10 June 1997: Al, A28.

Voigt, David Q. *American Baseball; From Gentleman's Sport to the Commissioner System.* 1966. Norman: U of Oklahoma P, 1983.

_____. *Baseball, an Illustrated History.* University: Pennsylvania State UP, 1987.

Whole Baseball Catalogue. Edited by John Thorn, Bob Carroll, and David Reuther. New York: Simon and Schuster, 1990.

SECTION III:
MONEY, MANAGING, AND MYTH

11

Here's the Pitch:
Baseball and Advertising

Roberta Newman

Since the mid-nineteenth century, two powerful institutions have played a significant role in shaping American culture, one, strictly a business, the other, ostensibly only a game. From the outset, the two have been inextricably tied to each other. The game, baseball, the national pastime, America's game, as the MSG cable sports network regularly assures us in its promotional ads, is, in fact, "more than just a game." Baseball is so fundamentally American, so permanently etched into American speech, the American psyche, American culture, that it may even be defined, however broadly, as America's secular religion, the American Church of Baseball. The business, advertising, James B. Twitchell asserts, is the central institution in contemporary American culture (Twitchell 1). Indeed, it would be difficult to argue that advertising does not permeate virtually every aspect of American life, that it does not dominate American cultural production. The advertising business, as with baseball, may have existed in embryonic form in England prior to taking root in the United States. But it took a nation of hustlers, a nation of hucksters, a nation of snake-oil salesmen, to turn it into a major industry. And it took the major industry to turn us, first and foremost, into a nation of consumers.

The love affair between professional baseball and advertising has endured for well over a century. Rather than souring with time, it grows stronger with the passing years. Where would professional baseball in the twenty-first century be without the beautiful new ballparks named by and for a variety of corporate entities such as Bank One, Enron, Pacific Bell, and the Coors and Miller brewing companies? Where would these major corporations be without baseball? Certainly, corporate sponsors would still have football, hockey, basketball, and stock car racing to fall back on in order to advertise their products. But the importance of the connection between professional baseball and the mainstays of sports advertising, the breweries, telecommunications giants, and energy providers, as well as the manufacturers of sports drinks, soft drinks, breakfast cereals, snack foods, and even demon tobacco, cannot be dismissed. Before the NFL, the NHL, the NBA, and NASCAR, that bastard child of Prohibition, were even glints in the eyes of their founders, or their sponsors, the marriage between professional baseball and advertising was entering middle age.

The most routinely criticized practice involving baseball and advertising, by media and fans alike, is the naming of new ballparks by and for corporations, thereby serving to connect specific corporate identities to the very fabric of the professional sport. Baseball purists long for the old days, when they could go out to the old ball game without invoking a corporate sponsor simply by mentioning a stadium's name. But this practice, reviled for taking the romance and tradition out of the national pastime, for debasing the great cathedrals of the American Church of Baseball, the naming of ballparks as a means of creating corporate name recognition, of advertising, of commercializing an already fundamentally commercial sport, is very much in the American baseball tradition, dating back, if not to the very origins of the professional sport, then to the early decades of the twentieth century.

Given the long connection between baseball and advertising, it is no wonder that the first man to suggest this particular marketing strategy is considered to be the father of the modern ad agency, Albert Lasker. Lasker, who was, for a time, the largest minority owner of the Chicago Cubs, prior to selling out to William Wrigley Jr., had a considerable impact upon the professional game of baseball both inside and outside the advertising arena (Fox 63). As an ad man, Lasker handled various accounts that were either directly or indirectly related to baseball. Although, when Lasker first joined the agency he would later control, Lord and Thomas, in 1898, Lord and Thomas counted Wrigley's gum company among its clients, Lasker never personally handled the account. In 1925, when he sold his share of the Cubs to Wrigley, his close friend with whom he could not work effectively, Lasker, ever the advertising executive, suggested that the chewing gum magnate change the name of his ballpark from Cubs Park to Wrigley Field (Gunther 123). Lasker convinced Wrigley that by calling the park Wrigley Field, it would do his "chewing gum business a lot of good," increasing name recognition, and thereby, selling more gum (Gunther 119). Lasker is perhaps best known in relation to baseball for proposing the eponymous Lasker Plan, suggesting that the major leagues needed the oversight of a commissioner's office in the wake of the 1919 Black Sox Scandal (Light 179). However, it would be difficult to deny that Lasker's most enduring contribution to the sport lies not in the appointment of Kenesaw Mountain Landis as the first baseball commissioner, but in creating a new form of advertising by connecting the names of ballparks with corporate entities and corporate identities.

The earliest and most enduring link between baseball and advertising is ballpark signage. Traditional stadium advertising signs, such as the one which graced the right field wall of Brooklyn's late, lamented Ebbets Field, sponsored by Brooklyn politician Abe Stark's clothing store, reading "Hit Sign, Win Suit," are still very much part of the fabric of the American baseball experience. Indeed, archival photographs of nineteenth-century ballparks indicate that the practice of placing advertisements on ballpark walls and scoreboards is as old as the professional game itself. Virtually every professional ballpark in America is decorated with signs pitching some sort of brand name product, so much so that a ballpark without signage looks peculiar. Notable exceptions to this rule, for example, Fenway Park's Green Monster, from which the bulk of advertising was removed in 1947, are notable specifically because they are exceptions (Light 256). This is not to say that Fenway Park is without its on-sight advertising. Ample scoreboard advertisements make up for the absence of advertising on the outfield wall.

Naturally, technology has had its effect on this piece of visual Americana. Traditional signage is often augmented with videotaped commercials, initially produced for television, which air on scoreboard diamond vision screens between innings. After all, if the spectator won't go to the television, television must be brought to the spectator. Moreover, ballpark advertising signage, be it traditional or high tech, is no longer limited to outfield walls and scoreboards. While early ballpark signage was aimed only at those in attendance, and was thereby limited in its scope, its twenty-first century descen-

dent has a much broader audience. Rotating billboards positioned behind home plate, out of view of all but a very few attendees, have also
become ubiquitous. Unlike outfield and scoreboard advertising, aimed
primarily at spectators physically in the ballpark, the rotating billboards have been placed behind the plate for the benefit of television
viewers. As with product placements, these rotating billboards represent valuable commercial opportunities for television sponsors, not
dependent upon breaks in the action like more conventional television advertising. While viewers are free to leave the room during
commercial breaks between innings, as well as during those ubiquitous calls to the bullpen, sponsored by the local telecommunications
providers, the rotating billboards are inescapable. As a result, it is virtually impossible to watch a baseball game on television without simultaneously and continuously consuming advertising, as it is in the
ballpark. In this regard, television brings the ballpark experience to
the home viewer in more ways than one.

Given the costs of maintaining professional baseball teams and
their respective ballparks, it should not be surprising that every available inch of stadium space should be occupied with signage. After
all, professional baseball is, as the ads remind us, more than just a
game. It is and has always been a business. But the ubiquitous nature
of ballpark signage extends far beyond the venues in which the professional sport is played. It is even apparent in and around Little
League diamonds (Twitchell 60). Little Leaguers themselves have
long been connected with advertising, literally. Just glance at the average Little League jersey. Nine out of ten times, you will find the
name of the team's sponsor—a real estate office, a dentist, a local
lawyer—emblazoned across the back in bold letters. In this respect,
the Little Leaguers become ballpark signage.

The connection between children, baseball, and advertising also
has a long history. Before there were Little Leaguers, before Derek
Jeter encouraged children to eat Skippy peanut butter and Ritz crackers, long before Mickey Mantle whined "I want my Maypo" to television viewers, the American Tobacco Company, at the time a giant
trust, staked its first claim in advertising with the introduction of tobacco trade cards. Embellished with pictures of athletes, actresses, and
exotic locales, perhaps the most popular of these were baseball cards.
Looking like little billboards that fit in the pocket, baseball trade cards,
also called pack stiffeners, for the ability to do just that, were issued in

numbered sets in order to provide added incentive for repeat purchasing (Twitchell 79). Trade cards had been used to sell patent medicines prior to their introduction by the American Tobacco Company (Twitchell 78). But the earliest baseball cards were essentially the domain of Big Tobacco. In fact, at the outset, individual brands of cigarettes were not marketed based on taste, as they are today. Instead, they were sold based on the cards inside the pack (ATC 23).

While adults were certainly interested in collecting trade cards, it is impossible to ignore the fact that the demographic American Tobacco intended to reach was primarily that of children, most probably pre-adolescent and adolescent boys (Twitchell 79). In this light, the late twentieth-century introduction by R.J. Reynolds of its phallic cartoon character, Joe Camel, intended as a means to appeal to the youngest potential smokers, was nothing new. R.J. Reynolds was simply following in a long tradition of cigarette advertising to the young.

Eventually, other industries would follow the lead of big tobacco. Trade cards bearing the images of baseball players were also included with such items as candy, chewing gum, and soft drinks. Trade cards became increasingly rare as the twentieth century wore on, but they did not disappear. Although baseball cards have become consumables in their own right, they still appear as premiums, included in or on certain products intended to increase sales to children and their parents. Skippy peanut butter, that mainstay of the American child's diet, now comes topped with a round trade card, bearing one of five different images of Derek Jeter, Skippy's All-Star MVP pitch man. Joining Jeter's image, which also resides inside newly minted boxes of baseball-shaped Ritz Crackers, are trade cards featuring Ken Griffey Jr. Enjoining children to "collect all five" or to "collect them all," the producers of Skippy and Ritz rely on an advertising strategy as old as advertising itself, marketing to the young, turning today's baseball fans into tomorrow's mass consumers.

The connection between baseball and tobacco advertising runs deep. Trade cards may have all but disappeared from cigarette packaging after World War I, but the long association between the professional sport and tobacco has not. Show a pack of "Bull Durhams" to anyone, and they will at once conjure up an image of Kevin Costner in a baseball uniform. But before there was a film of that name, before there was a Kevin Costner, Genuine Durham Smoking Tobacco, with its familiar trademark, the bull, was closely identified with baseball. Bull Durham tobacco, originally sold loose rather than prerolled, was perhaps the most widely copied brand in tobacco advertising history (ATC 18).

In 1902, when more Americans were smoking Bull Durham than any other brand, the Durham Bulls of North Carolina State Professional Baseball League were founded. Although the league folded after just forty-eight games, the Durham Bulls were to reappear in a number of incarnations, and still exist today as the AAA affiliate of the Tampa Bay Devil Rays ("Team History/Milestones"). Naming a team after a region's most important product appears to have been a particularly effective form of advertising. After all, Durham, North Carolina, was the home of the American Tobacco Company. Calling a team the Durham Bulls is essentially different from simply naming a team after a local industry. The Milwaukee Brewers, for example, may represent the brewery industry, but until moving into Miller Park in 2001, they were not associated with a particular brand name. The Durham team was not, after all, named the Tobaccos or even the Cigarettes, but rather, the Bulls. This is an early example of "branding," connecting a given product, and everything associated with it, no matter how loosely, with a specific brand, thereby investing the object with symbolic value (Twitchell 13). In this regard, the Durham Bulls, the branded baseball team, is intimately connected with the product. One cannot exist without invoking the other.

The association between baseball and Bull Durham tobacco persists, despite the best antitobacco efforts. But even though tobacco advertising carries with it a certain stigma, the Tampa Bay organization seems to be in no rush to change the name of its farm team, thereby discouraging the connection. The Bulls have even installed a mural in their new ballpark, which opened in 1995, featuring Bull Durham's enduring bovine trademark as well as the legend, "Hit Bull, Win Steak," clearly a reference to the old Ebbets Field sign. The mural was originally constructed as a prop for the 1988 film, *Bull Durham,* which might be construed as one giant product placement, in and of itself. Here, the lines between fiction—the film, reality—the twenty-first century minor league team, and advertising becomes permanently blurred. In many ways, this has been, inadvertently, one of the most successful ad campaigns in history. Legend even has it that the Bull Pen is so named because, in the area where Durham pitchers warmed up, there was a giant billboard advertising the American Tobacco Company's best-selling product, complete with an image of the trademark bull. Whether this is true or simply an apocryphal story, the tale serves as a potent form of unpaid advertising. That the legend has been perpetuated is further evidence for the success of the trademark bull and the associated branding.

Given the enduring connection between baseball and advertising, it is no coincidence that baseball's first star pitcher was also its first star pitchman. Indeed, Albert Goodwill Spalding was a man of firsts. He was the first player to pitch a shut-out, the first pitcher to win 200 games, and arguably the first to tie his own name, the name of his sporting goods company, inexorably to baseball (Coombs, West x). In the late nineteenth century, before the advent of the advertising agency, or advertising as we know it today, Spalding was a genius of marketing and promotion. Already associated with baseball as a player in the early 1870s, Spalding's real impact on the professional sport began with his promotion of baseball, and himself, in order to sell sporting goods.

Perpetuating the Spalding myth, an American myth if ever there was one, in the twenty-first century, Spalding Worldwide's Web site offers its official version of its founder's tale, in language suitable to describe a bona fide American folk hero:

> When youngsters get together for a ball game on a sandlot field, it's often the child who brings the ball that gets to be the pitcher. That's the way it has been for generations. That wasn't usually the case, however, at the Major League Level . . . except where Albert Goodwill Spalding was concerned. Then again, AG Spalding wasn't your ordinary pitcher. ("Classic Name Revolutionizes Sporting Goods Industry")

Spalding began to manufacture baseballs and opened his first sporting goods emporium in 1876, his first season as a pitchman and his final season as a pitcher (Light 678). The pitcher turned pitchman paid the National League, which he was involved in establishing, a dollar for every dozen balls it used, thereby allowing him to advertise his product, bearing his name, as the Official Base Ball of the National League (Ward, Burns 27). Thus, Spalding may be seen as the father of the official sports tie-in. The Claritin commercials which air during broadcasts of Major League Baseball games, for example, using imagery specific to the American pastoral mythology with which baseball associates itself, are direct descendants of Spalding's Official Base Balls. In these ads, we see blond children playing ball in an impossibly green field, a proverbial field of dreams. We see eager young minor leaguers, to borrow the title of one of Roger Kahn's works, good enough to dream. We see fresh-faced middle-class American families bonding over baseball in the twilight, living the American Dream. Even the requisite inner city Little Leaguers are blond, if not in reality, in spirit. As these images scroll by, the narrator informs us in avuncular tones that Claritin is the official allergy medicine of Major League Baseball. The connection between sports tie-ins and baseball is more complex than the fairly simple relationship between baseball and ballpark signage, trade cards, or even the naming of teams for products or corporate sponsors. In the same way that those who used Spalding's Official National League Baseballs could share in the glory of the professional participants in the national pastime, we, who take the official allergy medicine, share in the game's glory. Just as the presumably allergy-free players who have made it to the show, just as the pastoral participants in this American myth, we too by virtue of the liberating force of Claritin, can become participants in the American myth.

That professional baseball has official balls, that there is an official allergy medicine of Major League Baseball, is hardly surprising. After all, balls are necessary to the game, and the game is played outside during allergy season. Less clear is the connection made through product tie-ins such as the one for the official real estate brokers of Major League Baseball, Century 21, for example. But upon close examination, product tie-ins and the commercials which publicize them tell a different story. One of Century 21's more recent TV ads features what might be defined as the typical American family, new home owners, being welcomed by neighbors to their clean, suburban community. Their introduction to the neighborhood is capped off by the appearance of Cal Ripken Jr., who was responsible for breaking Lou Gehrig's record for consecutive games played, asking if the resident child would like to come out and play catch. While this is intended as a stab at humor, this ad evokes an extremely important element of the American dream associated with baseball, the sacred nature of Home. After all, what is the aim of baseball, but the desire to return, safe at home? What sport would be better suited to a corporate tie-in with a national real estate brokerage chain than Major League Baseball? And who could possibly be better to represent this Official Licensee in the twenty-first century, Century 21, than the ever reliable Cal Ripken Jr.? After all, what does home represent if not stability? Of course, in the age of free agency, there is another possible subtext to these ads. It is the players themselves, with possible exception of Ripken and a very few others, who may frequently find themselves in need of an official real estate agency.

Along with introducing the product tie-in to baseball, Spalding was also the first to usher in the age of product endorsements by celebrity athletes. Aside from the occasional celebrity testimonial citing the miraculous curative powers of a patent medicine, product endorsements by celebrities, be they baseball players or other notables, were not commonly used in advertising prior to the 1920s (Fox 89). The possible exception, trade cards, were frequently produced without the consent of the ballplayers pictured. However, by deliberately tying his name, as a pitcher, to his original product, the baseball, Spalding initiated a practice that has become the norm. Stanley Resor of J. Walter Thompson, one of the architects of the boom in celebrity endorsements in the 1920s, noted that we wish to imitate those people whom we assume to possess taste and knowledge superior to our own. Thus, by using the product associated with a given celebrity, we display our own taste and knowledge (Fox 90). But when we use a product endorsed by a ballplayer, we may wish to do more than simply imitate, thereby displaying taste and knowledge. Not only do we wish to share in their knowledge of the game, and their good taste in choosing to play it, we wish to share in their superior, almost supernatural, physical skills. In effect, naming the Spalding ball after its talented producer invests the product with magical properties. Users, therefore, share or shared in Spalding's glory. It becomes a relic, an object handled by or closely associated with a saint, the possession of which brings the owner closer to the divine. The magic becomes even more potent when the product is identified as the official ball handled by all national leaguers. Nineteenth-century purchasers of the Spalding Ball, the official ball of the National League, participated not only in Spalding's divinity, but in the collective divinity of the National League.

But what makes a baseball player's product endorsement different from a product endorsed by an athlete who plays a different sport? Why, for example, is the endorsement of Amtrak by Alex Rodriguez and Nomar Garciaparra different from Michael Jordan's Nike endorsements? After all, there is arguably no more universally recognizable sports figure than Jordan. By wearing Nike sneakers, we participate in Jordan's majesty, becoming, to borrow a slogan from another of Jordan's endorsements, "like Mike" (Twitchell 132). But what does being "like Mike" suggest? It brings to mind Jordan's elegance, grace, and unequaled athleticism on the court, and, perhaps, his good looks, suave demeanor, and healthy bank account off the court. Jordan is certainly an effective role model not only to African-American youths, but to children and even adults everywhere. But there it stops. While organized basketball is certainly popular, it does not have the rich tradition and mythological weight of baseball. The name Bill Russell, for instance, conjures up the image of the Boston Celtics' outstanding center, and, by extension, the great Celtics teams of the 1960s as a whole, but the association does not go beyond the basketball court. Compare this with what a name such as Joe DiMaggio or Ted Williams connotes. Not only do these names call forth great ballplayers of the past, but images of American heroes, images of what it means to be American. Therefore, when we ride Amtrak along with the images of Rodriguez and Garciaparra, we not only participate in the majesty of the star shortstops, we participate in the majesty of the baseball tradition and mythos as a whole. We participate in America. This is particularly potent when the endorsers have names like Rodriguez and Garciaparra. These representatives of the American mythos, of America itself, have names that sound distinctly Hispanic. What this particular endorsement may suggest is that somehow by riding Amtrak, a product that in and of itself evokes America, we, immigrants all, become more American. Even if we are called Rodriguez or Garciaparra, we too can participate in America.

The connection among the consumer, the product, and the symbolic weight of the endorser becomes even more significant when the product is something that is somehow perceived to alter or contribute to the ballplayer's physical ability. While athletic equipment may fall into this category, balls, bats, and shoes don't carry the weight of products such as patent medicines. Early patent medicines such as Lydia Pinkham's Vegetable Compound, were for the most part promoted as cures for female complaints (Fox 17). Baseball players would not have been ideal endorsers to appeal to this demographic. Of course, there were exceptions. In 1886, a self-proclaimed doctor in the patent medicine business mixed up a batch of syrup containing two powerful stimulants, extracts of cola nut and coca leaf, from which cocaine also derives. Thus was born what would become Coca-Cola, one of hundreds of patent medicines containing coca, which was marketed as a "brain and nerve tonic" ("History").

Although by 1905, only spent coca leaves, largely devoid of their active ingredient, were used in brewing Coca-Cola, and the alcohol was replaced by caffeine, it continued to be marketed as an elixir capable of curing headaches, and providing drinkers with a quick lift, as Napoleon Lajoie and Rube Waddell attested to in a 1906 print ad for Coke, part of a larger ad campaign which ran for a number of years, featuring Miller Huggins and Owen Bush, among others. Of particular note are the combined testimonials of Waddell and Lajoie that Coke had more than once gotten them through difficult games, providing stimulation, but having none of the nasty after effects of beer (Ritter 88). Testimonials such as these go beyond mere product endorsements. They seem to suggest that by ingesting this magic elixir, the consumer might somehow become physically more like the star ballplayers. Once again, if baseball represents America, then the Coke drinker somehow becomes physically more American. This is particularly true in the case of Coca-Cola, a magic elixir as closely associated with what it is to be American as is baseball, perhaps at least in small part because of early associations between the product and the national pastime.

It is no wonder, then, that patent medicine testimonials similar to those represented in the Coke ads are rooted in American evangelical culture. In the very earliest days of American advertising, it was itinerant preachers, the snake oil salesmen, who offered testimonials for products that could offer deliverance from suffering (Lears 51). The product, as well as the pitchman with whom it was associated, thereby took on mythic proportions (Twitchell 129). This is particularly true when the pitchman was a celebrity as was Waddell or Lajoie. In fact, the very term celebrity comes from the Latin, *celebratus,* the condition of being honored, from which also comes the term, celebrant, or priest (Twitchell 131). Note that the celebrity is not the celebrant, or priest, but the celebrated, the object of belief, itself. Thus, in a broad sense, the Coca-Cola endorsed by the early baseball stars becomes something like American advertising culture's response to the Eucharist. By drinking it, the consumer symbolically merges with the endorsers. By drinking it, the consumer symbolically merges with America.

The patent medicine industry was dealt a seemingly near fatal blow by the Pure Food and Drug Act of 1906 (Fox 65), but baseball players continued to endorse Coca-Cola as a refreshing soft drink rather than as a magic, almost eucharistic, potion. They still do, today. Furthermore, baseball players and other sports figures continue to pitch another magic elixir, essentially a patent medicine, Gatorade. Indeed, Gatorade is the product that makes the drinker "like Mike." A particularly symbolically potent Gatorade campaign features baseball luminaries, most notably Ivan Rodriguez and Derek Jeter, depicted in black and white, presumably restoring their unbalanced electrolytes after rigorous workouts, with neon-colored Gatorade. Almost inevitably, this results in the production of neon-colored sweat. Even more than the Waddell/Lajoie Coke endorsements, these ads suggest that a direct connection exists between the product and the actual substance of the ballplayer. Gatorade is blood of their blood, sweat of their sweat. The eucharistic connotation seems quite clear.

The use of color in the Gatorade ads is particularly interesting. Rodriguez, as his name suggests, is Hispanic, from Puerto Rico, while Jeter is racially mixed, choosing to define himself as neither exclusively white nor black. Yet, in the ads, these men of color are essentially decolorized. Although the ad makes no attempt to deny their respective ethnicities, by depicting the ballplayers in black and white, the ad does not place importance on ethnicity. Jeter and Rodriguez are not represented in glorious shades of brown as are Alex Rodriguez and Garciaparra in the Amtrak ads. In the Gatorade ads, the colors that matter are the neon colors of the magic elixir, itself. It is almost as if Jeter and Rodriguez represent the American ideal, the melting pot. They may be members of ethnic or racial minorities, but there is a sense that they would sweat red, white, and blue as well as neon green and orange, if the Gatorade being pitched in a given commercial were those colors. Even more than the Coke ads, this suggests that the sweat of their sweat is not Hispanic sweat, African-American sweat, or even Caucasian sweat, but American sweat.

Accusations that America's game is being corrupted by commercialism, that the national pastime has been reduced to being nothing but big business, that it has been robbed of its purity, in part, by advertising, abound in the media. Even radio and television sportscasters, whose livelihoods depend upon the continued commercial support of professional baseball, can occasionally be heard to complain that the commercialization of baseball has gone too far. However, professional baseball is a business and has always been a business. That the professional sport has ever been pure, free from advertising, is as much a myth as baseball's invention in Cooperstown by Abner Doubleday in 1839. Even in baseball's adopted anthem, a young woman urging her beau to "Buy me some peanuts and Cracker Jack" invokes a branded snack food (Ward, Burns 97). Professional baseball, that most American of spectator sports, has always been linked to advertising, that most American of businesses, that most American of cultural products. Indeed, these two powerful American institutions will continue to be linked, serving, in part, to define what it is to be American for the foreseeable future.

BIBLIOGRAPHY

American Tobacco Company. *Sold American—The First Fifty Years*. Durham, NC: ATC, 1954.

"Classic Name Revolutionizes Sporting Goods Industry." *Spalding Sports Worldwide*. 14 April 2001. <http://www.spalding.com/history.html>.

Coombs, Sam, and Bob West. Foreword. *Base Ball: America's National Game, 1839-1915*. By Alfred Goodwill Spalding. San Francisco: Halo, 1991.

Fox, Stephen. *The Mirror Makers*. Chicago: U of Illinois P, 1997.

Gunther, John. *Taken at the Flood: The Story of Albert D. Lasker*. New York: Harper, 1960.

"History." *Soda Fountain*. 21 April 2001. <http://www.sodafountain.com/softdrink/cocacola.html>.

Lears, T. J. Jackson. "American Advertising and the Reconstruction of the Body, 1880-1930." *Fitness in American Culture: Images of Health, Sport and the Body, 1830-1940*. Ed. Kathryn Grover. Amherst, MA: UMP, 1989.

Light, Jonathan Fraser. *The Cultural Encyclopedia of Baseball*. Jefferson, NC: McFarland, 1997.

Ritter, Lawrence S. *The Glory of Their Times*. New York: William Morrow, 1966.

Sleight, Steve. *Sponsorship: What Is It and How to Use It*. Maidenhead, UK: McGraw Hill UK, 1989.

"Team History/Milestones." *Durham Bull's Page*. 26 April 2000. <http://www.dbulls.com/team/history.html>.

Twitchell, James B. *ADCULTulsa*. New York: Columbia UP, 1996.

Ward, Geoffrey C., and Ken Burns. *Baseball: An Illustrated History*. New York: Knopf, 1994.

Veeck, Bill, with Ed Linn. *The Hustler's Handbook*. New York: Fireside Books, 1965.

12

From John McGraw to Joe Torre: Industrial Management Styles Applied Throughout the History of Major League Baseball

Richard J. Puerzer

In many ways, the management styles used throughout the history of professional baseball have reflected those used contemporaneously in American industry. At first thought this may seem obvious and natural, as baseball is often regarded as a reflection of much of what has occurred in recent American history. In reality, however, professional baseball has lagged behind the trends in American industry in many substantial management matters, most notably integration and unionization. In fact, the developments in the on-field management methods found throughout the history of baseball are but one of the few ways in which management in major league baseball has accurately reflected trends in industry and society as a whole.

The purpose of this essay is to focus upon and describe a few of these specific management philosophies and their chief purveyors in baseball throughout the last one hundred years. In discussing these individual philosophies, the essay will also discuss the reasons necessitating their evolution in both industry and professional baseball. The goal of this essay is to illuminate this relationship between professional baseball and American industry.

John McGraw and Scientific Management

The first clear use of a specific management philosophy in the on-field management of a baseball team dates back to the application of scientific management to the game. Industry at the turn of the twentieth century, whether it be steelmaking, mining, construction, or textiles, was expanding at an unprecedented rate. In an attempt to address and satisfy this expansion, the management philosophy known as scientific management was embraced by a great many industries. Scientific management is a management philosophy describing the use of such tools as time study, standardization of tools and tasks, and bonuses for performance in order to improve business efficacy (Niebel and Freivalds 8). Frederick W. Taylor was responsible for developing many of the concepts of scientific management. As an engineer and manager with a Philadelphia-based steel company in the 1880s, Taylor was seeking ways to increase the productivity and efficiency of workers in the making of steel. He began his work in the development of time studies, the study of the time required to complete a job or task by following a set of defined standard methods. Taylor believed that by using measurements and standard procedures such as those defined by time studies, management would be able to better schedule and control work while improving the quality of that work. Using these scientific management methods, managers were thus responsible for all of the thinking necessary for their workers, while the workers were simply left to carry out the manager's specific instructions. Scientific management methods proved to be quite effective in the management of these rapidly growing industries. Taylor, who eventually earned the moniker "Father of Scientific Management," used a baseball team as a metaphor in the description of how an efficient company could use scientific management, when presenting his ideas before Congress in 1911 (Risker 1-11). Indeed, scientific management proved to be an influential philosophy of management for quite some time.

The term scientific baseball dates back to the time of the development of scientific management with the American passion to apply science to all fields of human endeavor (Voigt 1: 198-199). Scientific baseball, synonymous with the term "small ball" used today, describes using specific offensive strategies such as place hitting, the hit-and-run, and stealing bases in order to score runs (Voigt 1: 200). At the time of its development, the precision of scientific baseball was seen as the opposite of "the manly game" of slugging and aggressive play to power one's team to victory.

Scientific baseball had supporters in some of the elder statesmen of the game including Henry Chadwick and Harry Wright. Likewise, such high-profile players as Willie Keeler and John McGraw were seen as flag bearers of the scientific game. The best teams of the 1890s, the Boston Beaneaters and the Baltimore Orioles, were purveyors of the scientific game. The Beaneaters are credited as the developers of the hit and run play (James, *Historical Abstract* 48). Ned Hanlon, whom Bill James calls the great-grandfather of most modern major league managers, managed the Orioles in the late 1890s when they were renowned for their core of Keeler, McGraw, Wilbert Robinson, and Hughie Jennings (James, *Managers* 34). Hanlon's philosophy as manager of the Orioles was pure scientific management, a systematic plan of keeping the opponent guessing and studying the opponents so as to take advantage of their weaknesses (Solomon 56-57). Scientific baseball would remain the dominant strategic philosophy in the on-field management of baseball teams until the 1920s when the predominance of home runs and high-scoring games would force it out of widespread use. Its departure left many, including Hall of Fame player Ty Cobb and writer Ring Lardner, to lament the passing of what they considered real baseball.

In his time, John McGraw was perhaps the leading advocate and purveyor of scientific baseball. McGraw, who managed the New York Giants from 1902 to 1932, ruled his teams with an iron fist, requiring his players to follow his instructions to the letter at all times. He envisioned his role as manager as requiring him to keep control of and be accountable for all of the actions of his players. In fact, McGraw did his best to control every aspect of not only the on-field circumstances but also the off-field lives of his players. He was known to examine the meal tickets of his players to see what they had been eating. If they were not eating right, he would talk to the players about it. McGraw also was well known for hiring private detectives to trail some of his ballplayers, especially those who were known to drink too much. Two such players, both gifted pitchers who had a difficult time staying consistent in their pitching performance due to their drinking habits, were "Bugs" Raymond and "Shufflin' Phil" Douglas.

Douglas, a spitball pitcher who hailed from Georgia, was traded to McGraw's New York Giants in 1919. He had previously pitched with great success for the Chicago Cubs, but was traded away primarily because of his drinking and the resulting discipline problems (Clark 31).

For most of the three seasons that Douglas played with the Giants, McGraw either had someone serving as a traveling companion with Douglas or hired someone to follow him. The resulting tension in the relationship between Douglas and McGraw reached a head during the 1922 season when McGraw took it upon himself to have Douglas put into a sanitarium against his will for five days to be "put through a cure," in other words, to go through an alcohol detoxification program. Following his release from the program, a wearied Douglas was billed for the treatments and fined by McGraw for the games he had missed while forcibly detained. It is believed that these events caused Douglas to write a desperate letter to a friend playing for the St. Louis Cardinals. The message in the letter was construed by some as an offer to fix ball games against the Giants as Douglas' revenge against McGraw. Remember that this was 1922, just two years after the Black Sox controversy when eight players were banned after fixing the 1919 World Series. This letter quickly led to Douglas' ban from the major leagues by baseball commissioner Kenesaw Mountain Landis. Although he lost a gifted pitcher, McGraw appeared unfazed in the media, stating his need to exert absolute control over his players.

Not all of McGraw's methods were as harsh toward his ballplayers. Following the example of scientific industrial managers, McGraw did take responsibility for his players who followed his instructions and methods. A clear example of this was his defense of first baseman Fred Merkle, following Merkle's base-running error in a game against the Chicago Cubs at the close of the 1908 season. The mistake, which became known as "Merkle's boner," helped cost the Giants the pennant. Although all of the media attention at the time blamed the nineteen-year-old Merkle for the mistake, McGraw defended him to the end and attempted to divert some of the blame from his young player (Alexander 138).

The use of scientific management helped John McGraw to win ten pennants and three World Series in his thirty-one years of managing the New York Giants. He is considered by many to be the greatest manager of all time.

Although the prevalence of scientific management disappeared in industry by the 1920s, it was and is still widely applied in baseball in many ways, including applications that McGraw did not use in his time. One tenet of scientific management is to use the best worker at hand to accomplish a specific task. Platooning, or the use of left-handed hitters against right-handed pitchers and vice-versa, was used as a strategy as early as the 1870s by Cap Anson's Chicago White Stockings and also later by Ned Hanlon's Orioles. It fell into disfavor in the 1930s and 1940s before a successful revival in the 1950s by Casey Stengel and the New York Yankees (Light 575-576). Platooning is, of course, widely used today.

The use of relief pitchers is another recently employed instance of the specialization of workers to achieve a specific task. Although, by necessity, relief pitchers have always been employed in baseball, they were often seen as what Branch Rickey referred to as "a necessary evil" before the 1950s. In the 1950s they became widely used, with Jim Konstanty winning the National League MVP for the 1950 Philadelphia Phillies as a reliever, along with Joe Black, Hoyt Wilhelm, and Roy Face all having stellar seasons in the relief pitching role (Light 608-610). The use of relief pitching has continued to adapt and flourish, with the further specialization of pitchers as long-relievers, middle-relievers, and closers. Often, the middle reliever(s) and closer are seen as a specialty team within the team, such as the 1990 Cincinnati Reds' "Nasty Boys" of Rob Dibble, Randy Myers, and Norm Charlton.

Vestiges of scientific management can still be found in industry. Time studies and other work measurement methods are necessary in industry for scheduling and standardization. However, management is no longer able to treat workers simply as interchangeable parts. Likewise in baseball, McGraw's methods of management are no longer feasible. However, some of his and other methods associated with scientific management are irreplaceable strategies of modern baseball.

Connie Mack and the Human Relations Philosophy of Management

Although a contemporary and rival of John McGraw, Connie Mack, who managed the Philadelphia A's from 1901 to 1950, employed a method of management quite different from that of McGraw. Mack's methods, which predated but were quite similar in spirit to that of the human relations school of thought, encouraged independent thought on the part of the worker and sought collaboration and cooperation between workers and management. Whereas McGraw's system was completely dependent on absolute discipline, Mack wanted players who could think for themselves.

The human relations philosophy of management followed scientific management as a form of revolt against the constraints of the scientific management system. Workers felt inhibited by scientific management because they obviously had thoughts and experiences to apply to improve their work. The human relations school asked the workers to use their own ideas in cooperation with the direction of management in order to achieve their mutual goal of productivity. Management theories similar to scientific management are often referred to as Theory X management while those similar to the human relations school are known as Theory Y management. With Theory X, it is assumed that the workers cannot understand what it is that they are to do and it is thus up to management to use a proverbial stick to coerce the workers in the proper direction. With Theory Y management, including the methods employed by Connie Mack, the workers are motivated and simply require direction provided by management, so management uses the proverbial stick to hold a carrot in order to draw the workers where directed.

The human relations school of management became prevalent especially in industries such as light manufacturing, which began to experience a blur in the line between management and labor. This ambiguity was brought on in part by the promotion of laborers to management positions as the industries expanded. The unionization of labor, especially in industries such as mining and heavy manufacturing, also forced management to do away with many of the methods of scientific management. Through these changes, management learned that paying closer attention to and becoming more cooperative with labor, in turn, would bring about happier workers and the production of higher quality products. Improvements were made in wages and work schedules, and significant improvements were made in the workplace environment, providing a safer and more comfortable workplace.

Connie Mack managed his players while respecting both their physical abilities as players as well as their intelligence. In fact, he sought out players with college experience when such men were a rather rare commodity. He treated his players as gentlemen, never berating them in front of others. In all of his years of managing and in stark contrast to McGraw, Mack was never thrown out of a game.

Mack's players reacted positively to his methods as reflected by the respect that his many players granted him over his long tenure as manager.

Connie Mack managed for a very long time, and his teams saw great success as well as great failure. By comparing Mack's teams of the same time period as McGraw's, from 1901 to 1932, we can see that Mack was generally very successful. In that time period, Mack's teams won eight pennants, two fewer than McGraw; five World Series, two more than McGraw; and finished over .500 twenty-one times, six fewer than McGraw. However, in the middle of this period, from 1915 to 1924, were ten years of poor performance, including seven seasons in which Mack's team finished dead last in the American League. During this time the A's were simply unable to pay competitive salaries and therefore fielded terrible teams. Over the period as a whole, Mack's teams' performance was the equal of McGraw's. In fact, in head-to-head World Series competition, Mack's A's won two of the three contests over McGraw's Giants. Bill James points out that Mack's teams were essentially as successful as McGraw's, but that Mack's players did not drink themselves into an early grave (James, *Managers* 65).

It has been said that seldom in the history of baseball was there a closer affinity between labor and management than on Mack's A's teams (Bouton 137). He was an optimist who gave his players the opportunity to work through any problems they were experiencing. Mack's methods of management became more the norm in organized baseball as players on average became better educated and society moved to a more worker-friendly environment due to the introduction of unions and government regulation of industry.

Some twenty years after the retirement of Connie Mack from baseball, the Kansas City Royals Baseball Academy was developed. This academy, essentially a school for the teaching and training of baseball players, is another manifestation of the human relations philosophy of management brought to baseball. The academy, founded in 1970 by Royals' owner Ewing Kaufman, had three goals: first, to increase the supply of talent in the Royals organization; second, to develop the players as people by paying for their college classes taken while in the academy; and third, to test and analyze the skills and performance of baseball players. Kaufman's vision of worker development and task improvement is not unlike that of W. Edwards Deming, the quality guru who helped Japanese industry gain worldwide prominence based primarily on the quality of their manufactured goods. The success of Japanese industry can be attributed in part to the respect for and empowerment afforded to Japanese workers by management. The work at the academy was not limited to teaching and measuring on-field performance, as it also examined such areas as the psychological and physiological effects of a player's drug and alcohol abuse problems.

However, the academy lasted only three years. At an expense of four million dollars and after the evaluation of thousands of athletes, only fourteen players signed professional contracts and only one player, Frank White, went on to the major leagues (Voigt 3: 277-278). Although the experiment of the baseball academy was seen as a failure by many, its discoveries have had a lasting impact on many of the ways in which players are trained and in which the game is played. Likewise, the impact of the human relations school on baseball management, especially given the respect that modern players require, is everlasting.

Leo Durocher and Motivation

Although Leo Durocher did not necessarily champion any one definable management philosophy, he is considered by many to have been one of the most effective managers in the history of the game. Durocher, who managed intermittently from the 1930s to the 1970s, was a master at the motivation of players. The ability to motivate is, of course, one of the most important skills of any manager. Over a long baseball season, it may be the most important ability of a baseball manager.

Durocher believed that he could get more out of a player than any other manager could partly by teaching him and partly by getting better effort from him (James, *Managers* 122). Although obviously a good teacher, Durocher was a better motivator. However, one of the failings of his methods was that they were not a part of a long-term plan. He played to win the game that day, to motivate his players with the importance of winning now, which sometimes was to the detriment of the long-term success of his teams. For example, he gave his players freedoms that other teams did not have, specifically allowing them to hit the town at night without the fear of a bed check. However, he expected his players to perform the next day at game time. If a player were not ready to play, he would be in Durocher's infamous doghouse, relegated to the bench, to be made an example of to the other players, and often to the press and fans.

Durocher motivated his players with a mixture of friendship and fear. He made an example of players who he thought didn't give maximum effort or who made boneheaded plays. Simultaneously, he developed a synergy within his teams by joining them together to intimidate the opposition and the umpires. Durocher was a master of manipulating his players and his teams to win, and more often than not they did win. As has been said about many successful managers in baseball as well as in industry, it is difficult to argue with success.

It is difficult to find analogous examples of Durocher's methods of motivation in industry, save for in the military, where management is often forced into short-term thinking. Like a military officer, Durocher commanded respect, which distanced him from many of his players. Despite the difficulties his methods caused and the players whom he alienated, Durocher was well respected by many of his most gifted players. He helped such players as Pee Wee Reese, Sal Maglie, and most notably Willie Mays to become great players. Also, Durocher changed the way in which managers were regarded, allowing for other men known for their intensity and emotion to follow in his footsteps, including such successful managers as Billy Martin and Earl Weaver.

Joe Torre and Emotional Intelligence

Modern baseball managers face a wildly dissimilar set of circumstances than their counterparts of even twenty-five years ago. Due to free agency and the transient nature of players, managers simply do not have the power once exhibited by managers such as McGraw or Durocher. For this reason, managers no longer manage their team so much as they manage individual players. Likewise, today's managers are often required to manage up as well as down; that is, they must also manage up to their bosses, the team's general manager and owners. Managing up was obviously not necessary for Mack and McGraw, as they were part or full team owners. The most successful manager in recent years has been Joe Torre. Torre, who previously managed the New York Mets, Atlanta Braves, and St. Louis Cardinals for a few years each in the 1970s through the 1990s, more recently led the New

York Yankees to World Series victories in four out of five seasons as of the conclusion of the 2000 season.

Torre's success as a manager has been based in part on his ability as an organizational psychologist. Following the 1998 season in which his Yankees won 114 regular season games and the World Series, Torre set down his managerial strategies in a book aimed at businessmen and managers. In the book, Torre lists twelve keys for managing, including knowing, respecting, and communicating with your workers and striking a balance of assertiveness and respect with your boss. Torre's book reads as an organizational psychology field manual, teaching through example how Torre has established himself as a very successful manager.

By recognizing the needs of those whom he manages, Joe Torre exhibits emotional intelligence in how he deals with his players (Useem). Emotional intelligence is the newest school of thought in management theory, and is espoused especially by companies in the technology sector which compete heavily for the scarce number of educated and experienced employees available. Examples of the application of this theory range from flextime, which tailors a worker's schedule more to his or her liking, to encouraging employees to exercise or even nap while on the job in order to deal with the stress of their work. Management's approach to each worker is individualized as much as possible, in an attempt to maximize the output of each worker.

A manager using emotional intelligence does not spend as much time motivating his or her employees as a group. Instead, he or she strives to understand and approach each employee as an individual. With this individualized attention, the employees feel more important in the eyes of their manager and are thus more highly motivated. In its individualized approach, this method of management is the polar opposite of scientific management, which sought to quantify and standardize all tasks and thus all employees. In the high-pressure, ego-driven, "what have you done for me lately?" world of professional baseball and the New York Yankees in particular, Torre's methods have been nothing but successful. For example, his approach to pitcher Roger Clemens was to provide him with brief private confidence-building statements, knowing that the veteran Clemens had no need for extended meetings or public displays of the manager's support. Meanwhile Torre dealt with pitcher David Wells in a much different manner. Wells required meetings and the clear communication of Torre's confidence in order to stay in shape, let alone be motivated to pitch (Torre 60). Both pitchers have had great seasons under Torre.

Torre's success as a manager is also attributable to his delegation of authority to his coaches, especially Don Zimmer, Mel Stottlemyre, and Willie Randolph. In watching the 2000 World Series, one could see that Torre was in constant conversation with his coaches and particularly Zimmer as he was formulating strategy. Managers have long used coaches. John McGraw was the first manager to hire a coach. Since McGraw's time, however, the number and subsequent roles of coaches have been expanded. Usually selected by the manager, the coaches serve as specialists by the manager to supervise in particular the pitchers or the hitters. However, coaches are often called upon to aid in the communication with the players, necessary over the long and often grueling baseball season. Although the Yankees have had several hitting and first base coaches during Torre's tenure, Zimmer, Stottlemyre, and Randolph have been a permanent fixture, at least through the 2001 season. Their role as sounding boards in the decision/strategy-making process and in the communication with players is inestimable. Likewise they also apply their own emotional intelligence in their rapport with the individual players.

Of course, to successfully work with his coaches and to apply this style of management, one must be gifted in his or her understanding of people. Torre's years of experience as a player and his largely unsuccessful years as manager for other teams prior to joining the Yankees, have helped him to better understand and cultivate a sense of empathy with his players. His previous experience has served him well. This individualized emotionally intelligent approach to managing a team composed of rookies and veterans, superstars and role-players, recovering drug addicts, born-again Christians, Cuban defectors, and multimillionaires has brought the Yankees multiple World Series championships and a probable place in the Hall of Fame as a manager for Torre. In short, this approach has helped the Yankees to once again become a baseball dynasty.

Management Styles in Baseball

Over the course of professional baseball history, the full spectrum of management styles has been exhibited. From John McGraw, Leo

Durocher, and Billy Martin's confrontational and authoritative manner to Connie Mack, Chuck Tanner, and Joe Torre's more amiable and low-key style, players have responded positively in their play. Success as a team requires synergy between manager and players. With changes in the attitudes and beliefs of society and in turn of players, the management methods capable of developing that synergy often change. As Bill James has remarked, the way in which baseball is played is not largely defined by the rules; instead it is defined by the conditions under which the game is played including the expectations of the public, the players, managers, ethics, and strategies of the time (James, *Managers* 39).

Management methods in industry will evolve with changes in society and the economy, developments in technology, and the apparent success of certain techniques. Although it appears that many of the methods of management in baseball have been around as long as the game itself, change has occurred. With future changes in professional baseball and, more important, within society, baseball management will continue to evolve and, in all likelihood, mirror the trends in American industry.

BIBLIOGRAPHY

Alexander, Charles C. *John McGraw.* New York: Viking Penguin, 1988.

Bouton, Jim, and Neil Offen. *I Managed Good but Boy Did They Play Bad.* Chicago: Playboy Press, 1973.

Clark, Tom. *One Last Round for the Shuffler.* New York: Truck Press, 1979.

James, Bill. *The Bill James Guide to Baseball Managers.* New York: Scribner, 1997.

_____. *The Bill James Historical Baseball Abstract.* New York: Villard Books, 1986.

Light, Jonathan Fraser. *The Cultural Encyclopedia of Baseball.* Jefferson, NC: McFarland, 1997.

Niebel, Benjamin, and Andris Freivalds. *Methods, Standards, and Work Design.* 10th ed. New York: WCB/McGraw-Hill, 1999.

Risker, D. Christopher. "Baseball and Management Theory: Similar Concerns—Different Fields." *Nine: A Journal of Baseball History and Social Policy Perspectives* 5.1 (Fall 1996): 49-61.

_____. "Frederick Taylor's Use of the Baseball Team Metaphor: A Historical Perspective on Scientific Management and Baseball." *Nine: A Journal of Baseball History and Social Policy Perspectives* 4.1 (Fall 1995): 1-11.

Solomon, Burt. *Where They Ain't: The Fabled Life and Untimely Death of the Original Baltimore Orioles, the Team That Gave Birth to Modern Baseball*. New York: The Free Press, 1999.

Torre, Joe, and Henry Dreher. *Joe Torre's Ground Rules for Winners*. New York: Hyperion, 1999.

Useem, Jerry. "Joe Torre: A Manager for all Seasons." *Fortune,* 30 April 2001: 66-72.

Voigt, David Quentin. *American Baseball Volume I: From the Gentleman's Sport to the Commissioner System*. University Park, PA: Penn State UP, 1983.

_____. *American Baseball Volume III: From Postwar Expansion to the Electronic Age*. University Park, PA: Penn State UP, 1983.

13

The Hall of Fame
and the American Mythology

George Grella

In their stroll through the exhibits at the National Baseball Hall of Fame in Cooperstown, New York, visitors will inevitably come upon a handsome, dignified display in which resides a scruffy, torn black leather sphere, discovered many years ago in the neighboring hamlet of Fly Creek; the judicious and discreet official statement describes the ball as "the basis for the legend that Abner Doubleday invented the game of baseball in Cooperstown in 1839." That particular concrete object, which possesses a special history all its own, coupled with the careful description, suggests at least a little of the complexity surrounding the game, its origins, and the Hall of Fame itself. Contemplating that scruffy and ambiguous antique inevitably inspires the observer to further meditations—on baseball, America, folklore, legend, myth, even faith; in a sense, that ball and its mythological context inspired the Hall of Fame, the structure built to surround it. Because of that object, the Hall of Fame occupies a special position in American culture, more than simply a center for the study, display, and appreciation of the sport and its past, but as the central structure of the surprisingly far-flung Church of Baseball. Because of its history and purpose, the nature and scope of its holdings, and the sport to which it dedicates itself, the very existence and location of the Hall of Fame, and consequently of that black, battered, batted ball, stuffed with cloth, perhaps hand sewn by the legendary Abner's no doubt sainted mother, encourages both physical and metaphysical speculation.

Baseball by its very nature inspires such speculation. Although shrouded in the mists of prehistory, long before box scores could record hits, runs, errors, and paid attendance, the sport probably originates in the ball and stick-and-ball games of ancient cultures, contests that formed part of the primordial vegetation rituals of primitive peoples. These contests evolved into more elaborate activities, one element among many in the ceremonial songs, dances, pageants, and dramas that constituted the religious practices of any society intimately acquainted with the natural cycle—simply put, the people of various communities in innumerable areas of the globe created rituals designed to celebrate and ensure the continued fertility of the land, the rising of the waters, the triumph of spring over winter, the resurrection of the wasteland (Henderson 15 ff.; Decker 111 ff.; Weston 12 ff.). The ball itself originally may represent some abstraction, the sun, or even the head of some god-king; it seems entirely possible that some cultures in fact used an actual human head in their games and ceremonies. The connection of all stick-and-ball games with some possible *Ur*-game continues to provide a major source of inquiry for some investigators, including the present writer (Grella, titles cited); just as so much of Western civilization derives from an area in the Eastern Mediterranean, what the high school textbooks used to call the Fertile Crescent, so perhaps all those related sports—polo, golf, field and ice hockey, lacrosse, cricket, hurling, even billiards—that revolve around the striking of a ball with a stick—grow out of one vital moment in an ancient, complicated ritual. Even in our own time, of course, baseball follows the seasonal cycle, celebrating the coming of spring with appropriate ceremonies on Opening Day, marking Midsummer's Eve with the All-Star Game, and ending in autumn, the time of mists and mellow fruitfulness, with the World Series.

Strangely, whatever winding paths its history takes from its obscure beginnings through the present day, baseball never entirely strays from its powerful association with the supernatural, in particular with some belief system. As with all games, it occupies what some of the most insightful philosophers of sport term "a sacred space" (Huizenga 10), an arena set aside, marked off, bounded away from the ordinary world. Like any sport, once baseball draws its lines, assigns its bases, or in intellectual terms, establishes its rules, it separates itself from other activities. Consecrating its arena, it creates then that bright green field, intersected by the brown base paths, with its two great boundaries radiating out from home plate. The physical beauty of the baseball field, which the more rhapsodic commentators frequently mention, emphasizes its special position in American sport and American culture—quite simply, no other sports arena rivals its geography, geometry, and landscape. It is entirely appropriate that a book about stadiums is titled *Green Cathedrals* (Lowry), a term that could not conceivably describe the appearance, significance, and emotional potential of any other athletic terrain.

Its history in America also reflects a remarkable connection with some sense of the divine, so curious in fact, that even the most recalcitrant baseball atheist should suspect some supernatural intervention. As any historian will confirm, Alexander Cartwright and his Knickerbocker Baseball Club, from New York City, played the first documented contest in 1846; significantly, the teams conducted the game in accordance with more or less recognizable versions of modern rules, including the drawing of foul lines, stipulating ninety feet between bases, and making outs by means of throwing the ball to a base ahead of instead of at the runner. The game took place in a poetic space in the prosaic city of Hoboken, New Jersey, at a park marvelously named after the playground of the gods in Greek mythology, the Elysian Fields. Despite that remarkable reference to myths older even than Doubleday's, and the happy chance that Cartwright's middle name was Joy, some questionable coincidences and a widespread acceptance of the legendary Abner's alleged creation caused the Hall of Fame to be located in the bucolic hamlet of Cooperstown, where that famous baseball resides.

The actual sequence of events, involving recorded incidents, real people, some tall tales, and a powerful strain of nationalism, that landed the ball, the Hall, and all it contains and represents in Cooperstown has been recounted many times by many chroniclers (e.g., Seymour, Voigt, Springwood) but surely some divine hand guided it to Cooperstown. Eager to establish the entirely American nature of the game, despite a strong claim of its descent from European sources, A.G. Spalding, a former pitcher and formidable pitchman, argued on the side of the Doubleday legend. When an old Cooperstonian, suspiciously also named Abner (Graves), wrote about his friend Doubleday drawing the outline of a field and articulating the rules back in the two Abners' no doubt happy youth in 1839, it must have seemed to Spalding a gift from the gods; he promptly bullied through his conclusion that the game indeed originated in that spot, and the rest, as they say, no matter how false, is history.

Whatever the verdicts of actual history and common sense, the beauty of the village, possibly more striking than any possible alternative in downtown Hoboken, immediately qualifies it for special consideration. That peaceful, pastoral spot, to begin with, reflects something of the ideal vision that innumerable commentators discover in any deep and somber contemplation of the sport, sentimentally linking Cooperstown with the nation's agrarian past, the culture's own rosy vision of itself. The surrounding green hills, the glistening lake, the restored homes and quaint cottages recall a soft and dreamy yesterday, a simpler, purer time, a fitting period for the play of the national pastime. In a wonderful example of the sort of tautology that often surfaces in discussions of the sport, Abner Doubleday somehow possessed both the genius and the prescience to invent his game in just the right place in which to invent it, perhaps even in order that over the years organized baseball and millions of visitors could celebrate and commemorate it there.

More significant and more wonderful perhaps, Cooperstown, as every student of American literature must know, enjoys a special relationship with the most powerful and enduring of all the national mythologies. Founded by the land developer, magistrate, and entrepreneur William Cooper in 1786 (Taylor), the village occupies a cardinal point on the national cultural compass. Along with its West Coast sister city and polar opposite, Hollywood, the tiny, picturesque hamlet serves as the capital city of our dreams, surely one of the birthplaces for that cultural fantasy, that unifying myth we often call the American Dream. In a coincidence that no simply mortal mind could imagine, the Hall of Fame stands in the location previously immortalized in the novels of James Fenimore Cooper, son of the farsighted village founder. In a series of novels known as "The Leatherstocking Tales," comprising *The Pioneers, The Deerslayer, The Pathfinder, The Last of the Mohicans,* and *The Prairie,* Cooper in effect invented the character of the frontiersman as the archetypal American hero. His continuing protagonist, Natty Bumppo, roamed the deep woods of New York and fought the French and certain Indian tribes under various sobriquets, including Deerslayer, Pathfinder, Hawkeye, and Leatherstocking, which derive from his many adventures, skills, and attire. Natty Bumppo engendered all the later imitations and avatars of the brave, rugged, capable woodsman and sharpshooter who dwelled in the wilderness and eventually led the way West; in his later incarnation he metamorphosed into that quintessential American hero, the cowboy. (For further exploration of this concept, see Grella, "Baseball and the American Dream," and "White Lines and Green Fields.")

In Cooperstown, in fact, along with the Farmer's Museum, the Hall of Fame shares at least some of the tourist spotlight (and profits) with another museum, the Fenimore Cooper House. A bronze statue of the author occupies the center of a lawn opposite the library of the Hall, and another of an Indian hunter, who might well represent Uncas, the brave and tragic young Indian of *The Last of the Mohicans,* stands with his faithful dog, the two of them gazing alertly out over shining Otsego Lake forever. A number of business establishments take their names from moments, people, or places in the book, and literary pilgrims can still trek to Natty Bumppo's Cave. The lake itself, which Cooper beautifully named Glimmerglass in his novels, provides the name for a number of commercial enterprises in the region, and most notably for the Glimmerglass Opera House, located just outside the village; the highly regarded opera company of the same name presents a variety of performances with famous singers every summer season.

More important, however, with its own fascinating history, its rich and continuing heritage from "The Leatherstocking Tales," and its location as the birthplace of baseball, Cooperstown stands squarely at the intersection of the two grand, interpenetrating traditions of baseball and the West, and therefore of all they mean to the nation. As the central location where the two mythologies can happily copulate, it is truly a magical, perhaps even a blessed place, perfectly appropriate for the Hall of Fame, for a museum displaying the artifacts of the national game and honoring its heroes and their deeds. It is, in a sense, all of America's hometown, the game's and the nation's home plate. Because Cooper transforms the complex and troubled relationship between new Americans and Native Americans, the actuality of the hunters, trappers, adventurers of the country's early years, and the romantic landscape of forests, lakes, and green fields into a truly American mythology, the town seems the starting place, at least in the imagination, for the great Western journey, the bold, exciting adventure that impels so much of the nation's history, fiction, and cinema. And again, because the founders of the Hall of Fame, the various sportswriters, baseball executives, and generally dubious and untrustworthy chroniclers promulgated the legend of Abner Doubleday, his game, and that famous ball, the town also becomes the starting place for baseball.

Both creations (and both creation myths) suggest so many layers of what one could unkindly call falsehoods amid their beauty and power that they come to seem myths about myths, a complex of entities entirely suitable for the magic, mysticism, and miracle of baseball. The presence of the Hall of Fame, in a sense, acknowledges and solidifies the story of creation. In a well-known essay, curiously ("The Creation Myths of Cooperstown" [Oates 520-531]), Stephen Jay Gould spends a good deal of time on the hoax of the Cardiff Giant, who resides at the Farmer's Museum, but pays very little attention to James Fenimore Cooper. Concentrating on the hoax of the Giant, which he compares with the establishing of the Hall of Fame, he virtually ignores the writer's contribution to the creation of the West, entirely missing the fact that the author and his novels, after all, occupy a far more important place in the town and in the national imagination than the Giant that so delights him.

Gould acknowledges the primacy of myth, but concludes with an extended rhetorical question that exhibits a profound misunderstanding of the game he professes to know and love. A dedicated Darwinian, of course, he wonders why "we prefer creation myths to evolutionary stories? . . .Yes, heroes and shrines are all very well, but is there not grandeur in the sweep of continuity?" (531). That evolutionary sweep that baseball Darwinians like Gould miss confirms their essential failure to grasp the genuine history of the game, which not only develops out of those apparently universal stick-and-ball games that provide a form of recreation and entertainment for virtually all cultures, but also in fact celebrates a variety of beliefs and certainly a variety of creation myths. Even the true history of the game, insofar as we know it, constitutes a sort of ongoing creation myth. In rejecting that creationism, theorists such as Gould neglect the game's important religious component, forgetting that other possibilities beyond the Doubleday legend generate their own peculiar understanding of the origins and meanings of the game; false prophets claiming to preach the faith of baseball, they might as well be baseball atheists or agnostics, and certainly not, as they loudly proclaim, true believers.

Whatever the particular facts or the reports of the chronicles, the Hall of Fame grows out of the long, slow unfolding of a rich and complicated history. It stands, not only as the deliberate, though presumably well-intentioned, fabrication of a group of people intent on establishing a national heritage for the game, however inaccurate, but also as the concrete symbol of an evolution the baseball atheists refuse to acknowledge. In a sense it represents the culmination of all those forces and elements that combined in the primordial stick-and-ball games, in the pageants, songs, and dances, the rituals and ceremonies that the human community created to venerate some god or to rejoice at the wonders of the great shining ball in the heavens or to guarantee the successful cycle of the seasons. The institution quite naturally and appropriately amalgamates in itself untold centuries of ball games, the patent falsehoods of the Doubleday legend, even the pastoral romance of the West, along with at least a consideration of the varieties of baseball practiced in other lands at other times.

The most passionate devotees of the game would no doubt echo the opening sentence of Annie Savoy's narration in *Bull Durham:* "I believe in the Church of Baseball." Most fans indeed speak of the history of the game, the spacious beauty of its fields, the occasionally monumental splendor of its stadiums, the lyrical quality of play, of particular teams and individuals, and inevitably, of the Hall of Fame itself with a certain reverence; the powerful emotional response the game evokes additionally explains the discernible religious undertone pervading so much baseball discourse. If, as many students of the game believe, such an entity as the Church of Baseball exists, then its members practice and worship in major and minor green cathedrals all over the land. As with any faith, some of these consecrated spots display some strains of unorthodox belief or even heresy—decorated perhaps with such abominations as artificial turf, for example, or showcasing the presence of the designated hitter, or even sharing their sacred space with other, lesser sports, such as football, soccer, or tractor pulls (talk about worshiping at the altars of strange gods!). The Hall of Fame then assumes an even more special place within that church, becoming itself a kind of holy structure to center the history and meaning of the game, to maintain some link with a fundamental theology and worship. Cooperstown then becomes, not only a special place in the great cultural fantasy of America, but also a holy city, a destination for pilgrims, perhaps even exerting for the faithful some healing power; one book, by a director of the Hall of Fame (Smith), even titles one of its chapters, "The Shrine."

For true believers in the Church of Baseball, Cooperstown, that blessed spot on the shores of Lake Glimmerglass, represents the church's Vatican City, and the Hall of Fame its St. Peter's Cathedral.

Entering the actual Hall of Fame, that Valhalla where bronze plaques honor and enshrine forever the game's immortals, the visitor immediately understands the religious elements of the game and the place. The Romanesque arches, the sepia light that bathes the Hall, the serried rows of smiling faces from the past, forever young in the glory of their time, who return the visitor's gaze, all suggest the interior of a church. The hushed reverence with which the visitors regard those heroes, some pausing to touch the plaque of a favorite player, echoes the behaviors of devout observers of any faith. At St. Peter's in Rome pilgrims kiss the foot of a bronze statue of the saint, and the lips of millions keep the spot polished; no doubt in the Hall of Fame in Cooperstown some plaques of great ballplayers testify by their gleam to the devotion of the faithful.

Among its many exhibits, both permanent and temporary, the Hall of Fame famously displays some of its countless, perhaps unclassifiable artifacts of the game, objects associated with historic figures and events or with history itself, some important, some decidedly not. One of its publicity brochures asserts that the Hall "has stood as the definitive repository of the game's treasures," which translates into an enormous collection of items associated in manifold ways with baseball. (For serious students of the game, the Hall's library offers an important archive of baseball history, lore, records, and arcana.) Many, naturally, mark historic events in baseball, such as the statement that officially transfers Babe Ruth's contract from the Boston Red Sox to the New York Yankees, for example, or the gloves, bats, balls, spikes, uniforms, etc., used by particular players in important moments in the game—a ball that Sandy Koufax threw in a no-hitter, or the bat with which Mark McGwire struck his seventieth home run. Others memorialize the past in special ways, with objects and exhibits dealing with women in baseball, the Negro Leagues, or baseball during World War II, providing a concrete sense of a fascinating and sometimes little-known history.

Other objects underline the religious aspect of the Hall and therefore of the game, emphasizing its identity as a shrine. Visitors are invited to gaze into Babe Ruth's locker or see the shoes of Shoeless Joe Jackson—himself banned from the Hall for his involvement in the Black Sox Scandal of 1919—or view the quaint old-fashioned equipment from the infancy and youth of the game. Those objects, including the countless numbers not on public view, suggest of course that the Hall provides something like an immense reliquary, a receptacle to contain items made precious or even holy by their attachment to some figure. Anyone who has observed in some Roman Catholic church, especially in Europe, the bodies or body parts of saints—fingerbones, heads, vials of blood, etc.,—encased in special, often beautiful containers, will understand the Hall's most recent major acquisition, of the famous Barry Halper Collection of baseball artifacts, which includes, among innumerable remarkable, significant, unique objects, Ty Cobb's dentures. Although the curators of the museum neither advertise nor display that particular article, in a sense their possession indicates the true meaning of the Hall and its association with baseball. It is the clearest, fullest, most distinctive expression of the complexity, the beauty, and the divinity of the game. Standing squarely in the nexus of American mythology, located at America's home plate, it truly deserves to be recognized as a shrine, as the supreme cathedral of the Church of Baseball. I would remind the literalists and the Darwinians, the baseball skeptics and atheists, that most of the visitors to the Sistine Chapel probably understand that God probably did not create mankind exactly as Michelangelo shows it on that magnificent ceiling, but most of them, I am sure, will find the representation, the metaphor, the myth glowing with truth if not fact, and entirely beautiful. The Hall of Fame reminds us that we must all believe in the Church of Baseball.

BIBLIOGRAPHY

Decker, Wolfgang. *Sports and Games of Ancient Egypt*. Translated by Allen Guttmann. New Haven: Yale UP, 1992.

Gould, Stephen Jay. "The Creation Myths of Cooperstown." In *The Best American Essays of the Century*. Ed. Joyce Carol Oates. Boston: Houghton Mifflin, 2000. 520-531.

Grella, George. "Baseball and the American Dream." *The Massachusetts Review* Summer 1975: 550-567.

_____. "Solarball: Baseball, America, Time, and the Sun." *The Cooperstown Symposium on Baseball and American Culture*. Ed. Peter M. Rutkoff. Jefferson, NC: McFarland, 2000. 9-21.

_____. "White Lines and Green Fields: A Meditation on Baseball and the West." *The Cooperstown Symposium on Baseball and American Culture*. Ed. Alvin L. Hall. Westport, CT: Meckler, 1990. 211-229.

Henderson, Robert W. *Ball, Bat, and Bishop: The Origin of Ball Games*. New York: Rockport Press, 1947.

Huizenga, Johan. *Homo Ludens: A Study of the Play Element in Culture.* Boston: Beacon Press, 1970.

Lowry, Philip J. *Green Cathedrals.* Reading, MA: Addison-Wesley, 1986.

Seymour, Harold. *Baseball: The Early Years.* New York: Oxford UP, 1960.

Smith, Ken. *Baseball's Hall of Fame.* New York: Grosset and Dunlap, 1974.

Springwood, Charles Fruehling. *Cooperstown to Dyersville: A Geography of Baseball Nostalgia.* New York: HarperCollins, 1993.

Taylor, Alan. *William Cooper's Town: Power and Passion on the Frontier of the Early American Republic.* New York: Knopf, 1995.

Voigt, David Q. *American Baseball.* Vol. 1. Norman: U of Oklahoma P, 1966.

Weston, Jessie L. *From Ritual to Romance.* Garden City, NY: Doubleday, 1957.

SECTION IV:
BASEBALL AND THE ARTS

14

Politics, Patriotism, and Baseball On-Screen

Rob Edelman

Baseball films often are about much more than horsehides being hurled at hitters, or fans obsessively following the Great American Pastime. They have served as bywords for patriotism, for mom's apple-pie Americana, for unabashed flag waving. In an ever-changing, ever-more complex world, they show how the sport has remained a cultural barometer, integral both to the American scene and the American Dream.

Take, for example, two films of the early 1990s, both of which feature baseball in a supporting role: *It Could Happen to You* (1994) and *Dave* (1993). The central character in each is an amiable, all-American nice guy who finds himself facing an extraordinary situation. *It Could Happen to You* is the story of Charlie Lang (Nicolas Cage), a cop who wins the New York lottery and honors his promise to share the winnings with a waitress (Bridget Fonda). Dave Kovic (Kevin Kline), the title character in *Dave,* just so happens to be a presidential look-alike. When the real Commander in Chief is felled by a stroke, Dave is drafted as an impersonator.

You do not have to wait for the plot to evolve to know that Charlie Lang and Dave Kovic are good guys. In *It Could Happen to You,* this is apparent in the imagery selected for the opening credits: Charlie is shown tutoring a neighborhood kid in the fine art of stickball. So it is not surprising when, later on in the story, he rents Yankee Stadium for a day. He escorts all the neighborhood kids there, who spend a joyous day clowning around and playing ball in the House That Ruth Built.

Before the character of Dave Kovic is sufficiently unveiled, how do we know that he is patriotic enough to double for the President?

For no other reason than he adores baseball. As Dave is introduced, we know he is A-OK because he has stashed a baseball and glove in his office desk drawer. Later on, garbed in a warm-up jacket with "PREZ" stitched on the back, President Dave throws out the major league season's first pitch: a role this Everyman especially relishes.

Baseball movies tell us that diamond heroes are among the most recognizable figures in all of American history, right up there with presidents and patriots. In *The Big Picture* (1989), an executive at a schlock movie company tells a young wannabe moviemaker (Kevin Bacon) that the public is hankering for buddy pictures. "Who do you think are the two most beloved figures in American history?" he asks. Why, they are Abraham Lincoln and Babe Ruth. Cut to a movie-within-the-movie, called *Abe and The Babe.* Abe is seen whittling away on a bat he is fashioning for The Babe. "Hey, Abe, how's that bat comin'?" asks Ruth. "I wanna hit some baseballs." After being presented with the club, Babe remarks, "She's a beaut. Thanks, kid." The President then tosses a pitch to the Ballplayer, who bashes the horsehide a country mile—and, fittingly, Abe then tells Babe to make sure the Yankees win.

Baseball as a reflection of Americanism has long been depicted in the movies, and has consistently transcended the different periods of American filmmaking and the manner in which those periods mirror history. For example, in Frank Capra's populist parable *Meet John Doe* (1941), journalist Ann Mitchell (Barbara Stanwyck) attempts to fire up her newspaper column by falsely claiming to have received an anonymous letter from "a disgusted American citizen, John Doe." This Depression-era victim has been jobless for four years, and promises to commit suicide by jumping off the City Hall roof. The column causes ripples and, after aggressive prodding from Ann, her editor decides to continue the charade. First, however, her John Doe must be produced.

Enter Long John Willoughby (Gary Cooper), a vagrant. After he informs the columnist that he "used to pitch" in the "bush leagues, mostly" until his "wing went bad," Ann pronounces, "He's perfect. A baseball player. What could be more American?"

What could be more American, indeed! Long John Willoughby starts out as a man looking only for a meal. He has no opinion on taxes, foreign affairs, or government corruption. Yet he is animated, and refreshingly American, when it comes to baseball. Long John does not express emotion until Ann irritates him by asking how he would feel if one of his pitches cut the heart of the plate, and the umpire called it a ball.

Meet John Doe, released nine months before Pearl Harbor, is decidedly pre-World War II in its sensibility. In his joblessness, Long John Willoughby is a very real holdover from the Great Depression. Meanwhile, *Woman of the Year* (1942), George Stevens' sharply observed comedy that was the first celluloid union of Spencer Tracy and Katharine Hepburn, came to theaters three months after America's entry into the war. At the time, the United States was digging in for the duration and here, too, baseball plays a small but significant role in the scenario. Hepburn plays Tess Harding, world-renowned journalist who speaks a hundred tongues—but none is the language of baseball. "I really don't know anything about American sports," she acknowledges. To her, a runner sprinting around the bases "seems like a frightful waste of energy." Why, during wartime, Tess Harding would advocate the banning of baseball!

Her position irks sportswriter Sam Craig (Tracy). "Say, look, we're concerned with a threat to what we like to call our American way of life," he declares. "Baseball and the things it represents is part of that way of life. What's the sense of abolishing the thing you're trying to protect?"

These sentiments are pure and true, and are further emphasized in one of the seminal American films of the postwar years: William Wyler's *The Best Years of Our Lives* (1946). From a baseball standpoint, *Best Years* bookends *Woman of the Year* by measuring the pulse of the changing face of World War II-era America.

In the film, the war has ended and a trio of veterans (Fredric March, Dana Andrews, Harold Russell) meet while flying to their hometown of Boone City. In the first, brief sequence after they arrive—it lasts all of twenty seconds—they share a taxi that drives them past the local ball park, home of the Boone City Beavers. One of the ex-GIs asks the cabdriver, "Say, how're the Beavers doing this season?" "Agh, they're in sixth place," is the sour response. The men then shake their collective heads and smile knowingly as if to declare, in unison, that some things never change.

From now on, the "enemy" they will be rooting against will not be the German U-boat commander or Japanese kamikaze pilot, but the slugging first baseman and slick-fielding shortstop who star for the

Beavers' opponents. As these vets drive past the ballpark and express their baseball passion, they now are officially home.

By 1955, when *Three Stripes in the Sun* came to theaters, the war had been over for a decade. The United States and Japan had become trusted allies, and what better way to unite them cinematically than to stage a game between Japanese ballplayers and American GIs? As the contest is played out, the cultural differences between the two nations are entertainingly contrasted via the aggressive on-field mentality of the Americans and the polite formalism of the Japanese.

Three Stripes in the Sun, The Best Years of Our Lives, and *Woman of the Year* utilize baseball as a metaphor for the nation's changing political and social climate. Yet all also illustrate how baseball has remained a constant on the American scene. For after all, the baseball season begins at a time of rejuvenation, when the snow is melting and flowers are blossoming, just as the title of a 1949 baseball movie tells us: *It Happens Every Spring.*

Springtime surely must be Dave Kovic's favorite season, if only because his glove and ball need no longer remain in his desk drawer. However, politics, Americanism, and baseball were linked decades prior to *Dave.* In *Remember the Day* (1941), set in the early twentieth century, a bright twelve-year-old boy, Dewey Roberts (Douglas Croft), is the star pitcher of the Auburn Grammar School baseball team. In class, Dewey is absorbed not in his textbook but in a Christy Mathewson-authored volume on how to pitch. In preparation for the big game against Rome, he practices hurling by throwing an eraser into a wastebasket. He is destined to become the centerpiece of the contest, a spirited affair played to a throng of avidly cheering children.

Unfortunately, our hero wrecks his knee while sliding into third base. And so this all-American boy, who loves baseball and boats, does not grow up to be Christy Mathewson. But he does mature into a nominee for the United States presidency. If a man is to be president, we are told in *Remember the Day,* one of the prerequisites is a love of baseball.

Conversely, bad boys never are ballplayers. To a juvenile delinquent, a ball or a bat is a weapon, rather than a piece of athletic equipment. In *The Blackboard Jungle* (1955), novice New York City high school English teacher Richard Dadier (Glenn Ford) completes writing his name on a blackboard. As he begins explaining its pronunciation, an unidentified student hurls a baseball at the board, smashing it and partially obliterating Dadier's name. The teacher picks up the ball, as the students peer at him silently and intently. Finally, Dadier announces, "Whoever threw that, you'll never pitch for the Yanks, boy."

Dadier's declaration is accurate, given the time period of the film in which he appears. Back then, the myth of the ballplayer was that of an all-American role model. A young punk who employs a baseball to badger a teacher *never* could play beside Mickey Mantle, Whitey Ford, and Yogi Berra! However, with the publication of Jim Bouton's *Ball Four* in 1970 came the revelation that not all New York Yankees were clean-living heroes. Such disclosures have had a sobering effect on society and popular culture; thus, in the more cynical 1990s, not all baseball lovers are super-patriots like Dave. In *Clear and Present Danger* (1994), a friend of the President of the United States and his family are killed by drug traffickers. "What are they going to do, come after me? Arrest me?" proclaims the defiant Colombian drug lord responsible for the murders. It is not without irony that, as he makes this pronouncement, he is swatting baseballs pitched to him in a makeshift batting range located on his haçienda.

However, a film such as *Clear and Present Danger* is the exception, rather than the rule. The majority of modern-era films that reference baseball, such as *It Could Happen to You, Dave,* and *The Big Picture,* offer pure, sweet, old-fashioned visions of the sport.

Throughout film history—including the post-*Ball Four* era—the myth of the idyllic American boyhood also has been a constant in baseball movies. *The Sandlot* (1993), set during the summer of 1962, spotlights a band of preteens who play ball by themselves on a makeshift field and have honed themselves into a crackerjack unit of hitters, runners, and fielders. As these youngsters share a simple, pure camaraderie, *The Sandlot* poignantly captures the essence of American boyhood as it depicts the playing of baseball as a sacred rite of youth.

This union of baseball and growing up in America is unabashedly melting-pot patriotic. Revealingly, the full name of Benny Rodriguez, the boys' leader and best player, is Benjamin Franklin Rodriguez: he may be Latino by background but, in the everyday reality of his life, he is a baseball-playing Latino American. Furthermore, in a poignant sequence, Benny and his pals play the summer's lone night game on the Fourth of July, under the glare of fireworks, with Ray Charles' soulful version of "God Bless America" on the soundtrack.

As a portrait of boyhood and baseball, *The Sandlot* is one in a long line of films. Their essence is captured in the Billy Wilder comedy *A Foreign Affair* (1948), set amid the rubble of postwar American-occupied Berlin. Here, a congressman notes, while watching some German kids play baseball, "One thing they don't have to worry about around here is breaking windows."

How many baseball biographies begin by showing their subjects as youngsters who are denied their places on the sandlots by bigger, louder kids, but when given their chance smash baseballs through windows? Young Lou Gehrig belts one out in such a manner, in *Pride of the Yankees* (1942). So does young Babe Ruth, in *The Babe* (1992). Or they make solid fielding plays, as does young Jackie Robinson in *The Jackie Robinson Story* (1950).

The Jackie Robinson Story is a simple, insightful screen biography that is both a relic of its era and a valuable social history. Granted, it (as well as other social justice films of the time) was designed for white audiences, with African-American culture noticeably absent. Yet it remains a significant first step upward from the shuffling racial celluloid stereotype.

Included in *The Jackie Robinson Story* are several pull-no-punches scenes depicting what Robinson suffered through in his quest to break baseball's color barrier. He is threatened by redneck fans and mercilessly mocked by opposing ballplayers who yell at him, "Hey, Jackie, gimme a shine" and "Hey, sambo, you wanna wash your dirty ears?" In response, Jackie (who plays himself in the film) lets his bat do his talking as he smashes base hits—proving that, in the words of Branch Rickey, who signed Robinson for the Brooklyn Dodgers, "We're dealing with rights here. The right of any American to play baseball, the American game."

Even though *The Jackie Robinson Story* acknowledges the racism of the era, it is by no means a radical polemic. Its scenario is over-loaded with fair-minded white men, as if to stress that not every white American is a bigot. A couple of whites acknowledge young Jackie's ability, and give him his first baseball glove. An athletic department employee at UCLA, where Jackie attends school, declares, "Colored boys are all right with me if they're the right color. I like a good, clean American boy with a B average." A former athletic rival recognizes and happily greets Jackie's brother Mack, himself a talented athlete who finished second to Jesse Owens in the 100-meter run at the 1936 Berlin Olympics. A Dodgers first baseman offers Jackie pointers on playing the position, even though it might mean his demotion from the starting lineup. Many of those who are against Robinson—minor league manager Clay Hopper, and a loud-mouthed baseball fan—come to favor the ballplayer once they see he is willing to dirty his uniform.

At the finale of *The Jackie Robinson Story,* Robinson has become established enough so that Rickey allows him to speak out on racism. However, Jackie does not lambaste bigotry. Instead, in a reflection of the anti-Communist rhetoric then becoming commonplace on screen, in the wake of the House Un-American Activities Committee hearings and the Hollywood Blacklist—Robinson testifies in Washington about how

> democracy works for those who are willing to fight for it, and I'm sure it's worth defending. . . . I'm certain that I and other Americans of many races and faiths have too much invested in our country's welfare to throw it away or to let it be taken from us.

The primary purpose of *The Jackie Robinson Story* is to reflect the reality that, despite his skin color, Robinson was allowed to live out his American Dream. The essence of the film is evident in its opening sequence. Here, a narrator proclaims, over the image of a young black lad walking down a road, "This is the story of a boy and his dream. But more than that, it is the story of an American boy, and a dream that is truly American."

Contrast such patriotic asides to the content of *The Court-Martial of Jackie Robinson* (1990) and *Soul of the Game* (1996), Robinson-related made-for-television movies. The first film tells the story of an attempt to court-martial Robinson (Andre Braugher) after he refused to move to the back of an army bus while stationed at Camp Hood in Texas during World War II. The Robinson portrayed here is a proud, defiant man who elicits a justifiable anger as he refuses to conform to life in a segregated military, and who speaks up clearly and loudly when confronted by any sort of discrimination.

Meanwhile, *Soul of the Game* is the story of three Negro League players at a pivotal point in their lives, and in the history of baseball:

Robinson (Blair Underwood) and the legendary Satchel Paige (Delroy Lindo) and Josh Gibson (Mykelti Williamson). In one sequence, Paige, Gibson, and Paige's wife Lahoma are on the road. They stop at a modest backcountry store, looked after by a disheveled young white girl thumbing thorough a movie fan magazine. The three blacks are well dressed, and compared to her are glamorous and prosperous. Lahoma offers the girl some tips on how to fix her hair. After paying for his purchase, Paige tells her to keep the change. As they are about to leave, Lahoma notes that she and the men have been driving all day, and she sure would appreciate it if she could use the washroom. Ever so innocently, the girl tells her, "Daddy don't let no niggers inside the house."

The child means no harm. But she must obey her father, and not allow a simple favor to these human beings who have treated her in such a friendly fashion. As they drive away, Gibson asks, rhetorically, "When does it end?"

With regard to the union of baseball and Americanism, *Soul of the Game* and *The Court-Martial of Jackie Robinson* are exceptions to the rule—just as Jim Crow has been an aberration in relation to the content of the Constitution and Bill of Rights. At the same time, their scenarios do not so much spotlight Jackie Robinson's accomplishments as the American tragedy of segregation and racism.

Still, as Robinson is a mythic figure in American history, his on-screen presence lends an automatic air of importance to a film. Such is the case in *Smoke* and its follow-up, *Blue in the Face* (both 1995), which are set in and around a Brooklyn cigar shop. In both films, characters wax nostalgic about the Dodgers, and the impact the team's abandoning the Borough of Churches for the orange groves of California had on Brooklyn and its citizens. In *Blue in the Face,* the ghost of Jackie Robinson even makes a cameo appearance.

In *Smoke* and *Blue in the Face,* baseball is intrinsically linked to civic pride, and civic identity. Meanwhile, on-screen images of ballparks are monuments to their cities. The Chicago location of the romantic comedy *While You Were Sleeping* (1995) is established via a series of shots of the city. One is of Wrigley Field, as much a symbol of the town as the Statue of Liberty or Empire State Building—or Yankee Stadium—are monuments to New York.

Unsurprisingly, perhaps the most beloved of all modern-era baseball films—Phil Alden Robinson's classic *Field of Dreams* (1989)—

is steeped in Americana. The film is the *It's a Wonderful Life* of baseball movies: a wistful fantasy about recaptured innocence and the timelessness of the game. Here, even baseball's villains find forgiveness as the spirits of Shoeless Joe Jackson and his fellow defamed Chicago Black Sox teammates come to play in an eternal, pastoral ballfield constructed in the middle of an Iowa cornfield by farmer/ex-1960s flower child Ray Kinsella (Kevin Costner).

Since his teens, Ray has been alienated from his now long-deceased father, and one of the film's most eloquent moments comes when he gets to meet his dad. Here, John Kinsella is a strapping young ballplayer, with his future in front of him. Ray can face him, and tell him what he was unable to as an angry young child of the 1960s. The men shake hands. As they play catch—a rite of camaraderie shared by father and son—their differences melt away, and their relationship is completed.

In *Field of Dreams,* anything is possible. Back in 1922, old Doc Graham (played by Burt Lancaster, and loosely based on a real-life one-game big leaguer named Archibald Wright "Moonlight" Graham) appeared in a single major league game, without getting a turn at bat. He went on to study medicine, and settled into a quiet but productive life as the town doctor in Chisholm, Minnesota. Graham died in 1972, and Kinsella is transported back in time where he meets the old man, whose sip of coffee in the majors was "like coming this close to your dreams."

Doc Graham's youth is restored. He is now Archie Graham, and he gets to play with Joe Jackson and the others. But young Archie fulfills his destiny by becoming old Doc Graham when Ray's daughter falls out of the bleachers and needs quick medical attention. The point, which is most meaningful in our celebrity-obsessed age, is that Graham need not have shined in the show to have lived a full, useful life. "If I'd only gotten to be a doctor for five minutes," he says, "*that* would be a tragedy."

Of all the characters in baseball films, perhaps the ones that are the most identifiable are the fans: Ray Kinsella, Charlie Lang, Dave Kovic, and even the Abraham Lincoln of *The Big Picture.* Even though there is nary a ballfield in *City Slickers* (1991), the film features average American males to whom every statistic-spewing baseball nut can relate. They are radio ad salesman Mitch (Billy Crystal), grocery store manager Phil (Daniel Stern), and sporting goods store owner Ed (Bruno Kirby).

While on a cattle drive vacation, the one woman in the group says she does not understand how men can obsessively memorize baseball trivia. She does not dislike baseball, she claims, but it is not "real life."

Phil forever disproves her statement when he chimes in, "I guess it is childish but, uh, when I was about eighteen and my dad and I couldn't communicate about anything at all, we would talk about baseball. That was real."

City Slickers may be linked to *Mr. Hobbs Takes a Vacation,* a 1962 comedy. Here, an invisible wall separates banker Hobbs (James Stewart) and his television-obsessed son, and so they bond by spending the day together on a boat. Almost immediately the boy asks his dad a series of baseball trivia questions regarding Bob Feller, Rogers Hornsby, and other Hall of Famers, culminating in the $64 one: "Did you really see Babe Ruth play?"

Yes, in 1928, responds Hobbs (whose first name is Roger, rather than Roy, of *The Natural* fame). And you can bet your 1952 Topps Mickey Mantle card that father and son are bonded for life—or, at least, until the escalation of the Vietnam War.

15

Writing Their Way Home:
American Writers and Baseball

Connie Ann Kirk

It's a strange time right now to be thinking about baseball, America, and writers' fascination with the game. As I worked this October weekend, Barry Bonds hit his seventy-third home run of the season, Cal Ripken retired, and the Mets closed their season singing "God Bless America" in a rocky chorus of off-key voices to a bundled crowd waving American flags on a cold, New York night. In a phone call to House Minority Leader, Dick Gephart, who sat in Camden Yards watching Ripken's last game, the same game at which former President Bill Clinton was also in attendance, President George W. Bush, former owner of the Texas Rangers, told Gephart that military strikes would begin the next day against terrorist targets in Afghanistan. As I write, smoke still rises from the death pyre in lower Manhattan. Thousands of bodies and remains have yet to be recovered and properly buried. The smoke and smell of that horrible scene, labeled Ground Zero, still weighs heavily at the bottom of the island, threatening to pull everything down with it into the sea. Oddly, that may be the only way that any sense of relief could be achieved from the black hole of grief that grips the nation at this particular moment.

Upstate, in the Finger Lakes Region just west of Cooperstown, the air prickles as usual with cooler temperatures and the crackling leaves of fall, but this time American flags curl and snap over pumpkins and cornstalks on countless porch steps in an unfamiliar mix of images from the summer's patriotic holidays held over to an autumn of unease. Everyone here knows somebody, or knows somebody else who knows somebody, who is among the missing downstate. Missing is still the word that is used. In this time of quick and confirmed information, it is inconceivable to most people that a loved one's body could simply disappear into thin air after just settling down at the desk with coffee and sports page, booting up the computer while catching a quick glimpse at the weekend's box scores.

The juxtaposition of America and baseball still works in these contexts; they are inextricably linked, and as I explore the connections American writers have made over the years to the game, I can already see the new stories coming. The stories from this season will be about lost innocence and new heroes, survivors and victims; they will be about doing one's job under extraordinary circumstances, staying focused in the midst of indescribable sorrow and distraction; they will be about the new battle between freedom and fear, and yet marvel will be there, too. There will be wonder in the stories about the interdenominational prayer service held in Yankee Stadium a couple of weeks ago, and how these things somehow all tie together even down to the cries of the widows and children in the half-full stands, and the fresh young faces of the Boys and Girls Choir of Harlem, who brought down the House that Ruth Built with the vitality of their voices. Writers will tell that story because they know it is part of who we are as Americans, how we cope. The history of baseball has run parallel with the history of the nation since before the Civil War (Honig 2-3). It has been played in one form or another through world wars and catastrophes, and not only sportswriters and historians but also novelists, playwrights, humorists, and poets have mined this metaphor many times for its richness and complexity of ideas, its concrete details that backdrop an abstract search for meaning. Americans talk baseball when they can't speak the unspeakable. It has always been the case, and this will be another one of those times.

What is it about baseball that makes scribes such as Roger Angell call it "the writer's game" (x)? What is it that fascinates writers about the beauty of the double play or makes them ponder an engrained image of the way a certain pitcher tipped his cap in the 1950s? Surely during most seasons there is not a national crisis of current proportions that makes writers look at the game more intensely as a metaphor. Not all of the connections writers see or feel are patriotic or nationalistic ones either. Most, in fact, are quite personal, even philosophical. Some are intellectual; few are academic. Writers are drawn to the game from their love of the sport itself, their player heroes, or the game's unique qualities, or from their own memories, like Annie Dillard's in Pittsburgh, of playing backlot ball. For writers as diverse as historian Doris Kearns Goodwin and comedy writer Billy Crystal, the lure of writing about the game is the same pull they feel to think about their childhoods and how their childhood experiences shaped the way they look at and function in the world. Videographer and writer Vanalyne Green calls it the "Mother Game" and sees the playing field in the shape of a womb (Nauen 224). Other female writers such as Kearns Goodwin and Ann Hood and countless male writers can't see a game without calling up memories of quality time spent with fathers. Others, such as Hemingway with his Santiago and DiMaggio in *The Old Man and the Sea,* did not grow up with the game. Still, they are drawn to write about it from a perspective of loss and longing for an American experience in which they were not privileged to share at a young age but that they recognize holds some kind of importance that they should not ignore as they mature. Still others, for example, the self-described "Baseball Wimp," Anna Quindlen, seem to write about the game out of respect, if not disdain, as though it is such an important institution of American life that an American writer must, at least, tip a hat to the playoffs and World Series out of guilt for walking blithely past the game the rest of the season.

Certainly one attraction to the game for writers must be that it reminds many of them of their principal passion, the act of writing itself. Poets Marianne Moore and Holly Prado wrote poems such as "Baseball and Writing" and "The World Series Is About Writing Poems," explicitly about this theme. Moore explains that both are exciting, hard work where "You can never tell . . . how it will go" (Nauen 3). Prado writes that in both, "all you want to do is connect" (271). Other baseball literature, of which there is a rich heritage and history, is more metaphoric about its similarities to the writer's art. Philip Roth's alliterative protagonist, Word "Smitty" Smith, for example, writes his version of *The Great American Novel* as the story of the lost, mythical Patriot League that no one will believe existed. As much as the League is mythic and unbelievable, so is a single novel, Roth seems to be saying, that can capture the American Dream to perfection. Even if it did exist, there would be too much disagreement about its authenticity for it to get the credit it deserved. Bernard Malamud's *The Natural* is as much about the success and failure associated with innate talent in sport as it is about a wonderboy kind of pen in America. When does the pen lose its charm? How long can natural talent stay true to its calling under the temptations of ambition? Robert Coover's *Universal Baseball Association, Inc., J. Henry Waugh, Prop.* sports a statistic-wielding protagonist playing an omniscient god with characters disguised as ballplayers and words disguised as numbers until he descends into madness in the hazy world that blurs what's real from what's fantasy. Baseball is a metaphor for life, as the speaker in Linda Pastan's poem "Baseball" finally agrees, and as such it is an irresistible subject for writing. Ready-made metaphors make writing about a subject easy and natural.

Another connection between the game and writing is in the important role that context plays in both. Writers know that context is everything. Shoot off a line of fiction or poetry; fire up a spray of dialogue in a dramatic moment for the stage. Writers know that all of these are nothing without the context in which the lines play out. It's context that gives the line life, a world in which to live. What has happened before is vital to the line's understanding for readers, but what writers know is that what's gone before is vital to the line's creation as well. Writers write in context before the reader reads that way, and they know that the creative act builds upon context, whether the words will keep moving in the same direction, or suddenly rebel against it. As with managers of baseball teams, writers must make choices, play out probabilities and possibilities in the mind before or while they are playing them out on the page. This is the thinking part of writing, the seven-hour part of a typical eight-hour day, where observers might see only one hour of the writer physically putting words down on paper or typing them up on a screen. This thinking about context and plotting the next move is the backdrop against which the miracles of the unexpected happen, the home runs and perfectly pitched games of the creative process. It's context and the long haul that builds the relationship between the game and the true fan, and a similar relationship exists between the page and the writer. The casual fan will cheer a good play but get bored between highlights. A casual reader may smile at catchy quotes in the Cliff's Notes version, but not read the whole book. What's missing for both of them is context.

Most writers who are fans of the game admit that demographics and timelessness play big factors in their emotions. A baseball player can be tall or short, thinner or fatter, as long as he or she has good eye-hand coordination and can run. Other attributes help as well, a good sense of judgment, for example, but those are the main qualities. The democratic nature of the players' backgrounds and physiques adds to the Americanness of it, too, and many writers are as attracted to that as is any other serious fan. Players' narratives attract storytellers, as evidenced by Susan E. Johnson's tales of the Rockford Peaches in *When Women Played Hardball.* Jackie Robinson's bravery attracted biographers, and historians have related many stories of various players in the so-called Negro League. It seems each player has overcome a major hurdle to earn the right to play ball for an audience. This is especially true in America, where industry and usefulness are almost requirements for citizenship, certainly for social acceptance. Writers, dreamers by nature, can relate to the obstacles met in American society by doing what one loves, *playing* an occupation, and getting paid for it, or at the very least, trying to make a suitable living. There are minor and major league writers, too, to be sure, and the movements back and forth between those subcultures is as dramatic as it is in baseball. Long-held claims of selling out from the purism of the small town minors to join "the show" of the majors persist in both worlds.

As with other serious fans, baseball writers lose themselves in the timelessness of the game. While each season of play marks the passing of years with remarkable clarity—the hope of spring openers, the intoxication of summer double-headers, the fire of October's World Series, the reflection of winter—each game in itself operates on its own internal time. As Roger Angell suggests, the game isn't called the national pastime for nothing:

> Within the ballpark, time moves differently, marked by no clock except the events of the game. . . . Baseball's time is seamless and invisible, a bubble within which players move at exactly the same pace and rhythms as all their predecessors. . . . Since baseball is measured only in outs, all you have to do is succeed utterly; keep hitting, keep the rally alive, and you have defeated time. You remain forever young. (351)

Concentrating on the subject of one's writing is like that, too. A writer at work, when it's going well, loses all track of time. The writing paces itself by how it's going, too, is measured in outs, too, if truth be told, stopping only when it's over or when life interferes, like a never-ending series of rain delays. And forever young? Who among us in this young nation wouldn't recognize that as a mantra in our homeland?

As one who has written in other settings about the metaphor of house and home in American literature, I conjecture that another reason many writers love baseball may be that the game represents the American inner struggle between contentment and restlessness, of longing for home while at the same time refusing to stay put once we get there. After all, the batter begins at home and strikes out taking a risk. His sole purpose is to get a wild, free run around the bases and back home before he's caught. There's something childlike about this, as well as something American. As a nation populated primarily of immigrants and their descendants who were orphaned from a Motherland looking for a new home, we bear an inherent restlessness in our national psyche. We keep looking for a better place. We move to the frontier, whether it be out West or outer space. We move out rather than stay in family homes and inherit aging property from our elders. We build new houses rather than remodel old ones. This is beginning to change, but only in the past few decades. Home is a loaded word anyway, but the American home carries with it the added burden of the American Dream. Home can stand for success or failure, accomplishment or deadweight, depending on the circumstances. We need to be able to leave it at will and return to it only on our own terms. If we cannot leave, we're unhappy; if we cannot return or make a new home somewhere else, we drift. Can it be any accident that America's pastime is about sticking your neck out, blasting a successful hit out of the ballpark, and then making it safely home? They may not realize it, but American writers probably feel this impulse in their bones, both from their own experience and from reading the work of their colleagues and predecessors.

As historians and baseball "literatoors" tell us, Cooperstown native and namesake descendant, James Fenimore Cooper, got it wrong in his autobiographical novel about a man who returns to town to rebuild the family home. In his 1838 novel, *Home As Found,* the protagonist meets with grief from the townspeople when he puts up no trespassing signs around his land where boys have begun playing a "ballgame" with stick and ball in his absence. Just as we might want the other hometown myth to be true, Abner Doubleday's inventing the game in that same town a year later, our desire to have this ball game of Cooper's be baseball is also deflated by history. It appears, from the rest of the description, that the game he wrote about is something more akin to field hockey (Zoss 257). Still, there is something classically un-American about both of Cooper's efforts here. The first is that he discouraged boys from playing any type of ballgame on his long-ignored property, and the second is that he would try to establish a medieval sort of family dynasty out of that property, a trait that is condemned by American society at large and described by countless American writers. Just think of Poe, Hawthorne, Faulkner, Fitzgerald, and Jane Smiley, to name a few.

If Cooper missed the ball about inaugurating baseball as the homegrown American sport from his own village, other writers, less known for singing the sport's praises than for singing about other things, were quick to pick it up. Walt Whitman, for example, that well-known songster to himself and his homeland, swept up what he called the "beautiful hurrah game" this way:

> Well—it's our game; that's the chief fact in connection with it: America's game; has the snap, go, fling, of the American atmosphere; it belongs as much to our institutions, fits into them significantly, as our constitution's laws; is just as important in the sum total of our historic life. (qtd. in Zoss 258)

As usual, old Walt knew a good American tradition when he saw it. It didn't hurt either that the players looked good to him doing what he called in section 33 of "Song of Myself" this "manly activity."

If Whitman claimed the game for the home team crowd, Mark Twain took it on the road. In 1889, he made a speech in Hawaii at a banquet held for the round-the-world teams that were on tour. He had this to say:

> They have carried the American name to the uttermost parts of the earth—and covered it in glory every time. That is a service to sentiment; but they did the general world a large practical service, also—a service to the great science of geography. . . . I drink long life to the boys who ploughed a new equator round the globe stealing bases on their bellies! (qtd. in Zoss 260)

Typical of Twain, he found a way to commodify the game, to make it something useful to the world. It would grow to become one of the great exports of the United States.

The notions of America and baseball, house and home, go together in our collective consciousness. Home is both the starting point and the final destination. Kids playing backlot ball have to be in the house before dark. Teammates holler "Go home!" or "Throw home!" depending on where they are in the top or bottom of an inning. Home can be stolen. The best hit possible is a home run. It's the *House* that Ruth Built, not the stadium. As Vanalyne Green notes, "And what is home anyway? Home is a white surface in the shape of a house" (Nauen 228). When you think about it, that is exactly what it is.

It's been a long time since baseball playoffs took place during wartime in the United States. During this, the end of the 2001 season, they sing solemn renditions of "God Bless America" instead of the playful "Take Me Out to the Ballgame" during the seventh-inning stretch. Players wear small flags sewn on their uniforms, and there are more American flags than team pennants in the stands. Most recently, a poison powder called anthrax is showing up in envelopes in government and media offices across the country; and a new government agency, called the Agency for Homeland Security, has been established for citizen protection. Blimps and planes are not allowed to fly over stadiums, or they risk being shot down by F-16 fighter jets on high alert, guarding the homeland. Fans are searched extensively at the doors, but they don't mind and wait patiently. The battle between freedom and fear continues. Unlike Stephen Crane, possibly the best-known ballplayer to have written classic American fiction (*Red Badge of Courage* about the Civil War), contemporary American writers look at the game for what it reflects about American life here and now. The only certain thing about these stories at the moment is that they will be worth writing home about, but their outcome is unknown.

BIBLIOGRAPHY

Angell, Roger. *Once More Around the Park: A Baseball Reader.* New York: Ballantine Books, 1991.

Cooper, James Fenimore. *Home As Found.* 1838. New York: Stringer and Townsend, 1855.

Coover, Robert. *Universal Baseball Association, Inc., J. Henry Waugh, Prop.* New York: Random House, 1968.

Honig, Donald. *Baseball America: The Heroes of the Game and the Times of Their Glory.* New York: Macmillan, 1985.

Johnson, Susan E. *When Women Played Hardball.* Seattle, WA: Seal Press, 1994.

Malamud, Bernard. *The Natural.* New York: Farrar, Straus, and Giroux, 1952.

Nauen, Elinor, ed. *Diamonds Are a Girl's Best Friend: Women Writers on Baseball.* Boston: Faber and Faber, 1993.

Roth, Philip. *The Great American Novel.* New York: Holt, Rinehart, and Winston, 1973.

Zoss, Joel and John Bowman. *Diamonds in the Rough: The Untold History of Baseball.* New York: Macmillan, 1989.

16

Baseball As a Second Language: The Impenetrability of Our National Pastime

Seth Whidden

It has become almost commonplace, when writing about the role of baseball in American culture, to quote Jacques Barzun's half-century-old statement about baseball from *God's Country and Mine*. In the middle of a comparison between baseball and cricket, Barzun writes, "Whoever wants to know the heart and mind of America had better learn baseball, the rules and realities of the game . . ." (159). While Barzun's comments certainly place a great importance—and pressure—on foreigners who want to learn about America, David Halberstam hints that the bar might be too high, saying that baseball

> is the sport that a foreigner is least likely to take to. You have to grow up playing it, you have to accept the lore of the bubble-gum card, and believe that if the answer to the Mays-Snider-Mantle question is found, then the universe will be a simpler and more ordered place. (qtd. in Mungo 167)

Gerald Early's accurate contextualization of Barzun's remarks not-withstanding,[1] it seems clear that the stakes are indeed high for any foreigner who sees the sport as a window into a slice of American culture and who thus attempts to learn the game of baseball. What are the obstacles confronting foreigners when they try to understand baseball? To what extent do the vocabulary and the complicated nature of the rules of the game hinder a newcomer's appreciation? On a larger scale, what does the impenetrability of baseball say about the difficulty of learning the greater American culture in general? This study will attempt to answer these questions, based in large part on my experience from English As a Second Language classrooms in France and in the United States, as well as on trips to the bleachers of Fenway Park with baseball neophytes.[2]

The Pregame: Learning the Game

From a pedagogical standpoint, baseball is surely difficult to explain, and anyone who believes otherwise is welcome to try to explain the essential aspects of the game in fifty words or less. A recent article about baseball idioms in American English that appeared in a German linguistics journal went so far as to include the *New York Public Library Desk Reference*'s definition of baseball (Probst). While succinct (just over four hundred words) and doubtless useful for the article's readers, one can only imagine their confusion upon reading, in the opening sentence of the definition, that "Baseball . . . has nine or ten players on each side" (qtd. in Probst 214). Nine *or* ten?

Before worrying about such confusing matters, the first thing that must be considered is the sheer amount of vocabulary involved.[3] Some baseball words are straightforward, others more difficult, and the game's many facets require that Baseball As a Second Language lessons be built around specific elements of the game. For starters, there are the defensive positions and the field itself; some terms, such as first base, second base, and third base, follow a certain pattern, as do the outfield (left, right, and center). Most of the defensive positions are equally logical (as are, for that matter, "deep" and "shallow" positions in the outfield). Other aspects of the field, such as the pitcher's mound, pitcher's rubber, and batter's box, all make sense once the students learn where the pitcher and batter are normally positioned. Even the designated hitter, although not universally appreciated, at least bears a name that accurately presents its role.

Lest the students think that baseball is always this predictable, I teach them some words that seem to have neither rhyme nor reason: shortstop, dugout, and bullpen. While the latter two are eventually accepted as comprehensible—a dugout is dug out of the ground, a bullpen holds awaiting relief pitchers as a pen would hold bulls—the idea of a shortstop is clearly one of the most bothersome terms in the first lessons of Baseball As a Second Language. Breaking the word down into its components does little good; although the position could be interpreted as a short stop between second base and third base (as its name might suggest), it is no more a midpoint between second and third than the second baseman's position is between first and second. And what about the second baseman, anyway? If the first baseman and third baseman play a couple of steps away from first and third, respectively, why doesn't the second baseman play just a couple of steps away from second?[4] More to the point: Why does the second baseman seem to be positioned no closer to his namesake base than the shortstop?

Once students begrudgingly accept the explanation that there is no explanation (to which they have already grown accustomed in learning English grammar), we move on to the general vocabulary governing how baseball is played. Some words are as straightforward as can be: "single," "double," "triple," and "home run"; even "ground-rule double" is easy to pick up. Other words need simply be learned; while the word "inning" is a new one, most students are familiar with games being divided up in some way, often into quarters, halves, periods, or sets. With its sets, tennis is particularly useful, for students who know tennis will be able to compare the service, which alternates by game, to the notion of an inning being divided into a "top" half and a "bottom" half.[5]

Another word that defies easy explanation is "bunt." While some might find it interesting, most students would get too confused with the fact that the word is derived from the word "butt": "to strike or push with the horns or head; BUTT <the ram *bunted* the boy so that he sat down with a jolt>" (*Webster's* 297). Similarly, it is best that the students simply accept the fact that three of the bases are called "base," while the fourth, pentagonal-shaped one is "home *plate*," and that the pitcher can throw pitches called "curveball," "fastball," "knuckleball," and "slider."[6]

The last words of vocabulary bridge the gap between learning the lingo and the actual play of the game: that is, calling balls and strikes. One important consideration to explain to students is when base runners are forced and when they are not (and, consequently, when fielders have to tag the runners out and when they can simply step on a base to get an out). Also, as with much of the vocabulary already discussed, students must simply accept the fact that a pitch is considered a "strike" *not* when the batter strikes the ball with his bat (as the verb "strike" might suggest) but rather when he misses it completely. The difference between a ball and strike is easily made clear by a brief explanation of the strike zone (and it is strongly recommended to stick to the theoretical "knees to the letters" definition, rather than discuss the subjective and ever-changing nature of this fundamental aspect of the game).

If only calling balls and strikes were that easy! Students are positively flummoxed to learn of all the different kinds of strikes (and which strikes can be a third strike and which cannot). Called strikes and swinging strikes make sense, but the following rules are not so logical:

1. Foul balls can be the first and second strikes against a batter, but not the third and final one;
2. Bunted balls, when foul, can be the first, second, and third strikes;
3. A dropped third strike is played like a ground ball in fair territory; and
4. A pop-up in foul territory is a simple foul ball if not touched by a fielder. If a fielder catches it, it is played as if it were in fair territory—but if the fielder tries to catch it and drops it, it's just a foul ball.

Most other aspects of the game—that is, those that one could reasonably expect to see at most baseball games—are easier to get a handle on. Runners tagging up before advancing after a fly ball to the outfield and the different types of double plays are very visual in nature and thus are easily explained with a chalkboard and some Xs and Os.

Warming Up: Watching a Game on Television (with the Aid of a Pause Button)

Explaining a batter's motivation—to hit the ball and reach base safely—is easy. But a pitcher's motivation—to get the hitter to hit a bad pitch or, ideally, to get him to strike out—is not self-evident. To really understand what a pitcher is trying to do, the students need to understand what he has to work with. Although the names of the different kinds of pitches can be learned, and although students can watch a teacher grip and pretend to throw a curveball, a knuckleball, a split-finger fastball, etc., these pitches are very hard to imagine. So, once students have a comfortable understanding of the general play of the game, watching a video of a couple of innings—pausing regularly for discussions and explanations—can be most helpful. Unless a pitcher has an extraordinary amount of movement on his pitches, and depending on the camera angles used by the broadcast crew, students must most often learn to accept the movement of an eighty-five mph curveball on faith alone (that is, unless the class can play with Wiffle balls).

For the most part, the video phase of the Baseball As a Second Language lessons serves to reinforce the students' basic understanding of the game and its vocabulary. Furthermore, the use of videotape can be used to point out colorful home run calls, comprehensible baseball expressions, and even local accents (e.g., Jerry Remy, colorful announcer for the Red Sox television broadcast and former Red Sox second baseman, who offers his viewing audience a relatively thick, and very recognizable, New England accent[7]). Once students can watch an inning or two of a typical ball game (a couple of hits here, a strikeout there), they are ready for the real thing.

Out with the Crowd: Watching the Game from the Bleachers at Fenway

A foreigner's first few experiences at a baseball game usually elicit reactions that fall into one of two categories: comments on the pace of the game and comments on the crowd. The pace of the game is considered to be excruciatingly slow, as one might expect. It should be noted that foreigners are not alone in this opinion, and that many people who understand baseball perfectly find its pace too slow.[8] For some, in fact, baseball's strength lies in its lack of action, relative to other sports:

> Many people say baseball is boring, and they're right. That's what's great about it. A spectacular play stands out vividly, an individual achievement, after minutes or hours of nothing happening. Baseball is the only game in which the Perfect Game is one in which nothing happens at all—no hits, runs, walks, errors, no men on base. (I met an eighty-year-old man who had

seen only one major league game in his life, Don Larsen's perfect game in the 1956 World Series. "Nothing happened," he
complained, "but everybody went crazy.") (Mungo 3)

Criticisms from newcomers to the game are certainly understandable; not only has the average length of a nine-inning baseball game
increased dramatically in the past twenty years, but no one who is
watching their first baseball game will understand all the strategy behind every leaning outfielder, every pitch, and every batter's stance.
While these nuances are the subject of fascinating in-depth studies
found in recent books by former players Keith Hernandez and Tim
McCarver (see bibliography), they are well beyond the grasp of the
typical Baseball As a Second Language student (and even beyond
that of many casual baseball fans, it should be noted).

It is precisely because of baseball's slow pace that, as with many
ticket-holders in attendance, most students spend as much time observing other people in the stands as the game itself. While they risk missing the third and fourth throw a pitcher might make to first base to
keep a base runner close, they often gain valuable insight into the average fan's attention level and thus enrich their comments in the post-
game discussion. For one thing, many first-time attendees are quick
to mention the amiable atmosphere in the stands; much unlike the hoo-
liganism that is a part of being a soccer fan in Europe, for example,
there are many more families with children than some Baseball As a
Second Language students usually expect. In addition, students are often surprised—and distracted, and certainly entertained—by all the di-
versions in which fans participate, as if passing the time while waiting for something to happen on the field. Many bleacher-goers at
Fenway Park are treated to a number of beach balls (smuggled in by
fans), which are punched and slapped around the outfield sections
until they (unfailingly) fall onto the playing field, stopping play and
causing an attendant to rush out and pop them. Also at Fenway, the
bleachers almost always seem to be the source of "the wave," which
wraps around the stadium a couple of times every game. Similar dis-
tractions from the actual play of the game occur when a fan interrupts
the game by running onto the field to slide into a base and when
fans—drunken or not—get into fights or otherwise distinguish themselves in ways that require their removal from the stadium. Last, stu-

dents argue, the very necessity of a seventh-inning stretch—what they see as distraction par excellence—is made possible by the slowness of the game itself. Of course, rain delays further try their patience.

A category of student reactions that should perhaps be added to the above two includes all the questions about things not discussed in class prior to the game, but which arise during a trip to the ballpark. To be sure, a Baseball As a Second Language teacher must decide which aspects of the game to teach and which to pass over, for one would need to spend months discussing every situation that might possibly come up during the course of a single game. Luckily, some things—a manager arguing a call, for example—need little or no explanation. Even if that manager is ejected, most students can figure out what is going on from the manager's body language, the umpire's signal of ejection, and the general crowd reaction. Similarly, one can quickly explain that a hit batsman is entitled to first base, and students can certainly understand—given the blazing speed of pitches and their thoughts of how it must feel to get hit—why some batters choose to charge the mound rather than go directly to first. By extension, most students of Baseball As a Second Language need no explanation as to why players otherwise sitting in the dugout feel compelled to rush the field and support their teammates in such altercations. Strategic moves—pinch hitters and runners, overshifts against pull hitters, etc.,—can be explained on the spot, if and when necessary, to the most attentive students; for other students, such deviations from the norm are either ignored or thought to be inconsequential. And finally, a teacher has to hope that scuffed balls, spitballs, and pine tar irregularities just don't come up during the game—such infractions are barely visible from bleacher seats, happen very infrequently, and would be difficult to explain quickly.

The Postgame: Consequences for Foreigners

If anything, this brief discussion of a possible approach to Baseball As a Second Language has shown just how much is involved in learning about baseball—not to the point of understanding which pitch counts are good for the hit-and-run, but even to follow a typical game in person. It's little wonder that many foreigners quickly lose interest when faced with the daunting task of sitting through numerous lessons in order to follow a game that seems to offer very little action. What, then, does baseball's impenetrability say about the larger question of the accessibility of American culture, what Barzun calls "the heart and mind of America"?

The answer, for students of Baseball As a Second Language, is simple: As with American culture, baseball is a tough nut to crack. The game seems simple—even boring—on the surface, only to reveal myriad layers of strategy and nuances upon closer examination. In today's increasingly complicated American society, no one aspect—be it political, economic, literary, or otherwise—can offer the single key into American culture the way Barzun suggested. In order to familiarize themselves with "the heart and mind of America," the task for foreigners is infinitely more difficult than it was fifty years ago and grows more so by the day. To some extent, the numerous facets of modern American culture are so intertwined that any one of them, branching out in practically every imaginable direction, reveals much of the best and worst that America has to offer. One has only to consider Jackie Robinson's impact on baseball, the numerous films, songs, and stories written about baseball, and the next labor dispute between the owners and the players' union to see how American baseball is intrinsically linked to American race relations, artistic production, and the economy, respectively.

No, they need not understand the importance of Halberstam's "Mays-Snider-Mantle question," nor today's "Nomar-A-Rod-Jeter" equivalent, in order to understand much of American culture. But they would be hard pressed to find a more enjoyable way to learn about it.

NOTES

1. Recently, Early has quite correctly situated Barzun's words, pointing out that they come from "the age of the Marshall Plan" (9) and that ". . . by the middle of the twentieth century, baseball as an unquestioned symbol and performance-ritual of the best qualities of something called Americanism was an entrenched truism" (10).

2. As a result, these observations would not be possible without the curiosity and keen insight of Hervé Hilaire, Keith Martin, and others, as well as the generous support of the English Language Center in Boston, Massachusetts. In addition, assistance with lesson plans and with an earlier draft of this study came from Chris and Harley Gorton and Andrew Seewald.

3. Such linguistic concerns do not even include the numerous idiomatic expressions related to baseball ("caught in a pickle," "suicide squeeze," etc.), the importance given to nicknames, or to expressions from famous baseball personalities (such as Casey Stengel and Yogi Berra), all of which are well beyond the capacity of most students of Baseball As a Second Language. Similarly beyond the scope of this study are the numerous phrases in American English that come from baseball; see Probst for a study of these idiomatic expressions.

4. This discussion is obviously based on the most traditional defensive positions—a first lesson in Baseball As a Second Language is not the time to point out the overshift employed by some managers against left-handed pull hitters such as Ken Griffey Jr., for example.

5. For French students, even the vocabulary is the same—the French use the word "une manche" to designate a set in tennis and the same word also means an inning of baseball, as anyone who has ever heard a Montreal Expos' radio broadcast will confirm.

6. Just as expressions such as "caught in a pickle" are beyond the scope of the first lessons of Baseball As a Second Language, it would be too confusing to delve into the numerous slang terms for pitches ("cheese," "cheddar," "high heater," "brushback," etc.) at this stage.

7. Remy was born in Fall River and grew up in nearby Somerset (both in southeastern Massachusetts).

8. In addition, attempts by Major League Baseball in the last few years to speed up the game indicate that this observation is far from limited to newcomers to the sport. "In February 1998, a memo was sent to teams outlining a series of speed-up measures, with the goal of cutting the average by fifteen minutes" ("Average Baseball Game"). These measures were in large response to the third game of the 1997 World Series, which lasted four hours, twelve minutes and which prompted commissioner Bud Selig to say, "The 'Unfinished Symphony' had a better chance of finishing before that game last night" (qtd. in Blum). A year and a half later, in October 2000, the sport set a new record for game time: "The average length of a nine-inning game was two hours, fifty-eight minutes, according to the Elias Sports Bureau, baseball's statistician. That makes a five-minute increase from 1999 and an eleven-minute increase from 1998. It breaks the previous mark of 2:54, set in 1994" ("Average Baseball Game"). Sandy Alderson, Executive Vice-President of Baseball Operations in the Commissioner's Office, indicated between the 2000 and 2001 seasons that shortening the average length of a game was a priority: "The time of game is an issue that we need to address, not one we need to highlight. We can get the time down appreciably without making major changes" (Dubow). Apparently not; despite whatever efforts may have been made, the average game time during the 2001 season was only down four minutes, to 2:54. In March 2002, Vice President of On-Field Operations Bob Watson discussed the matter with twenty of the thirty teams during spring training and reemphasized baseball's desire to speed up the game, saying "Things have kind of slipped through the cracks. What we want to do is basically cut down the dead time" (qtd. in Blum).

BIBLIOGRAPHY

"Average Baseball Game Up Five Minutes." *AP Online,* 2 Oct. 2000.

Barzun, Jacques. *God's Country and Mine: A Declaration of Love Spiced with a Few Harsh Words.* Boston: Little, Brown, 1954.

Blum, Ronald. "Bob Watson Looking to Speed Up Games." *AP Online,* 20 March 2002.

Dubow, Josh. "Baseball to Restore Strike Zone." *AP Online,* 8 Nov. 2000.

Early, Gerald. "Birdland: Two Observations on the Cultural Significance of Baseball." *American Poetry Review* 25.4 (1996): 9-12.

Hernandez, Keith, and Mike Bryan. *Pure Baseball: Pitch by Pitch for the Advanced Fan.* New York: HarperCollins, 1994.

McCarver, Tim, and Danny Peary. *Tim McCarver's Baseball for Brain Surgeons and Other Fans.* New York: Villard Books, 1998.

Mungo, Raymond. *Confessions from Left Field: A Baseball Pilgrimage.* New York: E. P. Dutton, 1983.

Probst, Gerhard. "American English and Baseball." *Neusprachliche Mitteilungen aus Wissenschaft und Praxis* 50.4 (1997): 214-223.

Webster's Third New International Dictionary of the English Language, Unabridged. Ed. Philip Babcock Gobe. Springfield, MA: Merriam-Webster, 1993.

17

Baseball Poetry:
Society's Overlooked and Underestimated Literary Art Form

Dan Zamudio

> There is not only fun and relaxation in baseball for a boy. There is also a poetry about the game. And the poetry of the game constitutes part of its appeal. It becomes a part of ourselves.
>
> James T. Farrell
> *My Baseball Diary*

Between 1990 and 1999 a surge occurred in the publication of baseball poetry books throughout the United States. More baseball poems were published during this time span than in any other decade since the development of the sport. Why had interest in baseball poetry grown so dramatically in the latter part of the century? Poet Gene Fehler believes "baseball has had an incredible impact on public consciousness throughout the twentieth century; the poetry of baseball is mostly simply a mirror reflection of that public consciousness." What was happening to the "public consciousness" between this time period that would provoke people throughout the country to begin writing poetry about a game? One explanation can be that poetry by definition possesses "a tenderly pleasing quality" (*DK* 628) in a way other literature may not be able to capture. It is this "tender quality" that compels baseball fans to write about a childhood sport. Although there have been many scholarly books and articles written about the baseball literature and its impact on society, very little has ever focused on baseball poetry. Due to the popularity of baseball poetry in the later part of the century, I believe this type of print culture is important as a form of expression for all baseball enthusiasts and plays an intricate role in the history and popularity of the sport.

During the 1990s baseball had become a corporate-sponsored megamillion-dollar industry. Player strikes and astronomical salaries had replaced box scores as headlines. Old ballparks had been demolished and replaced with new "Mall-parks." Ticket prices had been raised to a level that prevented many fans from being able to afford to attend a game. Slowly, the average baseball enthusiast had become excluded from the national pastime and became nostalgic for the way things used to be.

Why then is baseball poetry important? The increase in baseball poetry could be considered a direct response to a "separation anxiety" many people may be feeling toward the game. Often, a common theme in baseball poems is a reminiscing of a simpler time when the public felt it was "their" game and the sport was truly a mirror reflecting society. During baseball's heyday of the 1920s and 1930s, professional ballplayers were considered almost part of one's family. Hometown teams and players were used to help define their cities from the rest of the country. Baseball was something the average person could grasp, understand, and take pride in as a community.

How has the baseball poetry evolved with the changes in society and what is the cultural impact of baseball poems? The best way to approach these two questions is to begin with a brief history of the published baseball poem.

According to Don Hall in his book *Fathers Playing Catch with Sons,* H. L. Mencken traced the origins of the first mention of baseball in print to a poem in a children's book published in 1744. The poem, titled "Base-Ball," appeared in *A Little Pretty Pocket Book* published in England by John Newbery:

> The Ball once struck off
> Away flies the Boy
> To the next destin'd Post
> And then Home with Joy. (57-58)

One interesting aspect about baseball's first published reference is that it was written as a poem. This simple nineteen-word verse sets the tone for all baseball literature and establishes the game as a "tenderly pleasing" form of relaxation.

Besides a scattered few poems such as "Epitaph on a Base Ballist" (1872) and "Slug the Ump" (1886), baseball poetry seemed to be virtually nonexistent in any form of print for the next 144 years. During this time frame baseball was considered predominantly a children's activity. Then, in 1871, the National Association of Professional Base Ball Players formed the first professional baseball league which lifted the children's activity to another level. A few years later Albert Spalding wrote the *Spalding Official Baseball Guide* which laid out the ground rules to this "new" sport.

On June 3, 1888, the *San Francisco Examiner* published a long rhyming baseball poem titled *Casey at the Bat: A Ballad of the Republic* written by "Phin." Author Martin Gardner describes the public's first response to this poem in his book *The Annotated Casey at the Bat:*

> No one paid much attention to *Casey.* Baseball fans in San Francisco chuckled over it and a few eastern papers reprinted it, but it could have been quickly forgotten had it not been for a sequence of improbable events. (3)

The success of Casey can be attributed to Archibald Clavering Gunter, a novelist who would often cut articles out of newspapers to use for future story ideas. Nearly one year after "Casey" had appeared in print, De Wolf Hopper (a young comedian/singer and friend of Gunter) was to perform in front of an audience that consisted of baseball players from the Chicago White Stockings and New York Giants. Gunter gave the poem to Hopper who quickly memorized and performed it during the second act. Hopper describes his first reading of the poem in his memoirs *Once a Clown Always a Clown:*

> When I dropped my voice to B flat, below low C, at "the multitude was awed" I remember seeing Buck Ewing's gallant mustachios give a single nervous twitch. And as the house, after a moment of silence, grasped the anticlimactic denouement, it shouted its glee. (81)

The poem was an overwhelming hit and has since served as an "inspiration for films, cartoons, an opera, a ballet, a novel, paintings and hundreds of parodies, not to mention millions of spirited oral recitations in parlors and school auditoriums" (Regan 91). One of the most important impacts *Casey at the Bat* had on society was how it showed that baseball was more than just a relaxing pastime. Baseball was also worthy of poetic verse. Even though *Casey*'s author Ernest Lawrence Thayer, a Harvard graduate, believed the poem was "not poetry at all ... but merely a simple rhyme with a vigorous beat" (Isaacs 20), millions of people disagreed. Mr. Thayer, along with *Casey,* had opened a door for all avid baseball fans to become would-be poets.

Baseball poetry has evolved dramatically since the days of *Casey at the Bat*. Early in the twentieth century, sports reporters would often write short baseball-themed poems to fill newspaper space. These poems were often rhymed poems with more "word play" than actual poetics. A good example is "Baseball's Sad Lexicon" by Franklin P. Adams:

> These are the saddest of possible words:
> Tinker-to-Evers-to-Chance.
> Trio of Bear Cubs and fleeter than birds
> Tinker-to-Evers-to-Chance.
> Ruthlessly pricking our gonfalon bubble,
> Making a Giant hit into a double,
> Words that are weighty with nothing but trouble
> Tinker-to-Evers-to-Chance.

Eventually, well-respected poets began to express their opinions toward the game. Writer Tim Peeler believes that baseball poetry has "followed much the same route as other poetry in that it has become less formal, more proselike and often more personal."

Carl Sandburg, in the poem "Hits and Runs" published in 1918, uses a free-verse style of poetry to share his impressions of watching a ball game. This poem was written only eight years after "Baseball's Sad Lexicon" was published and is an excellent example of how baseball poetry was evolving from a sing-song ditty to a respected art form:

> I remember the Chillicothe ball players grappling the
>   Rock Island ball players in a sixteen-inning game ended
>   by darkness.

> And the shoulders of the Chillicothe players were a red
> smoke against the sundown and the shoulders of the
> Rock Island Players were a yellow smoke against the
> sundown.
> And the umpire's voice was hoarse calling balls and strikes
> and outs, and the umpire's throat fought in the dust for
> song. (*Hosannah* 41)

Concerning the changes in baseball poetry after Sandburg's "Hits and Runs," one of the most interesting observations is how nearly all the baseball poems published after 1918 were written in a free-verse style without the use of rhyme. It seems that rhyming baseball poems nearly disappear from the publishing world. Of course people were still writing poems in rhyme, but the standard for published work was changing. Sandburg brought an intellectual quality to baseball poetry that helped lift it from newspaper filler to the world of literature.

Books entirely dedicated to baseball poetry were scarce in the early part of the 1900s. Prior to the second half of the century, baseball and other sport-themed poems were often found printed inside poetry chapbooks, academic literary journals, or anthologies. Two rare books, *Base-Ball Ballads* by Grantland Rice (1910) and *Baseballogy* by Edmund Vance Cooke (1912), are early examples of the type of baseball poetry that was popular during that era. Both books consist of long rhymed poems whose topics range from women wearing big hats at ball games and "Casey" parodies to the umpire's bad calls and politics. In "Batter Up" from *Baseballogy,* Mr. Cooke writes:

> Who cares which politician leads the band?
> Who cares who'll be the coming White House tenant?
> We only know the season's coming, and
> We know our club is going to win the pennant. (17)

Although this poem was written over ninety years ago, the sentiments expressed for baseball and politics could easily describe many people's responses today toward presidential elections versus baseball.

Not many baseball poetry books were published between 1912 and the late 1960s. In the early 1970s baseball poetry books once again began to re-emerge. One of the first books published during that decade consisting solely of baseball poetry written by a single author is *Fan Poems* by Tom Clark.

Fan Poems consists of thirty-three poems that focus mostly on players from the 1970s era. All of the poems were written in a free-verse style that reads like letters to the players. In the poem "To Reggie Jackson," Mr. Clark expresses fondness for Jackson despite the player's loquaciousness.

These poems express a fan's enthusiasm not just for the game but also for the players. The detailed knowledge he shares with the players about their backgrounds, careers, and interests, helps him to develop almost a friendship with his heroes. For instance, in the poem "To Ken Holtzman," Mr. Clark's friendship allows him to joke about one player to another, in this case sharing a laugh with Holtzman at Reggie Jackson's expense.

The most interesting aspect about this book is how it was "partially supported by a grant from the National Endowment for the Arts." Could this mean the government had now accepted baseball poetry as a "true" art form that should be supported? In some historical way, 1976 can be considered a milestone year for baseball poetry.

By the mid-1990s, there were approximately thirty baseball poetry books published. Of those thirty, nearly half were produced within that decade. McFarland and Company, publishers best known for their general reference books and scholarly monographs, helped to increase interest in baseball poems by becoming the leaders in the publication of baseball poetry books during the 1990s. Many of the McFarland books, such as *Center Field Grasses* by Gene Fehler, *Green Fields and White Lines* by Robert L. Harrison and *Romancing the Horsehide* by Gene Carney, are now out of print and often sell at used bookstores or online for double their original price. Despite this demand, author Gene Carney thinks that "baseball poetry has a very tiny readership . . . its impact is no doubt minimal on the culture." I couldn't disagree more with this statement.

During baseball's "tough times" of the 1990s, I believe people began to write baseball poetry to remember how and why the sport was important in their lives. In the midst of this turmoil, Mike Schacht (baseball enthusiast, painter, and cofounder of *Fan Magazine*) placed an ad in a writer's magazine requesting submissions of haiku to his baseball journal. Hundreds of haiku arrived expressing pleasant memories of the game.

Other baseball literary journals such as *Spit Ball* and *Elysian Fields Quarterly* have always included a number of baseball poems inside each issue. In 1994, *Elysian Fields Quarterly* even published a special issue titled "The Poet's Game" which featured nearly twenty baseball poems, some written as parodies on poems of Shakespeare and W.B. Yeats. By writing parodies, baseball fans were encouraged to read the original poems and gain a better appreciation for all different types of poetry.

One small moment in baseball poetry's cultural impact was when former President Bill Clinton used it as a token of affection toward his wife Hillary. In 1996, before his infidelity scandal became national news, Clinton gave Hillary (an avid baseball fan) a collection of baseball books for Christmas. One of the books, *Mudville Diaries: A Book of Baseball Memories,* consists of short stories and baseball poetry.

Finally, college students in Harrisburg, Pennsylvania, participating in a seminar titled "Poetry Matters," read aloud *Casey at the Bat* prior to a college baseball game. Mark C. Aldrich, the professor conducting the seminar, stated that "the crowd listened intently and applauded loudly after the reading" ("Mighty Casey" 8). *Casey at the Bat,* the world's most famous baseball poem, was now being used as a means to help students gain confidence in their ability to speak in public.

In conclusion, baseball poetry does have a cultural impact on society. Despite the problems that often arise in the professional leagues, baseball will always spark that personal tender quality that can often inspire poetry. Baseball's greatest essence is safe with the works of these poets.

BIBLIOGRAPHY

Carney, Gene. Electronic interview with author. 10 October 2000.

Clark, Tom. *Fan Poems.* Plainfield, VT: North Atlantic Books, 1976.

Cooke, Edmund Vance. *Baseballogy.* Chicago: Forbes, 1912.

DK Illustrated Oxford Dictionary. Dorling Kindersley Limited and Oxford University Press, 1998.

Fehler, Gene. Electronic interview with author. 14 October 2000.

Fleming, Alice, ed. *Hosannah The Home Run! Poems About Sports.* Boston: Little, Brown, 1972.

Gardner, Martin. *The Annotated Casey at the Bat.* 3rd ed. Chicago: U of Chicago P, 1984.

Hall, Donald. *Fathers Playing Catch with Sons.* San Francisco: North Point, 1985.

Hopper, De Wolf, with Wesley Winans Stout. *Reminiscence of De Wolfe Hopper: Once a Clown Always a Clown.* Boston: Little, Brown and Company, 1927.

Isaacs, Benno. "Casey Hits 100." *Saturday Evening Post,* 260.4 (May-June 1988): 20.

"Mighty Casey Is a Hit." *The Chronicle of Higher Learning,* 25 Oct. 25 1996: A8.

Peeler, Tim. Electronic interview with author. 13 October 2000.

Regan, F. Scott. "The Mighty Casey: Enduring Folk Hero of Failure." *Journal of Popular Culture* 31 (Summer 1997): 91-109.

Sandburg, Carl. *Cornhuskers.* New York: Holt, Rhinehart, and Winston, 1918.

18

Eiron Men, "You Know Me, *Alazons,*" and Pixies: Baseball Humor As American Humor

Thomas L. Altherr

With all due respect to sports commentator Joe Garagiola, the typical baseball fan hardly needs Joe's reminder that baseball is a funny game. Everywhere the fan looks in the modern game, there are the funny men, the jokers, the braggarts, the irascible but loveable characters (usually managers of the Earl Weaver school), the mascots, and the "hairdos," the television announcers and sportswriters with their steady patter of puns, wiseacre talk, and fishing stories. Bob Uecker and Garagiola wink and chatter at the fan from their various media venues. Humor even arises from unintentional sources: Harry Caray, Jerry Coleman, Ralph Kiner, George Steinbrenner, and Marge Schott come to mind (Taaffe 90; Liebman [1994]117-120,169, and 177; Liebman [2001]130-133; Nathan 69-70 and 72-73). The Diamondvision scoreboards regularly show videos of bloopers, botched plays, fielding flops, and other assorted on-the-field oddities. Both "juniors," Ken Griffey and Cal Ripken have played themselves puckishly in mock "presidential" and U.S. Postal Service commercials respectively. The late perennial crowd favorite Max Patkin clowned his way across the country in stadia major and minor (Wulf). The post-1984 crop of baseball films have all depended heavily on humor. The burlesquery of the three major league flicks is obvious, but try to imagine *Bull Durham* without eyelid breathing, garters, voodoo, Bulls mascot beanings, and the flooded ballfield, or even *The Natural* minus Pop Fisher muttering "I shoulda been a farmer." Nearly every "as-told-to" or "kiss-and-tell" baseball book, with the notable exception of Hank Aaron's *I Had a Hammer,* feasts on the obligatory amount of comic incident. Just at the time when computerization, player salary and strike wrangles, fan bitterness, and tendentious stadium negotiations threaten to wring the joy out of the game, baseball has upped its funnybone quotient, its capacity for humor.

Baseball historians will recognize that this burst of buffoonery is not new. The sport is rife with humorous characters and events, many of them the stuff of legendary and near-epic tragedy (for Red Sox and Cubs fans). Whoever set fire to the first hotfoot or first nailed a rookie's spikes to the clubhouse is lost to the historical record, but it is little effort to recite a lengthy list of baseball's humorous personages and occurrences. Who could forget, for example, the 1962 Mets, Rube Waddell chasing fire engines, three Brooklyn Dodgers on third base in the 1920s, Dizzy Dean's country boy antics in the 1930s, Casey Stengel doffing his cap to let a bird fly free, Gabby Street and Gabby Hartnett catching baseballs thrown from monuments and buildings, and Wilbert Robinson getting splattered by a grapefruit dropped from a plane (Kavanagh 1-24)? Or Bill Veeck stationing Eddie Gaedel at the plate against Detroit (and harboring secret plans to send out nine midgets against the Yankees), Jimmy Piersall celebrating his 100th homer by running the bases backward (Pellowski 83)? Or Charlie Finley's A's riding mules into the game, Tommy Lasorda's Ultra Slim Fast commercials, King Kelly cutting from first to third base and inserting himself into the game from the bench to catch a foul fly (Okrent and Wulf 16)? Or Babe Herman and Jose Canseco mistaking the game for soccer and using their heads to attempt to field balls, Senators' clowns Al Schacht and Nick Altrock (Schacht; Amman)? Or Mark Fidrych conversing with the ball on the mound, Bowie Kuhn, any of a number of tales about Babe Ruth, and innumerable team clowns and bench jockeys? Indeed, baseball, in contrast to other major sports, has retained an overall lightheartedness. But what might explain this connection of humor and the National Pastime?

In a recent article, "Humor in Baseball: Functions and Dysfunctions," sociologist Michael Katovich suggested that humor has fulfilled five functions in the sport. First, according to Katovich, baseball humor has paid homage to the "character" and his type of "expressive" (some might say excessive) individualism. Second, because baseball is a game of complex social action, baseball humor has acted as a necessary contrast to define and reinforce that social interaction. Third, superstition-oriented baseball humor has emphasized "the importance of self-control." Fourth, baseball humor has cut across class and derided privilege and elitism and therefore upheld the worth of accomplishment over status. And fifth, humor in baseball has served as a psychodrama to permit players and fans to attempt to reconcile the paradox of play and violence inherent in the sport (Katovich 8).

Katovich made mostly persuasive cases for all of these functions. He noted the long tradition of adulation baseball fans and scribes held for such "characters" as Babe Ruth, Casey Stengel, and Yogi Berra, the concentration on their endearing idiosyncrasies and flouting of rules. Hilarious depictions of poor fielders and incompetent hitters served to remind participants and viewers of the competence and cooperation necessary to make the game function well. Serious attention to ritual and talismans, which often defy logic in humorous ways, similarly stressed the belief system that such are instrumental to success on the diamond. Moreover, as Katovich claimed, baseball humor catered to an anti-institutionalist streak among players and fans, who, suffused with pretensions to social democracy, celebrated the achievements of the player who overcame poverty and other adversities as well as those teams, such as the St. Louis Cardinals' fabled Gashouse Gang, which continued to thumb its collective nose at authority. Last, Katovich argued that baseball humor, especially in the format of the "rhubarb," the manager's argument with the umpire, provided some resolution of the tension between order and violence in baseball, followed a stylized set of theatrics that simultaneously dramatized distinct conflict but held the possibility of on-the-field violence and chaos in check (Katovich 8-12).

To Katovich's interesting analyses, it is possible to offer a sixth explanation of the prevalence of humor in baseball. Much as the game itself has paralleled the large sweeping trends of American culture, baseball humor has been American humor, squarely part and parcel of its grand types and themes. Far from being an isolated subgenre of American humor, in which, for example, Casey Stengel speaks in an arcane language about subjects pertinent only to baseball players and fans, baseball humor has transcended the game to speak to the mass of Americans conversant with humor in general. Baseball adapted styles of humor already in operation within American culture, and in turn provided Americans with anecdotes and proverbs that the larger culture would turn into sacred cornerstones of Americanness. It is no surprise then that when filmmaker Ken Burns sought to illustrate (over and over) the reasons for baseball's persistent appeal for Americans he had his narrator intone maxims from that esteemed modern proverbist Lawrence Peter Berra, chapter and verse. What is important to realize here is that Berra himself and other baseball raconteurs were hardly unique; instead they continued in the long line of "unintentional" witticists, masters of malapropism, wise fools, boasters, and storytellers that stretched back to the colonial and early national periods. Baseball humorists, however, freshened up these old themes, gave them the gloss of seeming novelty, and, whether purposely or not, underscored baseball humor's own inextricability from American culture.

Historians and other observers of American humor have located its peculiar Americanness in several themes. First, the incongruity of the promise of cherished American ideals and the harsher realities of American experience has been fertile ground for humor, especially of a self-deprecatory nature. Second, somewhat following from the first theme, a great deal of American humor has juxtaposed vernacular expression with more rigid hegemonic cultural codes, the hilarity resulting from the puncturing of pretentiousness. Third, the figure of the wise fool, not American in origin to be sure, has appeared frequently in American tales and parables. Fourth, incorporating indigenous humor strategies, the trickster character has popped up in the humor in several forms. Fifth, the tall tale, the "whopper," and the "shaggy dog" story, products of frontier populations, have all exhibited the characteristic American fondness for exaggeration and buffoonery. Sixth, but not least, there has been a variety of language-oriented jokes ranging from puns to comebacks to zingers, perhaps not as polished as European drawing-room insults, but reflective of peoples aware of the aggressive and protective properties of humor.

The nation that set such lofty conditions as the Declaration of Independence proposed was bound to fall short. As literary critic Louis Rubin Jr., wrote in his essay, "The Great American Joke,"

> Out of the incongruity between mundane circumstance and heroic ideal, material fact and spiritual hunger, democratic, mid-

dle-class society and desire for cultural definition, theory of equality and fact of social and economic inequality, the Declaration of Independence and the Mann Act, the Gettysburg Address and the Gross National Product, the Battle Hymn of the Republic and the Union Trust Company, the Horatio Alger ideal and the New York Social Register—between what men [and women] would be and must be, as acted out in American experience, has come much pathos, no small amount of tragedy, and also a great deal of humor. (Rubin, reprinted in Veron 260)

What arose among humorists was a type of self-denigration, humor that entered around an apology in advance for failures to live up to the promises. American *eirons* emerged in a number of formulations, particularly vaudeville-era comedians who specialized in self-deprecatory routines that attempted to soften the realities of immigrant experiences in the Promised Land (Barth, Chapter VI).

Often, however, American humor has reveled in that gap between the ought and the is, drawing on it to expose hypocrisy and pomposity, especially those fraudulencies that serve or reinforce the assumptions and status of dominant groups. Antebellum Southwestern humorists worked up the style that Mark Twain perfected after the war. In its classic formulas, an untutored youth or frontier rube saw through the transparent ruses of the real or pretender upper-crust characters, or a newly rich landowner or squire undercut this identification with his use of the diction and vocabulary of the lower class. High-falutin words, often misapplied or mispronounced, clashed with residual vernacular expressions as pretender desperately chased refinement. Or, conversely, the unlettered farmer or blushing bumpkin displayed more innate wisdom with more direct sentences and homely metaphors.

Indeed, many such wise fools rambled through American humor. Reminiscent of the medieval court jesters who occupied the precarious position as entertainer to and critic of the monarch, these shy-but-sly comedians honed their poses with American subjects. From Benjamin Franklin, who played the role of the simple backwoods American only to outwit the Europeans at the treaty table in Versailles in 1783, to Will Rogers, who, from behind a boyish grin, delivered a pointed if genial critique of the New Deal in the 1930s, the humor of the American wise fool has been a constant staple. In typical fashion, the wise fool allowed the intended target of the humor to feel superior by employing seeming nonchalance, confusion, misunderstanding, deference, and simplistic language, all the while leading up to dead-pan double-entendres or kickers that would show the fool much smarter or more moral.

The wise fool has always had certain parallels with the trickster figure of Native American tales. Although the image of the trickster, usually in the persona of Coyote, varied from tribe to tribe, the character often used humor, sometimes even malevolent humor, to effect a transformation in tribal life or alleviate the stress of some crisis affecting individuals, clans, or the whole tribe. In many versions, the trickster would resort to all sorts of ruses, charades, disguises, and practical jokes to gain its goal. The indigenous people, in turn, had to be wary of these tricks as part of the ritual and ordeal. This mutual tussle was supposed to result in a heightened awareness of natural processes and social dynamics; at the very least the trickster introduced a substantial measure of levity to temper the seriousness of daily life (Lincoln).

Euroamericans fashioned their own sorts of trickster tales in response to the conditions of colonial and frontier life. Encountering an unimagined abundance of natural resources, the explorers and settlers fell under the spell of fantasies of limitlessness. Nothing seemed impossible in the new lands. Even when actual experience acquainted the Euroamericans with definite sets of limits, the dreams of unboundedness persisted. As Walter Blair and Hamlin Hill wrote in *America's Humor,*

> Since peculiar things were always happening in America and uninformed newcomers always lusted for strange news, over the years merry fellows could unwind incredible yarns about flora, fauna, natives, and geography and then give true or untrue but more or less plausible explanations. (Blair and Hill, quoted in Walker 17)

In terms of humor, the tall tale, again not an American invention in itself but a form very well suited to the expansive landscape, symbolized these fantasies and dreams. Rife with hyperbolic assertions about size, strength, plentitude, and fearsome qualities, the tall tale also blended in other humor types of the confidence man, the wise fool, and the gullible and pompous civilized audience. All this blustering and boasting produced a number of celebrated *alazons* in the folklore and literature. Similarly the hunger for entertainment on the frontier spawned "shaggy dog" stories and long, drawn-out, even pointless jokes spun out for the pure fun of spoofery (Rourke, Chapter II; Brown).

Yet another area of identifiable American humor has been the hodgepodge category of shorter jokes, wisecracks, comebacks, quick gags, puns, and malapropisms that often depend on twists and turns of language. Even though cultural historian Louis Kronenberger took Americans to task in the early 1950s for what he considered American deficiencies in these types of humor—"in terms of cussing and repartee alike, our truck drivers are mere duffers in comparison with even the average cockney"—more recently Americans have developed a more finely tuned sense for language jokes (Kronenberger, reprinted in Veron 268). To be sure, much of this is still formulaic and still the window dressing of the business deal, the display of conspicuous consumption, and the sexual conquest. But a discernible appreciation of irony has emerged. Some regions, such as parts of the West, retain a relentless literal-mindedness, but the overall national acceptance of *Laugh-In, Saturday Night Live,* and their several "comedy improv" imitators have revealed a growing national taste for humor of a certain arched perspective normally absent in a relatively classless society.

Representative examples of all these categories abound in American baseball humor. Although Ring Lardner's characters "Alibi Ike" and Al Keefe of *You Know Me Al* were more *alazons* than *eirons,* that is, naive, self-unaware braggarts rather than knowing self-deprecators, they probably ushered in the tendency of self-deprecation in baseball literature. Red Sox left fielder Smead Jolley once excused a misplay on Duffy's Cliff in Fenway Park thus, "You smart guys taught me how to go up the hill, but nobody taught me how to come down" (Smith 18). Regarding his autograph, Tom Lasorda joked, "It's not worth much today, but in five years it will be worth even less" (Liebman [2001] 14). After a bad day at the plate, Andy Van Slyke lamented, "I couldn't have driven Miss Daisy home today" (Liebman [2001], 16). "You can't get rich sitting on the bench, but I'm giving it a try," Yankee infielder Phil Linz smirked (Liebman [2001], 25). The Dodgers' Billy Grabarkewitz claimed, "I have so many splinters from sitting on the bench that if somebody struck a match I might catch fire" (Nathan 164). Dodger pitcher Carl Erskine rued his pitching: "I've had pretty good success with Stan Musial, by throwing my best pitch and backing up third" (Rains 30). Hall of Famer Lefty Gomez once berated himself thus, "I never knew what Joe DiMaggio looked like until I roomed with him. All I ever saw was the back of his uniform after I threw a pitch." Years later Gomez returned to the theme: "When Neil Armstrong set foot on the moon, he found six baseballs that Jimmie Foxx hit off me in 1937" (Liebman [2001] 83 and 155). Another Hall of Famer, Reggie Jackson, said of his own fielding lapses, "The only way I'm going to win a Gold Glove is with a can of spray paint" (Liebman [2001] 88). After setting the dubious record for giving up the most home runs in a season, Bert Blyleven complained, "It's pretty hard when the family asks for passes to the game and want to sit in the left-field bleachers" (Liebman [2001] 100). Cardinals pitcher Joe Magrane struck a similar tone: "I knew I was in trouble when they started clocking my fastball with a sundial" (Liebman [2001] 208).

But it has remained for Joe Garagiola, Bob Uecker, and to some extent Jay Johnstone to perfect the posture in later decades. Garagiola, a good catcher with the Cardinals, Pirates, and Cubs in the 1940s and 1950s, capitalized on his friendship with Yogi Berra and his own personal glibness to launch a broadcasting career that eventually went beyond sports to morning talk show hosting. Garagiola's trademark, in addition to memories of Berra and the Hill section in St. Louis, became the running joke about his own career, especially the futility of the 1952 Pittsburgh Pirates, who dropped a pre-1962 Mets 112 games that year. In his 1960 book, *Baseball Is a Funny Game,* Garagiola mused with a bit of the bittersweet:

> Each year I don't play I get better. The first year on the banquet trail I was a former ballplayer, the second year I was great, the third year one of baseball's stars, and just last year I was introduced as one of baseball's immortals. The older I get the more I realize that the worst break I had was playing. (Garagiola 146)

Bob Uecker, however, a worse player than Garagiola, has managed to push the envelope of self-denigration. Uecker parlayed a .200 lifetime batting average and offbeat sense of humor into a lucrative post-baseball career as "Mr. Baseball." Well respected for his serious sportscasting, Uecker has become a national institution of sorts for his beer commercials and television and movie roles, especially that of Harry Doyle, the drunken announcer in the *Major League* films. His 1982 autobiography, *Catcher in the Wry,* distilled Uecker's penchant for humor at his own expense. The title, of course, conjured up Salinger's classic, and even in the preface, Uecker set himself within the hallowed tradition of Washington Irving and Mark Twain: "Some of what I have written might have happened, but didn't, and some could only have happened in the dark corners of my own imagination." Most of the rest of the book, however, is an extended series of variations on the main joke of self-deprecation. One example will suffice:

> In baseball the clues were more subtle. In my case, I began to get the hint when my bubble gum card came out and there was a blank space where the picture was supposed to be. Sporting goods companies offered to pay me not to endorse their products. I got to the park for what the manager had announced would be a night game, and found they'd started at 1:00 P.M. I came to bat in the bottom of the ninth, two out, the bases loaded, my team trailing by a run, and looked over at the other dugout and saw them already in their street clothes. (Uecker xi and 5)

Similarly longtime baseball man Charlie Metro tells Denver-area audiences that he stopped telling his sons that "193" was his playing weight when they were able to read and could see it was his lifetime major league batting average. Metro was also somewhat of a master of turning disaster into humorous advantage through deadpan self-deprecation. Managing the Tulsa Oilers in 1966, Charlie watched his eventual pennant winners lose nine in a row. Faced with a speaking engagement the next morning, the gloomy skipper brightened when he saw the headline in the sports section: "Oilers Drop Ninth: Pad Lead." The second-place Houston club had blown ten in a row, so the Oilers picked up a half game! Beaming, Metro chided the breakfasters for not knowing what a genius they had hired (Metro, Chapter 9).

Little League foibles have long been a source of humor for nonplayers who look back at their childhood ball with trepidation. One of the best expositors of this vein has been the Miami-based syndicated columnist Dave Barry. In a 2000 piece, Barry recounted how the organizers of the Joe DiMaggio Legends asked him to play in a charity event in Hollywood, Florida. Mistakenly assuming that the event would be "like one of those company-picnic softball games where beer is available in the outfield," Barry found himself plunged into a serious game. Hall of Famer Brooks Robinson gave him some advice: "Don't play in the infield. You'll get killed." This became important to Barry when he realized he didn't even own a cup, let alone have one on at that moment. The first few innings went well: "This is because I was not in the game." Then the manager sent him out to replace Mickey Rivers in left field, which was "like replacing Dom Perignon with weasel spit." Out in left field, Barry has "vivid Little League memories swarming in [his] brain—memories of praying for the ball not to come to me, and memories of falling down when it did." Of course, he misplayed a ball hit to him, making "a pathetic lunging gesture toward the ball as it zips past to the outfield wall," At bat, facing Al "The Mad Hungarian" Hrabosky, Barry struck out on three pitches. "I was still swinging at the last one when Hrabosky was in the showers," he moaned (Barry [2000] 5E). In another essay, Barry recalled, "[T]he coach put me in right field only because it was against the rules to put me in Sweden, where I would have done less damage to the team" (Barry [1996] 7).

Clashes over morality and rowdiness in baseball have also resulted in a substantial amount of humor. As baseball historian Warren Jay Goldstein described the 1845-1871 period in *Playing for Keeps,* baseball was always something of an arena for competing moral values. Fearing the breakdown of gentlemanly values of manliness and self-control in the face of overcompetitiveness, gambling, and professionalism, amateur baseball's keepers of the faith stumped for the preservation of baseball morality through stricter rules, stronger umpiring, and the expected calming influence of female fans (Goldstein). The British immigrant sportswriter Henry Chadwick spent forty-some years writing editorials and refining rules to regulate a game that was growing more and more rowdy. New York pitcher, shortstop, and union organizer John Montgomery Ward joined Chadwick in his campaign, and into the twentieth century, the didacticism continued in sententious books by Giants pitcher Christy Mathewson and general manager Branch Rickey. Baseball's league presidents and commissioners, especially Ban Johnson and Kenesaw Mountain Landis, sought to encode and enforce this morality from their high offices.

But many actual players ignored the pleas for morality, fashioned a rambunctious, rough-and-tumble game, and indulged in extracurricular hijinks to match. Coming from rural areas or lower-class city districts, many of these players owed little allegiance to the strictures of the middle class. Baseball stories reflected this discrepancy with rebellious characters speaking the dialect of the farms or inner cities. For every uplifting Frank Merriwell tale there were Lardner's Al Keefe, James Thurber's Squawks McGrew, and Mark Harris's overaged Huck Finn, Henry Wiggen, voicing Whitman's barbaric yawp in service of baseball. Later baseball fiction by W. P. Kinsella, Philip Roth, Robert Coover, John Sayles, and others added a panoply of oddball baseball figures who hardly reinforced the official pretentiousness of the sport's image-keepers. Other media, especially cartoons, *New Yorker* ones among the best of them, often gave visual form to this incongruity (Altherr 14-35).

From such stories and cartoons it was not much of a leap to the frequent presence of the wise fool in baseball humor. Yogi Berra, of course, springs to mind as baseball's quintessential wise fool. His sayings, collected in several anthologies, inspired William Safire to label them "bonapropisms" instead of malapropisms, because they veered so crazily close to profundity (Nathan 123-127). But Berra has had his rivals. The Cardinals' Dizzy Dean baffled sportswriters and grammarians alike with his wide-eyed country boy tales and fractured syntax (Okrent and Wulf 143-46). "Old Diz knows the King's English. And not only that, I also know the Queen is English," he once said (Liebman [2001] 67). Satchel Paige, mainstay of the Negro Leagues and later the American League, devised his own much-quoted, six-point philosophy that led many a batter to underestimate him as laid-back. Casey Stengel established his own dialect of English that also left scribes and a few Washington Senators, the ones asking him questions about baseball's antitrust exemption, scratching their heads (Stengel, "From The Congressional Record," reprinted in Schaap and Gerberg 120-123). "I'll never make the mistake of being seventy again," Stengel once said, proving he and his longtime catcher rubbed off on each other (Liebman [2001] 3). Lou "The Mad Russian" Novikoff qualified for this group when he once explained why he attempted to steal third base with the bases full, "I couldn't resist. I had such a great jump on the pitcher" (Liebman [2001] 220).

In the 1970s the somewhat counterculture personalities of pitchers Bill "Spaceman" Lee (Shlain 187-196) and Mark "The Bird" Fidrych didn't quite fit the mold of the professional athlete (Wisnia 154). Always viewing the baseball world from a different perspective, Lee once queried, "Do you realize that even as we sit here, we are hurtling through space at a tremendous rate of speed? Think about it. Our world is just a hanging curveball" (Liebman [1994] 50). After seeing the Green Monster, the left field wall at Fenway, for the first time Bill asked, "Do they leave it there during the games?" (Liebman [1994] 69). Asked to explain his flakiness, Lee countered, "What do you expect in a northpaw world?" (Liebman [1994] 110). Fidrych once offered an explanation for why he threw back a ball after the batter had gotten a hit: "That ball had a hit in it, so I want it to get back in the ball bag with the rest of the balls there. Maybe next time it'll learn some sense and come out as a pop-up next time" (Nathan 160). Mark had a brief and meteoric career as an effective pitcher, but he will always be remembered for talking to the ball on the mound, running to shake his fielder's hand after a good play, sprinting on and off the field, and other goofy mannerisms (Shlain 147-158).

But, as opponents quickly came to find out, these players and managers were hardly woodenheads. Beneath their offbeat images lay the cagey, expert baseball minds of winners. For example, Charlie Metro recounted falling victim to the Stengel mystique in 1962. During a Cubs-Mets game, Stengel appeared to have fallen asleep while Chicago threatened to tie or win the game. Suddenly, however, Metro heard Stengel shouting for his "glove" in the dugout. Underestimating the wise fool, thinking him addled, Metro figured the Cubs would surely win. But Casey's "glove" turned out to be the stellar-fielding Gil Hodges, whom Casey inserted for defense. Hodges promptly made two rally-crunching plays to preserve the Mets victory (Metro, Chapter 8).

Baseball tricksters supplemented the wise fools. Stories of practical jokers and jokes are legion throughout baseball history. Yankees reliever and journeyman pitcher Moe Drabowsky was among the best, but no one could possibly count up all the incidents of hotfoots, spikes glued to helmets, liniment rubbed in jockstraps, and misleading instructions to rookies throughout the career of Jay Johnstone alone, let alone the rest of the players, coaches, and managers (Schlossberg 68-69 and 76; Johnstone and Talley). Many teams have had

clowns who kept the mood loosey-goosey, dispensing humor to dis-
pel the tension that accumulates during long seasons and pennant
races (McGraw and Durso; Cataneo, Chapter 11). Milwaukee Braves
pitcher Lew Burdette, a right-hander, once posed as a left-hander for
his Topps baseball card (Obojski 92). Someone snuck a bat with a
common obscene four-letter word written on the bat handle bottom
into the hands of Oriole Bill Ripken during a card shoot. Jackie Price
performed so many antics with pet snakes, that he drove the irrepress-
ible Bill Veeck to release him from the Indians, but Price's acrobatic
maneuvers, bazookas firing baseballs, and other acts had made him a
crowd favorite (Metro and Altherr, Chapters 4 and 7). Other forms of
trickery abound in baseball. Indeed, the game fairly invites trick
pitches, foreign substances on the ball, corked bats, sign stealing,
field finessing by grounds crews, mind games, psych-out jobs, bench
jockeying, hidden ball tricks and other pick-off plays, decoy movements by fielders, anything to gain an advantage, get an edge on the
other guy. Hall of Famer Don Sutton once answered charges that he
employed a "foreign substance" on the ball by saying, "Not true at
all. Vaseline is manufactured right here in the United States of America" (Okrent and Wulf 330). Burdette himself combined the trickster
and self-deprecatory modes when he said of his decision to retire,
"They were starting to hit the dry side of the ball" (Liebman [2001]
189). Even attempting to use ventriloquism to throw voices onto the
field to disrupt fielders and misdirect throws as well as applying gra-
phology to the autographs of opposing managers were in at least one
manager's bag of tricks (Metro and Altherr 25). Baseball tricksters,
often referred to as "pixies," proudly polished their reputations for legal (and not-so-legal) chicanery. Perhaps the overly organized nature
of baseball may have stimulated such. As baseball historian David
Voigt once suggested,

> [I]f self-righteous baseball leaders from William Hulbert to
> Judge Landis to Bowie Kuhn labored hard to fit players into a
> neat mold of decorum, the institutionalization of individualism
> as a theme of our culture prompts many players to break out of
> imposed puritanic straightjackets. (Voigt 24)

Surprisingly the phenomenon of "tall tales" has survived in baseball humor despite the exposure of the players to the media, the video

and audio recording of virtually every contest, and the calculation (calcification?) of action into numerous statistical categories. Probably the best known "tall tale" in actual baseball history has been Babe Ruth's "Called Shot" in the 1932 World Series. Although recently discovered footage, broadcast on ESPN in 2000, pretty well disposed of the myth, the image has considerable staying power. And who better to accomplish it than baseball's own version of Paul Bunyan (Blaisdell 240-242)! More recent heroic efforts will always have to undergo the scrutiny of repeated ESPN replays. Yet there still seems to be a yearning for the trappings of the tall tale. Recall, for example, the instant legend-making that accompanied Kirk Gibson's home run in the first game of the 1988 World Series. Sportscasters and sportswriters are constantly verging on metahyperbolic vocabulary, so much so that the player or event balloons up to a much larger-than-life status. A need to believe in the fantastic, to expect enchantment in the realm of the ball field, persists despite the technological developments that undercut such expectations. The popularity of magical realism in baseball fiction and movies further attests to this trend. Readers and audiences want to believe that Roy Hobbs knocked the cover off the ball and smashed the clocks and light towers in *The Natural,* and that "Shoeless Joe" Jackson really did come back to play in Ray Kinsella's *Field of Dreams.* Nostalgia, of course, also contributes to the process, as aging fans hunger for the heroes and exploits of their own Golden Age of baseball. Perhaps the best indication of the pervasiveness of this penchant is how readily fans fell, on April Fool's Day, 1985, for George Plimpton's stunning tall tale about Sidd Finch, the Mets phenom who, with one foot bare and the other in a hiking boot, could fire a pitch 168 miles per hour with unerring accuracy (Plimpton).

The sheer number of language jokes associated with baseball humor has revealed the inherent verbal funniness within the game itself. As English professor Kenneth Pellow remarked in an article on literary baseball humor,

> "Funny language" may (indeed does) occur in the context of other sports; however, it is more relevant to baseball players partly because . . . they are involved in a more verbal game. So the writers who have made comedy out of baseball talk have had not to invent such language but rather to adapt it. (Pellow 79)

This type of humor has stemmed from several sources. The wise fools already mentioned purposely or naturally have mangled pronunciation and grammar on their way to hoodwinking the opposition and public. Occasionally the humor came from a reverse direction when a player such as Mark Harris's Henry Wiggen tried to sound literate: "Attendance went up to where the only seats left was standing room only" or "It was now my ball game to win or lose which we did in the bottom of the ninth." Baseball cliches have been another patch of fertile ground. Who could keep a straight face every time Sparky Anderson proclaimed that spring's Tigers squad the best team he had ever seen? Or when Crash Davis and Nuke LaLoosh ripped the traditional platitudes of the rookie called up to the Show in *Bull Durham*? Sometimes, however, it is hard to ascertain who is more the target of the humor: the interviewee spouting the cliches or the audience, aglow in the light of the celebrity, hanging on his every word.

Several announcers, most notably Vin Scully of the Dodgers, also have been proficient at the repartee and razor-sharp wit. "Bob Gibson pitches as though he's double parked," Scully once said (Rains 28). When Pittsburgh's Rennie Stennett prematurely distributed cigars for the birth of a boy, only to have the infant be female, Vin quipped, "He only missed by one" (Liebman [2001] 181). When Leo Durocher went to Japan to manage in 1976, Scully chuckled, "It took us 35 years to get revenge for Pearl Harbor" (Liebman [1994] 107). After Alejandro Peña came back from chicken pox, Scully noted, "You might say he's starting from scratch" (Liebman [1994] 165). But several announcers and players have been notorious for mangling the language. A couple of examples from Mets broadcaster Ralph Kiner and Padres' voice Jerry Coleman will suffice. "Third base is certainly a reactionary position," Kiner once intoned (Liebman [1994] 120). Another time Ralph remarked, "If Casey Stengel were alive today, he'd be spinning in his grave" (Nathan 73). Coleman once described an outfield play this way: "There's a fly ball deep to center field. Winfield is going back, back. He hits his head against the wall. It's rolling toward second base." Another time he reported on an infield play: "Ozzie Smith just made another play that I've never seen anyone else make before, and I've seen him make it more than anyone else ever has" (Nathan 69). Milwaukee Braves' shortstop Johnny Logan was another fount of malapropisms: "I will perish this trophy forever"; "I know the name but I can't replace the face"; "Maybe I can find some major league suspects"; and "I'll have to go along with the immoral Babe Ruth," when asked who was the greatest all-time ballplayer (Liebman [1994] 121).

Last but not least have been the wonderful nicknames, real and fictional, that have spiced up baseball's landscape over the years. When Robert Coover went to write *The Universal Baseball Association, Inc., J. Henry Waugh, Prop.*, his protagonist was so steeped in the lore of baseball nicknames that in his own ultimate fantasy league, he created some, such as "Hatrack Hines," that rivaled or outdid reality. Indeed so inventive have been baseball's vocabularians, as Paul Dickson's dictionary indicated, this type of baseball humor shows no sign of slowing down. The next set of baseball neologisms, some of them with a healthy dollop of humor, will come winging along any week now.

For it has been this very sort of flexibility that has given these various types of baseball humor their vibrancy and staying power. Americans have always loved to wallow (or watch someone else wallow) in self-derogation, pop the bubble of the pretentious with the needle of the vulgar, delight in the antics of the wise fools and the tricksters, fall for the tall tales, and wink along with the word games. Repeatedly American humor, including baseball humor, has provided the vehicles for these processes. Sadly, economic forces may submerge baseball irretrievably or alter it into something unworthy of the term "the National Pastime," but in the meantime baseball humor will continue to remind fans and the larger public that losing the seventh game of the World Series, or World Serious, as Al Keefe would have said, is not the end of the world as we know it. With better luck, baseball humor may help keep the game viable and invigorating as it taps into the very forces that have kept Americans laughing throughout even the most trying years of the grand experiment. Perhaps it is fitting to draw on Mr. Berra for the amen: "It ain't over till it's over."

BIBLIOGRAPHY

Altherr, Thomas L. "Eustace Tilley Draws the Game: The Image of Baseball in *New Yorker* Cartoons, 1925 to the Present." *Nine* 3.1 (1994): 14-35.

Amman, Larry. "The Clown Prince of Baseball." *The Baseball Research Journal* 9 (1982): 119-126.

Barry, Dave. "Big Leaguer: Baseball 'Callup' Stirs Memories of Little League." *The Denver Post* 5 March 2000: 5E.

_____. "Pirates-Yankees Series Baseball's Golden Age." *The Denver Post* 31 March 1996, *Empire Magazine:* 7.

Barth, Gunter. *City People: The Rise of Modern City Culture in Nineteenth-Century America.* New York: Oxford UP, 1980.

Blair, Walter, and Hamlin Hill. *America's Humor: From Poor Richard to Doonesbury.* New York: Oxford UP, 1978.

Blaisdell, Lowell D. "Legends As an Expression of Baseball Memory." *Journal of Sport History* 19.3 (1992): 227-243.

Brown, Carolyn S. *The Tall Tale in American Folklore and Literature.* Knoxville: U of Tennessee P, 1987.

Catataneo, David. *Peanuts and Crackerjack: A Treasury of Baseball Legends and Lore.* San Diego: Harcourt, 1991.

Garagiola, Joe. *Baseball Is a Funny Game.* New York: J. B. Lippincott, 1960.

Goldstein, Warren Jay. *Playing for Keeps: A History of Early Baseball.* Ithaca, NY: Cornell UP, 1989.

Johnstone, Jay, and Rick Talley. *Some of My Best Friends Are Crazy: Baseball's Favorite Lunatic Goes in Search of His Peers.* New York: Macmillan, 1990.

Katovich, Michael A. "Humor in Baseball: Functions and Dysfunctions." *Journal of American Culture* 16.2 (1993): 7-15.

Kavanagh, Jack. *The Heights of Ridiculousness: The Feats of Baseball's Merrymakers.* South Bend, IN: Diamond Communications, 1998.

Kronenberger, Louis. "The American Sense of Humor," reprinted in Veron 264-271, 1976.

Liebman, Glen. *Baseball Shorts: 1,000 of the Game's Funniest One-Liners.* Chicago: Contemporary Books, 1994.

_____. *Grand Slams: The Ultimate Collection of Baseball's Best Quips, Quotes, and Cutting Remarks.* Lincolnwood, IL: Contemporary Books, 2001.

Lincoln, Kenneth. *Indi'n Humor.* Berkeley: U of California P, 1993.

McGraw, Tug, and Joseph Durso. *Screwball.* Boston: Houghton Mifflin, 1974.

Metro, Charlie, and Tom Altherr. "Nostalgia: Weird Tricks of the Trade." *Baseball Weekly* 17-23 Jan. 1996: 25.

Metro, Charlie, with Tom Altherr. *Safe by a Mile: A Heart Full of Baseball.* Lincoln: U of Nebraska P, 2002.

Nathan, David H. *Baseball Quotations: The Wisdom and Wisecracks of Players, Managers, Owners, Umpires, Announcers, Writers, and Fans on the Great American Pastime.* Jefferson, NC: McFarland, 1991.

Obojski, Robert. *Baseball's Zaniest Moments.* New York: Sterling Publishing, 1999.

Okrent, Daniel, and Steve Wulf. *Baseball Anecdotes.* New York: Oxford UP, 1989.

Pellow, C. Kenneth. "Baseball Humor." *Humor* 3.1 (1990): 75-84.

Pellowski, Michael J. *Baseball's Funniest People.* New York: Sterling Publishing, 1997.

Plimpton, George. *The Curious Case of Sidd Finch.* New York: Macmillan, 1987.

_____. "The Curious Case of Sidd Finch: He's a Pitcher, Part Yogi and Part Recluse. Impressively Liberated from Our Opulent Life-Style, Sidd's Deciding

About Yoga—and His Future in Baseball." *Sports Illustrated* 1 April 1985: 58-62, 64ff.

Rains, Rob. *The Cardinal Fan's Little Book of Wisdom: 101 Truths . . . Learned the Hard Way.* South Bend, IN: Diamond Communications, 1994.

Rourke, Constance. *American Humor: A Study of the National Character.* New York: Harcourt, Brace, Jovanovich, 1931.

Rubin, Louis Jr. "The Great American Joke," reprinted in Veron 255-265, 1976.

Schaap, Dick, and Mort Gerberg, eds. *Joy in Mudville: The Big Book of Baseball Humor.*

Schacht, Al. *Clowning Through Baseball.* New York: A.S. Barnes, 1941; New York: Doubleday, 1992.

Schlossberg, Dan. *Baseballaffs.* Middle Village, NY: Jonathan David, 1982.

Shlain, Bruce. *Oddballs: Baseball's Greatest Pranksters, Rakes, Hot Dogs, and Hotheads.* New York: Penguin, 1989.

Smith, Curt. *The Red Sox Fan's Little Book of Wisdom: A Fine Sense of the Ridiculous.* South Bend, IN: Diamond Communications, 1994.

Taaffe, William. "Legends of the Err Waves: Jerry Coleman and Ralph Kiner Give Their Listeners Tongues of Fun." *Sports Illustrated* 20 May 1985: 90.

Uecker, Bob. *Catcher in the Wry.* New York: G. P. Putnam's Sons, 1982.

Veron, Enid, ed. *Humor in America: An Anthology.* San Diego: Harcourt Brace Jovanovich, 1976.

Voigt, David Q. "Reflections on Diamonds: American Baseball and American Culture." *Journal of Sport History* 1 (Spring 1974): 3-25.

Walker, Nancy A., ed. *What's So Funny? Humor in American Culture.* Wilmington: Scholarly Resources, 1998.

Wisnia, Saul, and Dan Schlossberg. *Wit & Wisdom of Baseball.* Lincolnwood, IL: Publications International, 1998.

Wulf, Steve. "Max: After More than 40 Years, the Clown Prince of Baseball, Max Patkin, Still Leaves 'Em Laughing." *Sports Illustrated* 6 June 1988: 98-102, 104-106, 108, and 110.

SECTION V:
BASEBALL AND RESOLUTION
OF CONFLICT

19

Baseball Labor Relations:
Is It Safe to Go Back to the Ballpark?

Karen Shallcross Koziara

The Texas Rangers stunned the baseball world in 2000 by signing free agent Alex Rodriguez to a contract worth $252 million over ten years. The signing prompted commentary, and even controversy. Commissioner Bud Selig said that the contract pointed out the "inequity in baseball's system," and that the system had to and would be changed ("Selig: System's Broken" 2000 D-4). Others wondered how it could be that a baseball player could earn that much money.

In contrast, how much was Jimmie Foxx worth? As did Rodriguez, Foxx came from a humble background. The son of a tenant farmer on Maryland's Eastern Shore, as a boy Foxx plowed and milked cows. One day a postcard from Home Run Baker asked him to try out for a Class D team and Foxx became a ballplayer. A Hall of Famer, Foxx hit a lifetime .325, was the American League Most Valuable Player three times, and is now the eleventh highest home run hitter of all time. In his autobiography, Ted Williams wrote that next to DiMaggio, Foxx was the greatest player he ever saw. In his last years Foxx went from job to job working in sales and restaurants. He had retired a year too early to be eligible for a baseball pension (Gildea D1). Later major league players would see pensions as a system that needed fixing.

Baseball is a game in which power matters. Meetings between power pitchers such as Curt Schilling and power hitters such as Mark McGwire are among baseball's most dramatic events. Baseball is also a sophisticated and complicated business in which economic power is the coin of the realm. Because baseball is a business, power struggles between owners and players have long characterized the sport.

The major league owners and players have one of the most widely discussed bargaining relationships in the United States. Further, the bargaining relationship between the owners and the umpires has its own dramas. Like most interesting power struggles, baseball labor relations is remarkable for volatility as well as visibility. From the sidelines fans have watched fierce disagreements, numerous strikes and lockouts, and the disastrous 1994 World Series cancellation.

When will it be safe for fans to go back to the ballpark without fears of labor disputes? This essay tries to answer this question by explaining the power struggles that underlie baseball's troubled labor history. To do this, it focuses on the 1994/1995 work stoppage and its settlement, and subsequent labor relations events and their implications.

Two separate bargaining relationships exist in major league baseball. The first involves the owners, The American League of Professional Baseball Clubs (AL) and the National League of Professional Baseball Clubs (NL), and the union representing the players, the Major League Baseball Players Association (MLBPA). The owners also have a bargaining relationship with the major league umpires, who are represented by the World Umpires Association (WUA).

Economic Power and Early Union Efforts: 1876 to the 1960s

Collective bargaining relationships do not exist in a vacuum in any industry. Economic, political, and technological pressures influence both labor and management and are key to understanding bargaining relationships. Prior to 1960, economic forces, and to a lesser extent public policy, had a major influence on the relative power of owners and players.

Two economic forces, the product and labor markets, are particularly important in the power relationship between owners and players. The owners face a product market in which baseball competes with other forms of entertainment for sales. As a product baseball has many substitutes, and the product cannot be made ahead of time and stockpiled for later use. Both factors make owners vulnerable to work stoppages. Revenue largely comes from ticket sales, broadcast fees, parking, and concessions. These revenues are all related to market size and club standing. A winning record increases revenue, and high performance players increase the odds of winning. Getting and keeping quality players is economically important to owners, and it is in their self-interest to reduce players' bargaining power by restricting their mobility.

Players face a labor market that calls many, but chooses few for the major leagues. Only the best players get to the minor leagues, and few minor leaguers ever reach the majors. Players who get to the majors for a cup of coffee in spring training are much commoner than ten-year veterans, and even major leaguers have relatively few income producing years. Players have few potential baseball employers, and their skills do not transfer easily to other occupations. The fewer the number of employers, the less bargaining power players have. Mobility, or the ability of players to choose to move from club to club, thus affects their bargaining power and income potential. Thus player mobility is economically important to both players and owners. Indeed, the players' earliest efforts at unionization focused on the owners' efforts to tie players to one team with the reserve clause.

The National League, formed in 1876, brought financial and organizational stability to professional baseball. The first effort to unionize major league baseball players followed shortly thereafter. Professional teams existed prior to 1876, but the National League established "organized" baseball both as a sport with a predictable structure and as a viable business. The league created stability by defining sets of competitors and allocating geographic jurisdictions to member clubs.

Prior to the league's formation, players could move from team to team, even during the season. The newly formed league allowed players to continue this practice. This resulted in salary competition between owners to attract the best players. The owners quickly recognized player salaries as their major cost and that unrestricted player movement raised salaries. This recognition led the owners to take steps to limit player mobility and bargaining power. Beginning in 1880 the owners included reserve clauses in the players' individual annual contracts. These clauses reserved, or guaranteed to the clubs, the service of individual players the following year. Owners much preferred this practice to salary competition. The reserve clause bound players to one club and prevented them from selling their services to the highest bidder. It also began the players' interest in unionization.

In 1885 John Montgomery Ward, a Hall of Famer who earned a law degree while playing for the New York Giants, led the formation of the first players' union, the Brotherhood of Professional Players. This unionization effort was aimed squarely at the reserve clause. Then, as now, players had short careers. The impact of the reserve clause on player mobility and bargaining power had a significant effect on potential earnings, as well as on player self-respect and dignity. As a Brotherhood manifesto described the situation, "There was a time when the League stood for integrity and fair dealing. Today it stands for dollars and cents. . . . Players have been bought, sold, and exchanged as though they were sheep, instead of American citizens" (Abrams 18).

This first effort failed due to the owners' determined efforts to defeat unionization. This experience set combative and adversarial expectations for labor management encounters far into the future. It also identified the reserve clause, and its impact on player mobility and the bargaining power of players and owners, as a central economic issue dividing owners and players.

The players made three other unsuccessful unionization attempts between 1900 and 1950. These efforts focused on the reserve clause and its chilling effect on salaries. In 1900 the brief-lived Players Protective Association unsuccessfully sought a salary minimum, changes in the reserve clause, and free uniforms. In 1912 Ty Cobb was suspended indefinitely for pursuing a heckler into the stands. His Detroit teammates struck in protest, and the incident ignited the Baseball Players' Fraternity. The Fraternity tried to raise salaries by providing its members the option of jumping to the newly formed Federal League. A brief bidding war ensued which raised salaries until the Federal League failed in 1915. In 1946 Robert Murphy, a lawyer, registered the American Baseball Guild as an independent union. Although the Guild was unsuccessful, its activity alerted the owners to the threat of unionization. An owner-sponsored commission concluded that better relationships with the players would discourage unionization, and the owners invited player representatives from each club to meet with them to discuss and formulate working condition reforms. This representation mechanism was the prelude to formal negotiations. It enabled the players to suggest changes in working conditions, and the owners agreed to some changes, including a minimum salary and a pension plan (Jennings 6-11).

Although the players could elect representatives for discussions with the owners, these representatives were neither independent from nor as powerful as the owners. The pension plan was particularly important to the players. In 1953 the player reps for both leagues, Ralph Kiner (NL-Pirates) and Allie Reynolds (AL-Yankees), were sufficiently worried about the pension plan's design and funding to hire an attorney as a representative in upcoming negotiations. This angered the owners, who urged the players to fire him. The players then agreed to hire an attorney chosen by the owners. The owner-chosen attorney did not allay the players' worries about the pension plan. With the plan due to expire in 1967, in 1965 players Robin Roberts, Jim Bunning, and Harvey Kuenn met with Marvin Miller, chief economist and assistant to the president of the Steelworkers Union, about representing the players (Miller 4-7).

The players' decision to hire Miller resulted in a new model for player interactions with owners. Prior to Miller, the players could make proposals to the owners, but were dependent on the owners for improvements in working conditions. Because of his union experience, Miller recognized the importance of the Major League Ball Players Association (MLBPA) being financially and philosophically independent from the owners. This facilitated the development of meaningful two-party collective bargaining in baseball. In 1966, with Miller as executive director, MLBPA negotiated a new pension agreement. In 1968 the first complete basic player contract provided many economic improvements for the players as well as a formal grievance procedure. A second contract in 1970 made binding impartial arbitration the final step in the grievance procedure. These grievance and arbitration provisions proved to be important to future relationships between the players and owners (Miller 63).

Public Policy and Bargaining Power:
1969 to the Present

During this period two major laws had a role in baseball labor relations. The earliest, the 1890 Sherman Antitrust Act, outlawed monopolies and other restraints of trade. In 1922 the Supreme Court ruled in *Federal Baseball Club, Inc. v. National League of Professional Ball Clubs* that baseball was exempt from the Sherman Act. The case, involving issues of player mobility, arose when a new league, the Federal League, began competing with the NL and AL for players. The NL and AL responded with suits against the players for violations of the reserve clause. The Federal League responded that the actions of the NL and AL were restraints of trade that violated the Sherman Act. The Supreme Court decided that the Sherman Act did not apply because baseball games were "purely state affairs" and neither trade nor commerce. This exemption protected the reserve clause from charges that it violated the Sherman Act. In doing so, it helped insulate the owners' economic power from player efforts to increase mobility among clubs. Subsequent court cases upheld this decision, and baseball's antitrust exemption continued until enactment of the Curt Flood Act in 1998.

The National Labor Relations Act (NLRA), which regulates most private sector collective bargaining, is designed to protect and encourage collective bargaining. It guarantees employees the right to form a union and to engage in collective bargaining over wages, hours, and terms and conditions of employment. The National Labor Relations Board (NLRB), the agency that administers the NLRA, has two primary functions. One is to determine when unfair labor practices, as outlined in the NLRA, have occurred. Unfair labor practices are actions that undermine collective bargaining, such as employer attempts to discourage unionization by threatening employees or discriminating against union activists. The NLRB also holds secret ballot elections to determine if a group of workers wants union representation. If a majority votes to have a union, the NLRA requires that the employer bargain in good faith with the union.

Prior to 1969 it was not clear that Major League Baseball was subject to the NLRA's provisions. This was because in *Federal Baseball* the Supreme Court ruled that baseball was not commerce, and was only indirectly involved in interstate commerce. This reasoning seemed to preclude baseball from the NLRB's jurisdiction, which was limited to employers in interstate commerce.

In 1969 the NLRB decided that the NLRA covered baseball in a case that began when the AL umpires, seeking unionization, filed an election request with the NLRB. This request was for an election to show whether a majority of umpires wanted union representation. AL management opposed the election based on baseball's long-standing exemption from the Sherman Act.

The NLRB decided that the NLRA covered baseball regardless of the antitrust exemption. It pointed out that neither the Congressional hearings on the NLRA nor the language of the law showed any intent to exempt baseball from the NLRA. If Congress had so decided, it could have included baseball along with the NLRA's other exemptions. The Board said, "There is persuasive reason to believe that future labor disputes—should they arise in this industry—will be national in scope radiating far beyond individual State boundaries." The NLRB further explained that although Congress had not passed specific legislation to end the antitrust exemption, there was no evidence of Congressional intent to sanction a government policy of noninvolvement in all baseball matters. To the contrary, Congress passed the NLRA to provide employees in almost every industry the right to unionize and bargain collectively (*The American League of Professional Baseball Clubs and Association of National Baseball League Umpires,* 1969).

This decision established the precedent that the Sherman Act did not remove major league baseball from NLRA coverage. Its immediate effect was to provide the AL umpires with protected bargaining rights. The long-term impact was broader and it provided NLRA protections for major league players as well as umpires. Prior to this decision the Sherman Act exemption had provided owners with a powerful weapon. The NLRB's decision that the NLRA covered baseball regardless of the Sherman Act provided the players with NLRA protections and increased their bargaining power. Due to this case, the NLRB was to play an important future role in a number of baseball labor relations situations.

Baseball Labor Relations: 1969 to 1995

The adversarial nature of baseball labor relations became apparent during this period. The 1968 and 1970 negotiations reached settlements without work stoppages. After 1972 work stoppages (strikes or lockouts) occurred, each time the existing collective bargaining agreement expired. Work stoppages in 1972, 1973, 1976, 1980, 1981, 1985, 1990, and 1994-95 gave the owners and players an unenviable eight for eight record. Economic issues, including minimum salaries, the pension program, and other employee benefits, were important topics in negotiations. However, these economic issues were usually less troublesome to resolve than were the intertwined issues of the reserve clause, salary arbitration, and free agency.

Curt Flood's legal challenge to the reserve clause provides an important backdrop to collective bargaining during this period. As explained earlier, the reserve clause historically tied players to one club indefinitely and sharply limited their bargaining power. Curt Flood, the St. Louis outfielder, challenged the legality of the reserve clause after he was traded unwillingly to the Phillies in 1969. In a 1972 decision the Supreme Court recognized that Major League Baseball was actually a business that was involved in interstate commerce. Nonetheless, it ruled that the reserve clause did not violate the Sherman Act due to the exemption created by the *Federal Baseball* case. The Court wrote that its reasoning might involve "inconsistencies or illogic," but that given the historic exemption, inconsistencies and illogic should be settled by Congress rather than the Court *(Flood v. Kuhn)*. After being declared legal by the Supreme Court due to baseball's antitrust exemption, the reserve clause became a negotiations topic.

Because of the previous history, the reserve clause, salary arbitration, and free agency became intertwined bargaining issues. It did not affect negotiations in 1972, although the players delayed the season with a thirteen-day strike over the pension plan and health care benefits. In 1973 the owners refused to operate spring training without a contract. The reserve clause was discussed in the 1973 negotiations, but it was not changed by the resulting contract. However, the owners did agree to salary arbitration. Salary arbitration increased player bargaining power by providing eligible players with a mechanism to combat the disadvantage of being legally tied to one club.

In 1975 an arbitration case, made possible by the grievance procedure developed in the 1968 and 1970 contracts, ended the reserve clause. In this case, the MLBPA asserted that the reserve clause provided for a one-time renewal only, not for unlimited renewals. The arbitrator found no contract language to support renewals beyond one year, and he ruled that the contract provided for only one-time renewals. A ruling by the Eighth Circuit Court subsequently enforced the ruling *(Kansas City Royals v. Players Association)*. This decision allowed players to become free agents after playing one year under the terms of their last contract and essentially did away with the reserve system. This set the stage for the terms of free agency and salary arbitration to become important in 1975 and subsequent negotiations.

During spring training in 1976 the owners instituted a seventeen-day lockout, which Commissioner Bowie Kuhn ended. The 1976 agreement provided players with free agency rights after six years. The terms of free agency were negotiated again when the players struck for the final eight days of spring training in 1980. Free agency continued as a contentious issue in 1981. When the owners announced their intention to implement their own free agency plan, the players began a midseason strike which lasted fifty days and caused cancellation of 713 games. A two-day strike occurred during the 1985 negotiations in which salary arbitration was a major issue. In 1990 the owners proposed major changes in the existing contract including salary caps, a pay-for-performance plan to eliminate the role of salary arbitration, and revenue sharing. Although the owners implemented a thirty-two-day lockout during spring training to support their proposals, none of these changes became part of the 1990 contract (Staudohar 50-51).

Collective bargaining, free agency, and salary arbitration led to increased salaries. Salary escalation and weak television revenues exacerbated financial tensions between the richer and poorer clubs. The 1990 contract expired at the end of 1993, and the 1994 partial season was played under the terms of the old contract. In June 1994, the owners formally presented MLBPA with a proposal to phase in salary caps, eliminate salary arbitration but reduce the time before players were eligible for free agency, and reduce the percentage of revenue available to pay wages and benefits. The owners saw these issues as important to preserving the economic viability of the "small market" teams.

The strike began August 12, 1994. The strike was timed to put pressure on owners at the point during the season when broadcast revenues are highest. Although the owners had given in to the players on many issues in previous negotiations, Acting Commissioner Bud Selig kept the owners united and firm even when faced with canceling the 1994 World Series. The strike had huge costs. Owners' costs were about $376 million, and the players lost $350 million in salaries (Holtzman 276).

Even given the punishing impact of the 1994 strike, there was no agreement under which to begin the 1995 season. The strike continued, and the clubs used replacement players in spring training. In early 1995 the owners unilaterally changed the terms of the expired contract. The NLRB found that these changes involved mandatory bargaining subjects, and that the owners violated the NLRA and undermined the bargaining process by changing them unilaterally. An injunction allowed the 1995 season to begin under the terms of the expired contract (*Silverman v. Major League Baseball* 1995).

The owners and MLBPA finally agreed to a new contract on January 1, 1997 (*Basic Agreement Major League Baseball and Major League Ball Players Association* 1997). The contract ran through October 2001. It contained no salary cap provisions. However, it did provide for revenue sharing through a luxury tax on club payrolls. Payrolls could be taxed on payrolls above $51 million in 1997, $55 million in 1998 and $58.9 million in 1999. There was no luxury tax in 2000 and 2001. This was a beginning effort at revenue sharing, but it did not have a dramatic impact on the economics of baseball.

The Basic Agreement: Similarities with Other Industries

The American labor movement is "bread and butter unionism" because it focuses on workplace issues rather than political or ideological issues. Collective bargaining in baseball follows this model. For example, the contract negotiated between the AL and NL clubs and MLBPA has compensation provisions such as minimum salaries and meal and spring training allowances. It also includes scheduling issues such as the length of the season, split doubleheaders, and one-day stands, and other workplace issues such as the provision of full-time trainers and parking facilities.

As with almost all collectively bargained contracts, the Basic Agreement includes a grievance procedure with specific steps including arbitration. This procedure resolves questions of what the contract means and what the parties' rights are under the contract. The case mentioned earlier which limited the scope of the reserve clause illustrates how the grievance procedure and arbitration define contract rights. Although the grievance procedure is common in other industries, in that case the issue was specific to professional baseball.

Discipline issues, or questions about whether an employee was disciplined fairly, are common grievance topics in baseball and other industries. In fact, discipline cases are so common that over time arbitrators developed "just cause" principles to determine the fairness of discipline. Fair discipline requires that employees be disciplined only for clearly communicated and consistently applied rules with known consequences, and that the punishment fits the crime.

The case involving John Rocker's discipline for injudicious speech illustrates the application of just cause principles. Rocker made disparaging remarks about his dislike of New York's ethnic diversity and riding the train to Shea Stadium with, among others, people having purple hair, AIDS, and prison records. These comments were published in *Sports Illustrated,* much to the embarrassment of Major League Baseball. Commissioner Selig said that Rocker had "offended practically every element of society," while bringing dishonor to himself, his team, and Major League Baseball. Selig suspended Rocker for seventy-three days and fined him $200,000. Rocker and MLBPA appealed Selig's decision and the arbitrator reduced Rocker's suspension to twenty-seven days and his fine to $500 (Chass March 2, 2000 D1). Although Selig and others criticized the decision, it reflected just cause principles. Baseball had no clear and consistent rules limiting player speech. Nor was it clear that some forms of speech would result in punishment. In fact, in 1988 a player reacted to a possible woman umpire with disparaging comments about women, but was not disciplined. In light of those factors, the punishment Selig meted out exceeded the crime.

Unusual Aspects of the Basic Agreement

The players' contract differs from most other bargained agreements in several interesting ways. The Basic Agreement provides a minimum salary for all major leaguers, but allows players to negotiate salaries and contract length individually. Most unions see individual bargaining as antithetical to collective action. However, MLBPA, similar to unions in the performing arts, represents people with varying experience, skill levels, and marketability. Stars with the ability to negotiate high salaries have little interest in standardized wages. The availability of individual negotiations accommodates the union's most sought after and least replaceable members, which in turn strengthens the union.

Salary arbitration is another unusual feature of baseball labor relations. Salary arbitration is available to players with several years' major league experience who are not yet eligible for free agency. These players can only negotiate with one club, and salary arbitration provides them with some bargaining leverage. Salary arbitration is irrelevant once players are eligible for free agency.

The contract provides for a particular form of arbitration, final-offer arbitration. In final-offer arbitration the parties present their final positions to the arbitrator, who chooses one of them, presumably the most realistic one. Arbitrators are unlikely to favor extreme positions, and the possibility of losing is real. This encourages the parties to make reasonable offers, which helps them move toward negotiated settlements. Baseball's experience with salary arbitration shows that the percentage of cases settled prior to arbitration has increased over time. In 1973, when arbitration was first available, about 45 percent of cases were settled prior to arbitration. During the 1990s the settlement rate rose to above 80 percent.

Although most cases get settled prior to arbitration, salary arbitration has increased the bargaining power of eligible players. It is one reason for the increased levels of baseball salaries. Because of its impact, the owners have made frequent proposals to modify or do away with it.

Another outgrowth of individual bargaining is the players' extensive use of agents. The contract allows players to have agents represent them, and MLBPA certifies those agents. Agents represent players in the initial signing process, in salary arbitration, and in free agent negotiations. Agent Scott Boras illustrates the range of activities. Besides traveling to Latin America in search of players unencumbered by the draft, he managed J. D. Drew's manipulation of the draft, presented novel and well-researched arguments in salary arbitration, and developed a sophisticated plan to market free-agent Alex Rodriguez.

Baseball Bargaining: Why So Confrontational?

From baseball's earliest days, the owners and players jousted in an ongoing power struggle. The heart of the struggle was the power to affect economic returns to the owners and players. The reserve system tipped the scales in favor of the owners. The NLRA, collective bargaining, the end of the reserve system, and the arrival of free agency and salary arbitration tipped some power back to the players. When one side gained power, the other side lost financially. Issues were cast so that a win for one side was a loss for the other, and there were few shared wins. Trust was a scarce commodity, and collaborative efforts to solve difficult problems were rare. Strong adversarial norms developed and helped create a self-fulfilling prophecy of antagonism, conflict, and confrontation. Distrust hampers bargaining because it inhibits management from sharing sensitive internal information with the union. Mistrust causes the union to suspect management's motivations and financial accuracy.

Personality issues exacerbated the mistrust between the owners and the players. To illustrate, former U.S. Secretary of Labor Robert Reich tried to mediate differences between the sides early in the 1994 strike. He found both Commissioner Selig and Donald Fehr, MLBPA's executive director, to be stubborn, pugnacious, and mistrustful. He described the dynamics of the meeting as both men talking endlessly in monologues and not responding directly to questions or comments. He concluded, "Each is convinced the other is out to screw him. Neither will budge. If there is a hell, it is a small room in which one is trapped for eternity with both these men" (Reich 190).

The complex finances of baseball ownership also complicate communication and understanding. Many major league clubs have multiple owners, and most owners have multiple financial interests. This makes evaluating a club's financial position difficult. Multiple owners also mean multiple perspectives at the bargaining table. Due to differences in finances and market shares, club owners have differing views on important issues such as revenue sharing. They also differ in philosophy. For example, although many owners have traditional management views of unions, Peter Angelos, principal owner of the Baltimore Orioles, has represented unions and even won an AFL-CIO human rights prize. He was the only owner to refuse to use replacement players in 1995.

Finally, the most problematic issues in baseball do not have easy win-win solutions. The owners face economic realities with the potential to continue to make labor negotiations difficult and conflict-ridden. Revenue sharing is particularly divisive. After the 1999 season, the thirteen clubs with the highest revenue provided the thirteen clubs with the lowest revenues a total of 100 million. Interestingly, several recipient clubs, including the Cincinnati Reds, Montreal Expos, and Oakland A's, actually lowered payrolls after benefiting from revenue sharing. Meanwhile, the Boston Red Sox, Los Angeles Dodgers, and New York Mets, all big revenue-sharing donors, lost $5 million each. In theory, revenue sharing provides poorer clubs with more ability to compete for players. In practice, it may punish clubs willing to spend to get quality players, and reward "cheapskate" owners (Badenhausen, Sicheri, and Pinto 112-115). In 1994 the owners tried to sidestep the tensions revenue sharing creates in their ranks by strenuous negotiating to get the players to accept salary caps. That experience suggests the likely futility of hoping the players will solve the problems market inequities create for the owners.

Recent Labor Relations Developments

The 1994-1995 work stoppage was an economic disaster and public relations nightmare. Clubs and players lost money, and disenchantment ran high among fans. Due to the strike's impact on the public's view of baseball, three Hall of Fame inductees addressed the situation in the 1995 and 1996 induction ceremonies. Richie Ashburn said it was "time to get this mess straightened out" (Ashburn 11). Jim Bunning admonished the owners to get their house in order. He said, "Figure out how you want to share your revenues without going to the players and asking them to foot the bill. Get an agreement . . . a long-term agreement, a minimum of 10 years" (Bunning 16). Mike Schmidt's 1995 comments were particularly heartfelt. He saw baseball at a crossroads, as evidenced by empty seats at every game and playgrounds empty of kids playing baseball. He said, "That concerns me, and baseball, it should scare you. Just a new agreement will not bring the fans back. . . . there must be a new level, a higher level of cooperation and understanding . . ." (Schmidt 14).

They were not alone in seeing the importance of change. In 1997, Fehr, in an appearance before the U.S. Senate Committee on the Judiciary, spoke of hope for a fundamentally different relationship in the next round of negotiations. Acknowledging the difficulty in changing the relationship between owners and players given baseball's bargaining history, he said, "Our task for the next go-round is to make sure that that record is broken, and broken with as large thump as we can manage" (Committee on the Judiciary 5). He warned that MLBPA would vigorously defend free agency and salary arbitration, but tempered that warning by saying, "Memories of what we went through four years ago remain reasonably vivid. If that remains when we get to bargaining, that should have a beneficial effect" (Blum 1999).

In 1998, the day after he was elected Commissioner, Selig stated that he did not believe it was possible for the clubs and players to think of a work stoppage in the next generation and that smarter ways to solve problems were needed. He said he was so sure that, "I told the clubs the same thing yesterday when I was alone with them.... If anybody thinks, . . . old-fashioned methods are going to work, they're wrong. I don't know how much more blunt I can be but that" (Knisley 16).

Several events provided evidence of a more cooperative relationship between the owners and MLBPA. The 1997 agreement provided for interleague play as a two-year experiment ending after 1998 unless the owners and MLBA agreed to an extension. They agreed to an extension with little difficulty. The contract also stipulated that the parties work together to get passage of the Curt Flood Act. A joint effort occurred, and the Curt Flood Act became law in 1998. This law ends baseball's antitrust exemption with respect to collective bargaining matters. The law protects the players from the owners resurrecting the reserve clause in the event of a bargaining impasse. For the owners, the law reduces the likelihood of subsequent restrictions on the antitrust exemption.

Commissioner Selig thinks additional revenue sharing is important to baseball's competitive balance. In 1999 he appointed a Blue Ribbon Committee to plan for increased revenue sharing. Headed by former Federal Reserve Chairman Paul Volker, the committee had no baseball administrators or players as members. In its 2000 report, the committee recommended the owners share 40 to 50 percent of local revenues, institute a 50 percent tax on payrolls above $84 million, and encourage clubs to have minimum payrolls of $40 million by withholding revenue sharing from clubs not reaching that level. This would encourage low payroll clubs to use shared revenues on player salaries. It also advocated sharpening competitive balance by instituting a worldwide, rather than U.S. only, draft of amateur players to prevent the richest clubs from outbidding the others for the best foreign players.

The plan's design may help middle-level clubs more than the poorest clubs, which might increase the plan's political acceptability to the owners. Yale President Richard C. Levin, a committee member, suggested that the midlevel teams would be able to see their playoff chances improve if they invest in players (Chass July 15, 2000 D2). However, owners of the richer clubs, such as Yankees' owner George Steinbrenner, have much to lose and may oppose the plan. That opposition could be in the form of efforts to affect the other owners' acceptance of the plan, or in the form of shifting financial assets to endeavors not covered by revenue sharing.

Future Implications

Historically baseball owners and players have had stormy and mistrustful relationships. The 1994-1995 strike was the most destructive event in that history. Since the strike, efforts were made to develop a more cooperative relationship. Economic inequities among the clubs remain a major unresolved issue. The Blue Ribbon Committee's report may help the owners resolve these inequities internally, and ease negotiations over a new contract. However, resolution of revenue sharing issues will not be easy. If the owners fail to agree, and demand salary caps and changes in salary arbitration from the players, negotiations will be contentious. On a hopeful note, contentious negotiations do not necessarily mean a strike. If the owners and players have learned this lesson, life will be easier for them and for the fans.

Editor's Note

As this book moved into production, the players' union and owners, perhaps exhibiting the improved relationship discussed in the essay above, reached a new labor agreement. The August 30, 2002, agreement came only hours before a union-set strike deadline. Although great revenue disparity will continue to exist among the teams, the two sides essentially decided to agree where they could agree. Changes from the previous agreement included increasing the percentage of locally generated revenue to be shared by teams from 20 percent to 34 percent, establishing a luxury tax on the portion of team payrolls above $117 million in 2003 (the threshold rising to $136.5 million in 2006), and increasing minimum player salaries from $200,000 to $300,000. In addition, owners agreed not to eliminate any major league teams before 2007, and players accepted some random testing for steroid use. Most importantly for fans, the threat of a players' strike or owners' lockout disappeared at least until the agreement expires after the 2006 season.

BIBLIOGRAPHY

Abrams, Roger I. *Legal Bases: Baseball and the Law.* Philadelphia: Temple UP, 1998.

The American League of Professional Baseball Clubs and The National League of Professional Baseball Clubs and Major League Baseball Players Association. 1997. *Basic Agreement.*

Ashburn, Richie. *Induction Ceremonies.* National Baseball Hall of Fame and Museum, 30 July 1995: 11.

Badenhausen, Kurt, William Sicheri, and Richard Pinto. "Baseball Games." *Forbes* 31 May 31 1999: 112-115.

Blum, Ronald. 1999. "Men Without Caps." *Sporting News* 1 February 1999.

Bunning, Jim. 1996. *Induction Ceremonies.* National Baseball Hall of Fame and Museum, Inc. 4 August 1996: 16.

Chass, Murray. "Plan Would Give Boost to Middle-Class Teams." *The New York Times* 15 July 2000: D2.

_____. "Rocker Permitted to Attend Camp, to Selig's Dismay." *The New York Times* 2 March 2000: D1.

Curt Flood Act. Public Law 105-297, Section 27: 1998.

Federal Baseball Club, Inc. v. National League of Professional Baseball Clubs, 259 U.S. 200 (1922).

Flood v. Kuhn, 407 U.S. 258 (1972).

Gildea, William. "Sudlersville Loves 'the Beast'; Eastern Shore Community Remembers Jimmie Foxx." *The Washington Post* 24 October 1987: D1.

Holtzman, Jerome. *The Commissioners: Baseball's Midlife Crisis.* New York: Total Sports: 1998.

Jennings, Kenneth M. *Balls and Strikes.* New York: Praeger Press: 1990.

Kansas City Royals v. Players Association, 532 F2d 615 (1976).

Knisley, Michael. "Wedded Bliss—for Now." *The Sporting News* 20 July 1998: 16.

Miller, Marvin. *A Whole Different Ball Game.* New York: Birch Lane Press: 1991.

NLRB. *The American League of Professional Baseball Clubs and Association of National Baseball League Umpires* (1969).

Reich, Robert B. *Locked in the Cabinet.* New York: Knopf: 1997.

Schmidt, Michael J. *Induction Ceremonies.* National Baseball Hall of Fame and Museum. 30 July 1995: 14.

"Selig: System's Broken, but 'How do we fix it?'" *The Philadelphia Inquirer* 12 December 2000, D-4.

Silverman v. Major League Baseball, 880 F. Supp. 246 (1995).

Staudohar, Paul D. "The Baseball Strike of 1994-95." In *Diamond Mines.* Ed. Paul Staudohar. Syracuse: Syracuse UP, 2000.

U.S. Congress. Senate. Committee on the Judiciary. *Hearings on S. 53.* Washington, DC: GPO: 1997.

20

God and the Diamond:
The "Born-Again" Baseball
Autobiography

Gary Land

Although the baseball autobiography dates back to the early twentieth century, the genre has become especially significant within the past three decades. Within this genre is a subgenre of books which combine the baseball story with a personal testament of the player's religious faith. In a sense, these works bring together the centuries-old tradition of spiritual autobiography, begun by Augustine (Hawkins), with the twentieth-century's sports autobiography.

As has been noted by several critics (Pascal 61-83, Eakin 181-278, Leibowitz 3-28, Olney), autobiography is a stylized literary form. Rather than being the unconscious product of raw experience, it is a consciously shaped story which attempts to bring order and meaning to one's life from the perspective of the present. As James Goodwin writes,

> An autobiography represents the writer's effort, made at a certain stage of life, to portray the meaning of personal experience as it has developed over the course of a significant period of time *or* from the distance of that significant time period. (11)

Hence, the degree to which the autobiography corresponds with that life as actually lived is problematic.

This essay is a revised version of a paper presented at the Conference on Baseball in Literature and Culture, Indiana State University, Terre Haute, Indiana, April 18, 1997.

The manner in which the baseball autobiography is written further complicates the nature of autobiographical truth. Rather than writing the autobiography himself, the baseball hero uses what might be called a "ghostwriter," except that he or she is usually named, to actually compose the book. This writer, normally an experienced journalist, interviews the player, then pulls the material together into a book. Although the player presumably approves what is ultimately published, the product of this joint effort must be recognized as something standing between a true autobiography, actually written by the subject, and a biography, written by a researcher who uses materials reaching beyond his or her subject's own statements. Furthermore, the book is written primarily for a commercial, rather than literary or historical, purpose, as both the publisher and author direct their efforts toward the sports fan who, it is hoped, will be interested to read the "inside" story of his sport.

While virtually all sports autobiographies must be approached with these elements in mind, it needs to be recognized that the Christian version of these works adds the element of testimony to the sports story. Usually introduced by religious publishers, these works are intended to appeal to both the sports fan and the Christian believer whose faith is bolstered by reading about famous people who share that faith. There is probably an evangelistic aspect to these works as well, namely the hope that the nonbelieving sports fan who reads the book for the sports story will experience a religious awakening through reading the athlete's testimony (Eitzen and Sage 92-101). To this end, these religious-baseball autobiographies have been almost entirely Christian, although Orlando Cepeda's recent discussion of his conversion to Buddhism (Cepeda) is perhaps a harbinger of the books that may arise from baseball's increasingly multicultural character.

Of the some twenty such books that have been written, I have chosen three representative works as a means of analyzing the content and structure of this subgenre. Brooks Robinson's *Third Base Is My Home,* published in 1974, was written near the end of a career. Orel Hershiser's *Out of the Blue,* published in 1989, appeared about a year after the pitcher's record-breaking 1988 season. And Dave Dravecky's *Comeback,* published in 1990, came out after a dramatic and very public battle with cancer that ended the player's career. Thus these books emerged out of very different situations that shaped the way their stories were told. Also, although more research needs to be done to establish its significance, Robinson's book appeared before the giving of personal religious testimonies became a frequent occurrence on the sports scene, something that may have affected the volume's style.

These books revolve around three elements, which might be called (1) the "baseball story," (2) the "conversion and testimony of faith story," and (3) the "baseball-faith story." These "stories" are not usually separate sections, but rather are intertwined themes that flow through an entire book.

The Baseball Story

As one would expect in a sports autobiography, each of these books recounts the player's athletic career, what I have called the "baseball story." Although this "story" is ultimately the book's reason for being and provides the organizational framework within which the other elements are developed, I will not spend much time in examining it, for it is held in common with all other baseball autobiographies. Robinson spends considerable time describing his experience in high school and the minor leagues, before recounting his major league career. While the first half of the volume is largely chronological, the second half is organized topically, addressing such issues as family life, relations with management, conditioning, and memories of great plays. In contrast to the lack of a central focus in Robinson's book, Hershiser's account, while also telling about his rise to the major leagues, is organized around the 1988 season when he pitched fifty-nine consecutive scoreless innings and helped the Dodgers win the World Series. Similarly, Dravecky's story revolves around his struggle with cancer during the 1989 and 1990 seasons in addition to recounting his baseball career.

The Conversion and Testimony Story

Within these contexts, the athletes present their religious commitment. Although the conversion story plays an important role in Hershiser's and Dravecky's books, for Robinson there appears to have been no dramatic moment of being "born again." He states that he has regularly attended church on Sundays and that his parents made Christianity a part of his life from early childhood (143-144). The style of religion in which he was raised appears to have emphasized nurture, or what Anne Huniker Hawkins calls the "gradual or *lysis* type of conversion," rather than a dramatic or *crisis* conversion experience (21). Similarly, Robinson does not detail his religious beliefs, stating that personal faith is more important than intellectual understanding. For him, "there is one absolute—Jesus Christ. The rest of us are still trying to reach his spiritual perfection, and that's the significant goal, no matter what form our worship takes" (144). His theological understanding becomes somewhat clearer when he speaks of Jesus offering forgiveness "and the promise that I may still become a new person through him" (146).

In contrast, Hershiser and Dravecky recount in considerable detail their conversion experience, which for both of them occurred in the minor leagues primarily through the influence of another player, and discuss at some length their religious beliefs. Hershiser was what might be described as a "nominal" Christian prior to his conversion, attending church on Easter Sunday and having a vague belief in Christian doctrine. But after meeting Butch Wickensheimer, a devout Christian on the Single A Clinton, Iowa, team, Hershiser's life took a new direction. Although he played the devil's advocate, challenging Wickensheimer's beliefs in an attempt, as he puts it, to look "for an out" (80), he began reading the Bible. For several months he stood on the edge of belief, recognizing that he must decide whether Christ was a man or God. Finally, one night he ran through a series of questions in his mind regarding God, the Bible, the nature of sin, and the person of Jesus. Not sure he knew how to pray, he knelt beside his bed and admitted to God that he knew little about him and probably never would. Nonetheless, Hershiser recognized that he was a sinner, wanted forgiveness, and desired to have Christ in his life. There was no dramatic emotional experience; he simply accepted Jesus as his savior and went to bed (82).

Dravecky, raised in a devout Catholic home, and active in baseball chapel (Kashatus) in the minor leagues, nonetheless regarded religion as something of a formality. Before meeting Byron Ballard in Amarillo, at the Double-A level, he believed in God's existence, regarded himself as a Christian, and accepted the Bible as God's inspired word. But despite these apparent commitments he had never read the Bible and seems to have had no deep religious experience.

Ballard's manner of living impressed him, however, and Dravecky began reading Scripture, a practice that changed his idea of God from an abstraction to a being who related to people personally, especially in his act of entering into human existence as Jesus, who had died for all human beings, including Dravecky himself. As with Hershiser, Dravecky took time before making his decision, but unlike the Dodger pitcher he does not describe a specific moment when he chose to follow Christ. Recognizing that because God is personal he requires a commitment, Dravecky and his wife, Janice, decided, "eventually" as he states, to follow the God of the Bible as revealed by Jesus. They accepted that Jesus had died for them and promised that they would depend on him as they sought to follow his will (66-69). Both Hershiser's and Dravecky's conversion stories contain elements common to much evangelical Christian teaching: the importance of personal influence, the role of Scripture in awakening a sense of God's presence, recognition of one's status as a sinner, an understanding of Jesus as God and his death on the cross as payment for sin's penalty, and a personal decision to both believe and commit oneself to living out that belief (Hunter 47). It is striking that both men, although in no sense describing themselves as intellectuals, went through considerable mental as well as emotional struggle before becoming believing Christians. Perhaps it is not surprising that they both earned the reputation of being "thinking" pitchers.

The Baseball-Faith Story

No matter how intense the Christian experience and conviction of these men, it is unlikely that they would have written their stories if they had not been ballplayers. Furthermore, few people would be interested in reading only their religious stories. It is the combination of both baseball and religion that attracts the reader. Consequently, the structural and thematic relationships between baseball and religion in these books play an important role in their audience appeal.

Much of Robinson's book, as noted earlier, is organized topically, particularly the recounting of his major league experience. Within this organizational structure, one chapter addresses religion. But that chapter revolves around his move from Protestantism to Catholicism as a result of marrying a Catholic and says virtually nothing about the relationship of religion and baseball (143-146). Elsewhere, he makes brief references to God giving him health and physical ability (157) and blessing him with a good income from playing the game (178). But he does not develop these comments into major themes.

Hershiser and Dravecky develop the baseball-faith story much more self-consciously. Both address the apparently frequently made charge that Christian athletes are not competitive enough (Kashatus 83-84). Hershiser, whom manager Tommy Lasorda nicknamed "Bulldog," says that his faith would have been a "crutch" or "a weak, sad alibi" if it simply made him accept defeat on the baseball diamond. "People who criticize Christians for being less competitive—and Christians who *are* less competitive—have missed the point of the faith." He observes that a Christian who does not do his very best is a hypocrite, for his religion demands his very best effort (25). Dravecky, asked by reporters about Christian players lacking "intensity and determination," similarly replied that he performed for Jesus, who was his example, glorifying God for the ability that he had given. Because he had the responsibility of representing Jesus, Dravecky played "with everything I have" (14).

The views expressed in these books seem to parallel, although there is no evidence of direct influence, the theology of "Total Release Performance," developed by Wesley Neal, which calls on athletes to make a complete effort, not only to achieve athletic victory but also to express thanks for their God-given talents. The consciousness that everything that they do is for the glory of God leads to a particular approach or attitude toward the game. While in the clubhouse prior to a game Hershiser thought, prayed, and read his Bible, stating that these activities relaxed him, for it was like talking to a friend. God, however, had nothing to do with the upcoming game's outcome which, according to Hershiser, is not related to the pitcher's faithfulness (48). After going to the mound it was Hershiser's custom to offer a silent prayer, thanking God for the opportunity to play and requesting that no one be injured. But apart from asking God to help his team do its best, he did not pray about the outcome (152).

During the 1988 World Series, while pitching the sixth game, Hershiser prayed, talked to himself, sang hymns, and yawned—an interesting combination of the sacred and mundane—all in an effort to relax (212). When he won the game and series, he looked upward and offered a quick thank you prayer (217). But Hershiser also notes a moment when thinking about God interfered with his play. Needing one more out to set the regular season consecutive scoreless innings record, he relaxed for a moment, taking in the situation and thinking about God's blessing. In doing so, he lost his focus and hit Lee Mazilli with his next pitch. This incident reminded him that a single pitch is important, that after victory he could celebrate and offer a prayer of thanks. But first he had to make a good pitch. Reestablishing his focus, he struck out Howard Johnson and "quickly dropped to one knee and breathed a prayer of thanks" (189).

While Dravecky does not describe a regular practice of praying before games, he does recount discovering while pitching in Hawaii that visualizing Jesus as his audience took off pressure. He states that one played to glorify God rather than oneself. Losing hurt, but has no ultimate meaning, for God was still there (83-84). He objects, however, to attributing success on the diamond to God. If God is truly the master of the universe, he must be concerned with more important things than a ballplayer's statistics. In Dravecky's opinion, to believe that God helps one win ball games is simply superstition (56).

The perspectives offered by Hershiser and Dravecky suggest that the most important function of religious faith in relationship to baseball for these players is the provision of perspective. Hershiser speaks of his faith being a balancing agent in his life, giving him both strength and humility (91-92). Although he disliked failure, it did not overly disturb him, for he knew that both his family and God would continue to love him. Life would continue. He comments that his faith reminded him that the ability to pitch successfully has no cosmic significance (25). References to the importance of family is characteristic of all three books, especially those by Hershiser and Dravecky, for the family provided support for the players' careers, a refuge from the pressures of baseball life, and a continuing reminder of what was truly important. Hershiser reports that his agent, Robert Fraley, talked with him about his priorities, saying that the success of his career should be measured, not only by the financial rewards, but by his marriage, family, friends, and community respect (97).

In addition to describing his great success in 1988, Hershiser writes about his relatively poor 1989 season, commenting that although it tested both his theories and his faith, his religious beliefs remained strong (236). About the same time, Dravecky's understanding of his faith passed through a test more fundamental than lack of success on the field. During the same season that Hershiser was getting his name in the record books, Dravecky learned that he had a malignant desmoid tumor in his left arm. A few weeks later a surgeon removed one-half of the deltoid muscle in his pitching arm and froze part of the humerus bone to reduce the chances of recurrence.

Although his life was not in danger, Dravecky's career appeared to have ended. While it would seem that such an experience might challenge his faith, Dravecky denies having had doubt. He states that he had always wondered whether he would be able to maintain confidence in God's love when facing difficult times (118). When that tough experience arrived in the form of cancer, he and his wife learned that their faith provided the resources to carry them through what might have been a valley of despair (126).

Looking back on the past few years, Dravecky believed that God had put him and his family through some difficult experiences, particularly while playing winter ball in Colombia, that had prepared him for this new situation (69-70). Essentially, he faced cancer and its consequences in the same way that he approached baseball, confident that God was caring for him no matter what happened. He seems not to have sought a theological explanation or justification for why cancer struck him.

Although a return to pitching seemed unlikely, he began to work toward that end. "My faith in a personal God released me from the fear of failing," he observes. "That's not fatalism. It's trust. Trust helped me to work hard and not to worry about the outcome" (126). When he returned to the mound during the 1989 season he asked God to help him have a proper attitude, no matter what happened. Prior to his August 10 comeback game in San Francisco, he prayed that God would give him a correct attitude and focus (180).

Five days after winning that comeback game, however, Dravecky's humerus bone—which had been frozen during surgery—broke. While on the ground in great pain, he thought of God's purpose. He states that instead of being filled with anger, he was both astonished and certain that God was directing him into a new, exciting phase of life (209). About two months later he learned that the cancer had returned, requiring an operation which removed his arm and forced his retirement from baseball.

In recounting his cancer story, Dravecky reaffirms the essential element of what I have called the "baseball-faith story," namely that Christian faith places baseball in perspective. Hence, the shattering of his career did not destroy his person. Reflecting on the experience of living with one arm, Dravecky concludes that he has had to learn to accept his physical limitations and trust that God would take care of everything else (265).

If, as noted at the beginning of this essay, autobiography brings meaning and order to the writer's life, these books do so by encircling the game of baseball, which nearly everyone would regard as rather insignificant in the grand scheme of things, with belief in the ultimate reality of God. The "baseball story," recounting games won and lost and amazing feats on the diamond, dominates the organization of Robinson's and Hershiser's books and establishes the dramatic background for Dravecky's account. This story thereby provides the primary attraction to the reader. But the books become more than sports stories through the "conversion and testimony of faith story" which draws the reader into the search for ultimate meaning and either provides confirmation of the believer's own faith or offers the nonbeliever a glimpse of an otherwise foreign religious experience. But the "baseball story" and the "conversion and testimony story" exist in tension with each other, a tension between the profane and sacred, between the trivial and the ultimate. The "baseball-faith story" helps resolve this tension by providing a thematic unity in which baseball is played for the glory of God. The resolving of this tension not only enables the player to justify his career on the diamond but also eases the conscience of the Christian baseball fan who may wonder whether an interest in sports is really compatible with his or her religious commitment. Just as the "invented" life of the secular baseball autobiography provides the reader with a vicarious sports experience, the Christian born-again autobiography enables the believing reader to identify with someone who bridges the gap between the worldly and the spiritual, achieving both earthly glory and heavenly salvation.

BIBLIOGRAPHY

Cepeda, Orlando, with Herb Fagan. *Baby Bull: From Hardball to Hard Time and Back.* Dallas: Taylor, 1999.

Dravecky, Dave, with Tim Stafford. *Comeback.* San Francisco: Harper and Row and Grand Rapids, MI: Zondervan, 1990; reprinted, New York: Harper Paperbacks, 1991.

Eakin, Paul John. *Fictions in Autobiography: Studies in the Art of Self-Invention.* Princeton: Princeton UP, 1985.

Eitzen, D. Stanley, and George H. Sage. "Sport and Religion." *Religion and Sport: The Meeting of Sacred and Profane.* Contributions to the Study of Popular Culture, No. 36. Ed. Charles S. Prebish. Westport, CT: Greenwood, 1993.

Goodwin, James. *Autobiography: The Self-Made Text.* Studies in Literary Themes and Genres No. 2. New York: Twayne, 1993.

Hawkins, Anne Hunsaker. *Archetypes of Conversion: The Autobiographies of Augustine, Bunyan, and Merton.* Lewisburg: Bucknell UP, 1985.

Hershiser, Orel, with Jerry B. Jenkins. *Out of the Blue.* Brentwood, TN: Wolgemuth and Hyatt, 1989; reprinted, New York: Jove Books, 1990.

Hunter, James Davison. *American Evangelicalism: Conservative Religion and the Quandary of Modernity.* New Brunswick, NJ: Rutgers UP, 1983.

Kashatus, William C. "The Origins of Baseball Chapel and the Era of the Christian Athlete, 1973-1990." *Nine: A Journal of Baseball History and Social Policy Perspectives* 7 (Spring 1999): 75-90.

Leibowitz, Herbert. *Fabricating Lives: Exploration in American Autobiography.* New York: Alfred A. Knopf, 1989.

Olney, James. *Metaphors of Self: The Meaning of Autobiography.* Princeton: Princeton UP, 1972.

Pascal, Ray. *Design and Truth in Autobiography.* London: Routledge and Kegan Paul, 1960.

Robinson, Brooks, as told to Jack Tobin. *Third Base Is My Home.* Waco: Word Books, 1974.

21

The Winter Meetings,
the King of Baseball,
and the Conscience of the Game

Larry Moffi

The office of Commissioner of Baseball has come nearly full circle. A few years ago, after more than eighty years of operating under the authority of a largely impartial commissioner, the owners of major league baseball's thirty teams appointed one of their own, Milwaukee's Bud Selig, to oversee the game. Their decision begs a few questions: Can a commissioner be an effective conscience of the game in this era of players' rights? Does baseball need an overseer? Is the position even appropriate?

The last time organized baseball was governed by team owners, they botched it. Penurious to a tragic flaw, they virtually caused the Black Sox Scandal of 1919; or if that's stretching the point, they at least had more than a few opportunities to force the players' hands, so to speak, halt the scam, and challenge them as mutual investors in a common cause known as success. The owners have been botching it ever since.

Back in 1920, the benighted owners invented the "proactive stance." They went out and hired a judge, anointed him High Commissioner of Baseball, granted him tenure, a salary of $50,000 a year, then built him a podium from which he preached with the fervor of an evangelist for two decades. Meanwhile, down in the cheap seats, the owners cried, "Save us!" responsively and in unison, to the judge's message that he would tolerate no evil, either among players or owners. "Save our game!" the owners cried out again, ". . . and keep us out of court."

More than a judge, the new commissioner was the Mountain, which they had moved unto themselves.

You don't have to be a student of either law or baseball to appreciate how off-the-wall the Landis decision concerning Shoeless Joe Jackson and the other seven White Sox players was. Landis reversed a court ruling, not as an appeals court judge but as a High Commissioner. It was a decision beyond "right" or "wrong" and based on a conscience that Landis felt obliged to exercise, and there would be many more under Landis and his successors.

Landis's ruling would never stand today—not with the players' union, the umpires' union, the agents, the arbitration clauses, and so on. But it worked back then. What Landis established was an authority of conscience, the last word in all matters of baseball—and the word was good and blessed by a man who once was judge and remained a mountain. In the language of the law he left behind, Landis was precedent setting. You can ask Bud Selig, who has set a few precedents of his own.

Every commissioner of baseball, Landis to Selig (including Spike Eckert), has invoked the call to conscience either by word or by action. While the deal the owners cut was with Landis, the Unrivaled Lucifer, the next seven commissioners were little devils, too. Each had his own peculiar tick or itch that, along with the times, influenced his expression of conscience.

Landis fulfilled his obligation to the owners: he kept baseball out of the courts. He was the last commissioner to do so. Today, after his brief and self-effacing stint as "interim commissioner," Selig, baseball's ninth official commissioner, "governs" a game of day in court that's rarely out of season.

Alan "Bud" Selig is about as different from Kenesaw Mountain Landis, as bud, indeed, is from mountain. Selig ran a car dealership in Milwaukee; his first brush with Major League Baseball was lending new cars to Braves players fifty years ago. Landis was welcomed to the game as a federal appeals court judge who had ignored the Federal League's antitrust action against organized baseball. The analogy here comes closer to the field: Selig being as different from Landis as William Bendix was from Babe Ruth. That said, not even World War II could force the cancellation of half a baseball season and the World Series; Bud Selig did. (I actually hoped Bill Clinton would step in and rule in favor of an American institution and its fans,

a gesture in the spirit of FDR's recommendation to Landis that baseball could best serve the war effort and boost public morale, not by
aborting the season but by playing it out.) Selig's decision to cancel
both the balance of the 1998 season and the World Series had to have
been as difficult as any Landis had made; certainly on a par with Bart
Giamatti's barring of Pete Rose for life.

Landis had a face that spoke good conscience. It was so unforgiving it might have been etched in stone, another profile for Mt.
Rushmore against the Dakota horizon. Selig's, at best, belongs in a
car commercial. Yet the robe of justice that Selig wears today is the
very one that Landis tailored for himself. I find it remarkable how
comfortable a man called "Bud" seems to be in it, though it's worn
and threadbare in spots, altered and re-altered to suit the conscience
of the eight others before him. Selig, who professes that he doesn't
have to try to make it fit, has probably entertained the thought that
maybe the best thing to do would be to retire the robe. (Surely the
owners—many, if not all—have wished often enough that Landis had
been buried in the robe, an appropriate shroud.)

As everyone on both sides of the equation knows today, the players
hardly need more protection. (Remember, it was the players' strike
that caused Selig to cancel the season.) Really, is anyone sympathetic
with the players? There is no longer anything anyone can do in behalf
of the players—not the courts, not the commissioner, not the league
presidents (even if they did exist). Everyone has had his day in court;
if not, there's always tomorrow.

Meantime, today, despite his mandate of conscience, the question
remains: Can a Commissioner of Baseball viably and impartially
oversee the game?

Perhaps a king would work.

I once met the King of Baseball and I can tell you this: the King of
Baseball is not the Commissioner of Baseball. That's what's good
about baseball.

In December 1985, I had dinner on the infield (it might have been
the outfield) of the Houston Astrodome along with hundreds of other
guests at the banquet of baseball's annual winter meetings. Unaffili-
ated with any official baseball organization, I was seated on a space-
available agreement with the "front office" of a California Angels
rookie league affiliate, Medicine Hat, if I remember right: a general

manager and his wife, the club's office manager and her husband, and three summer interns from the local community college. The highlight of the evening was the crowning of The King of Baseball 1985, Donald Davidson.

Davidson was a midget, the perfect size for a king, particularly the King of Baseball, it seems to me, but not in the Eddie Gaedel mode. Davidson, I realized, surely was a man larger than size alone, as his newly acquired pedigree required. You could say of him that he was a man unconstrained by his size. Isn't that what we want from a king? Would the crown even fit, otherwise?

Davidson had spent his entire life working in baseball, mostly for the Braves. As a kid he was batboy for the old Boston club. Then, via Milwaukee, he moved down to Atlanta working wherever he was needed, mostly in public relations. It was clear enough from Davidson's selection that the King of Baseball must unabashedly love the game—at all costs. (The previous summer I watched in awe as the longitudinally challenged Davidson frightened a 6'2", three-hundred pound electrician to tears in the press box after a ball game. Something to do with the latter's knocking a cup of ballpark beer onto Davidson's color-coded-with-felt-tip-pens scorecard. The colors ran like something biblical, the Red Sea after the Israelites had safely reached the other side.) That kind of passion.

All right, the King of Baseball is a titular role, an ambassador of goodwill, so to speak. But when I think of what he is supposed to represent—everything that is good about the game of baseball—I'm beginning to think that, given the absence of conscience in today's game, a king might be the right man for the job. The lineage of the King of Baseball embodies the spirit of the game. Bill Veeck reigned as King; Spike Eckert as king is unimaginable. If the King is the spirit of the game and the Commissioner is its conscience, I'm beginning to favor the King.

The Commissioner of Baseball that year in Houston was Peter Ueberroth, his first. The previous summer, just six months before, he had marketed the Summer Olympics from Los Angeles to international fanfare and acclaim. He won awards. His picture was on every magazine cover in the country. There was talk of him running for president. To major league baseball owners in search of a persona to replace Bowie Kuhn as commissioner, he was the prototype celebrity of the changing economic times. Ueberroth came across as a marketing genius with a Midas touch. He was a practical-minded yet imaginative man—also somewhat aloof, which the owners liked, aloofness being a quality they shared, to a man. I have no recollection of Ueberroth's presence at Davidson's coronation—although given his public relations acumen, I cannot imagine him not being there.

On the Friday night of those meetings sixteen years ago, I attended a party hosted by Jack Kent Cooke, the owner of the Washington Redskins, who was trying to lure a major league baseball team to DC. But most of the cocktail chatter that night involved Ueberroth, as in: Did you hear, the Commissioner is supposed to show up. And so he did. And everyone called him Mr. Commissioner.

Never had mister sounded so regal. While not The King, he was kingly indeed. He had an aura about him that seemed to emanate directly from his title, Commissioner of Baseball: Conscience of the game, if not the spirit.

As far removed as Ueberroth was from Landis, the office (as we like to say when we speak of presidents and other distant officials who rise to office) would be the measure of the man. Ueberroth in his own way was stepping up to the challenge, just as his five predecessors had done. This time the challenge, as always involving mostly money, would precipitate a climatic shift in both power and conscience.

Over the years, the commissioner's expression of good conscience has changed with the man and the times. For Peter Ueberroth, everything was measured at the bottom line. His employers applauded his vision even when he publicly offended or derided them.

Lyndon Johnson once said: "Bobby Kennedy couldn't pour shit out of a cowboy boot if the directions were written on the heel." Ueberroth's variation, which he voiced some years later, when baseball's owners were being hauled into court over the issue of collusion not to sign free agents, was much more accurate than L.B.J.'s one liner. "They aren't capable of colluding," Ueberroth said of the owners. "They couldn't agree on what to have for breakfast."

Publicly, Ueberroth, similar to every commissioner before him, believed his role was to better the game for all concerned: "Most important, for the fans," he lied. But when asked for his personal assessment of his tenure the night he announced his retirement a year and a half before his contract expired, he said, "When I took over, baseball wasn't healthy financially. Now it is." With the bottom line in the black, his conscience clear, Ueberroth rode off into his personal California sunset never to be heard from again (not unlike Eckert, although the general's exit was marred by his equally unmemorable entrance). Not surprisingly, Ueberroth is the only commissioner to leave office on his own terms.

It was at that low point in baseball history that the notion of Commissioner of Baseball as conscience of the game seemed finally to have rusted out beyond repair. Then Bart Giamatti, the president of the National League and the former president of Yale University, was named Ueberroth's successor. Conscience, it seemed, had drawn new life.

Bowie Kuhn once pontificated that it is the dream of every boy in America to grow up to be commissioner. But it was Bart Giamatti who spoke in royal eloquence when, in accepting the appointment as president of the National League, he said, "I am almost fifty years old, and I have fallen in love. I'm running away with a beautiful redhead with flashing eyes whose name is baseball." Being named commissioner must have been like waking on his honeymoon to the redhead and her twin sister.

Giamatti seemed to possess all the qualities a good king should possess. Just as Davidson, he was passionate about the game; just as Veeck, he was conscientious about retaining and enriching its goodness. (In expressing his desire to buy the Philadelphia Phillies in 1944, Veeck told Landis of his intent to sign black ballplayers to major and minor league contracts, at which point Landis nixed the sale. Civil rights did not fall within the scope of the Landis conscience.) Then, barely five months in office, the man who would be king and commissioner died. If ever there was hope for the office it seemed to die with Giamatti.

Giamatti's successor, Fay Vincent, never had a chance. Less than a month after taking office in 1989, he faced an immediate Armageddon in the form of the San Francisco earthquake, which resulted in a ten-day postponement of the World Series.

To appreciate why the Commissioner of Baseball has never been King of Baseball, you have to go all the way back to the beginning again, and the owners. Obsessed with antitrust legislation, they forgot to look over their other shoulder: civil rights, labor rights, arbitration, among other legal issues were about to blindside them, à la Pete Rose versus Ray Fosse in the 1970 All-Star Game. As with Fosse, the owners never fully regained their old form.

Landis's expression of conscience encompassed a number of aspects of baseball and its growth. Civil rights was not one of them. Born a year after the end of the Civil War and named for the battle where his grandfather, a Union Army surgeon, was wounded while tending to casualties, Landis had no interest in bringing black ballplayers into the majors. Yes, he ruled in favor of Marty Marion's minor league contract, despite the fact that it was written on a paper napkin. Yes, he deconstructed Branch Rickey's St. Louis Cardinals' monopoly of minor league teams. But while he ostensibly kept organized baseball free of gamblers, he also kept it free of African Americans. Baseball would wait until the judge's successor, a U.S. Congressman from the parimutuel state of Kentucky—below the Mason-Dixon Line, as well—to support Branch Rickey's signing Jackie Robinson to the Dodgers in 1947.

Understandably sensitive to the livelihood of the folks who once had been his constituents, A.B. "Happy" Chandler walked a very fine line when it came to gambling and behavior that was not "in the best interest of the game" (the phrase was actually first uttered by Commissioner Kuhn). On the one hand, Chandler banished Leo Durocher from baseball for a year for consorting with gamblers; on the other, he approved Dan Topping's ownership of the Yankees, knowing full well that Topping was affiliated with Las Vegas casinos. But it was the man from Kentucky, not the one from Ohio (Landis), who supported Branch Rickey's breaking of major league baseball's color barrier. The new commissioner had been schooled in politics, and the conscience of the game was on the verge of fifty years of dramatic and radical changes. But not before a fifteen-year interregnum known as the Ford Frick years.

Frick was a laissez-faire commissioner who all too frequently delegated his conscience to the leagues. As much as Happy Chandler was known to sing "My Old Kentucky Home" in public, commissioner Frick's mantra was monotone and much more direct: "It's a league matter," he said, over and over, regarding one impending ruling or another because, as he reiterated in his autobiography, "It was a league matter." But given the structures of the National and American leagues, "it" always seemed to become an owners' matter, a "fact" that pleased the owners to no end.

The owners made the most of the next seventeen years and four months: fourteen and one under Frick, three and one under Frick's successor, General William Eckert. If Frick was laissez faire, he was an ego-maniacal revolutionary compared to Eckert. The moniker he carried for his brief administration—"The Unknown Soldier"—says all you need to know. As comfy as the owners felt back in 1969, they should have known better. The end of all good things was near.

It was Dante, not John Grisham, who assigned lawyers their rightful place in Hell. And it was lawyers and what they stood for that organized baseball feared. Given the owners' penchant for shooting themselves in the foot, it's hardly surprising that prior to becoming commissioner, Bowie Kuhn, who succeeded Eckert early in 1969, was—what else?—a lawyer.

Kuhn had come of age as council for a private law firm that represented the National League. Indeed, he seemed to have been grooming himself for the job of commissioner. But as much as Bowie Kuhn knew about baseball—he hung numbers on the Griffith Stadium scoreboard as a kid—the law, not baseball, governed his conscience. It was Kuhn who coined the term "in the best interests of the game." And it was under Kuhn that the "best interests" took a seismic shift in favor of the players. About the time that "lawyer jokes" were regaining popularity the courts began to make a joke of baseball—organized baseball, that is. Organized baseball, as in the owners.

After managing to stay out of court for years, being in court had become as common as spring training. The owners kept losing and losing. In 1975, in a case brought to court by Andy Messersmith of the Dodgers and Dave McNally of the Expos, baseball's "reserve clause" was struck down, and the two pitchers were declared free agents. This reversal of the Supreme Court's ruling five years earlier against Curt Flood's similar claim was the first of many players' victories. Five years later the courts stood behind the players, refusing to issue an injunction that would disallow a midseason strike that lasted nearly two months. Later, in the mid-1980s, justice again weighed in favor of the players, when a judge ruled that the owners had "colluded" in refusing to sign free agents. Collectively, as the trend revealed, players began to sound as arrogant and self-serving as the owners.

As with all earthquakes, the one that hit San Francisco in 1989 came fiercely and violently from deep down under. For Fay Vincent, the new commissioner, managing to actually complete the World Series amid the tragedy and chaos was his singular triumph as commissioner. While he rose eloquently and righteously from those ashes, things just got worse in a hurry. It must have been quite clear to Vincent that the source that was rocking the commissionership was as unforgiving and long-brewing as that of any earthquake. Every which way Vincent turned he seemed to piss off the owners—there's no better way to say it. Three years after he took office, he was out. Even Spike Eckert outlasted Fay Vincent.

Which brings us to the present state of affairs, ironically similar to those of the past. The first commissioner of baseball was born from the owners' failure to exercise good conscience. Before Landis, organized baseball was governed by a National Commission of the National and American leagues, with a chairman, Cincinnati Reds' owner "Gary" Hermann, who functioned not all that differently from the way Bud Selig operates today. If the authority of the Commission and its chair was concerned with anything more than telling players which club owned their contracts, there is little evidence today.

Before the Commission was decommissioned in 1919, it had run organized baseball since 1903. There was no precedent for running baseball any differently. Eighty years ago, the decision to create the office of Commissioner of Baseball subject to Landis's absolute power was the only likely solution to getting organized baseball on track. Today, under Commissioner Selig, that "option" seems like fantasy.

As Commissioner of Baseball, Selig is a peculiar hybrid of Landis (and the seven men who succeeded him) and of Hermann, chair of the National Commission. But the position has been so inbred and so constrained by just decisions of the courts in favor of the players that the game can probably sustain itself without a commissioner. But not without a king.

I would like to suggest that the game's powers that be—the owners, the players, and even the agents and unions—anoint some good-hearted fan King of Baseball. But it would never work. Fay Vincent, as great a fan of the game as anyone I know, could not pull it off.

Maybe what we need is someone like Rick Dempsey, the ex-Oriole catcher, who during rain delays would run the tarp-covered bases and slide through the puddles of rain into home, just for the sheer joy of it.

Or maybe Joe Morgan, the Hall of Fame second baseman and ESPN broadcaster, whose knowledge of the game is surpassed only by his love for it. I'm not thinking of a king who would challenge the courts. I'm not thinking of a king who would threaten a ballplayer's right to earn whatever the market will bear or an owner's right to earn a profit from his investment.

I'm thinking of a king who would affect some basic changes in favor of all who love the game for its own sake. A king who would get rid of the designated hitter, say, or shorten the season so that the World Series was not played in winter conditions, or turn weekday Series games into afternoon affairs so that kids could watch. I'm talking about the basics. I'm talking about a King of Baseball who, when something was amiss on the field of play, would step down from his throneseat in the stands, march across the diamond, and in the kingly voice of Casey Stengel speaking of [to] his woebegone Mets of years ago, say: "Can't anyone here play this game?" And then make it right. That's the king for me.

22

Control Problems: The Limitations of Baseball As Metaphor

William W. Wright

If only life could be more like baseball.

Dave Dravecky

For many, there is no more obvious forum for the enactment of divine intervention than in sports.

Ira Berkow

Like many fans and critics of the game, I have an autographed baseball on my desk. Signed by my family, it rolls around between the mouse pad, the clock, and the piles of papers that grow and shrink with the seasons. When I look at it, I am reminded of the opportunities to connect with the people that I love. This baseball is a metaphor. This chapter is about baseball and metaphors, about how we use the game of baseball to examine and explain the more complicated parts of our lives. When countless commentators and players evoke the primal scene of fathers playing catch with sons or celebrate the permanence of baseball in America, they are engaged in metaphor. We use the game to describe and circumscribe country, family, effort, and life. The familiar cry of "Wait 'til next year" is a metaphor for hope, not just for our team or for the game, but for ourselves. Sometimes, of course, there is no next year. Sometimes life is nothing like baseball despite our metaphors to the contrary.

More specifically, this is an essay about the consequences of metaphor, the limitations that baseball metaphors enact and the disappointments that they engender. I am going to tell the story of my sister

259

and baseball, about how she used baseball as one of a number of strategies for responding to illness. Her husband, Scott, struggled with the pain, humility, and possibilities of cancer during the same time that our families were making it a point to meet at a major league ball game once or twice a year. When we talked and wrote to and about Scott, we often talked in the terms and metaphors of baseball.

As we know, an earthquake disrupted the 1989 World Series. At approximately 5:04 p.m. on October 17, 1989, the 60,000 plus fans awaiting game three of the series between the Oakland A's and the San Francisco Giants felt the rolling jolt of the Loma Prieta earthquake. My sister Donna and her husband Scott were among those fans. Much of the response to the earthquake in the days that followed and up to the present focused first on the reminder that baseball was just a game. Cameras focused on ballplayers searching for families. We got to see footage of Willie Mays being interviewed at the very moment of the earthquake, and for that moment Mays was startled on the ball field for perhaps the only time in his life. Video footage showed us broken bridges, smashed freeways, and burning buildings, while commentators reminded us that the earthquake put the game and our lives into perspective.

Later responses to the quake focused on baseball as a metaphor for renewal, persistence, and redemption. Once the initial shock of the event wore off, we started looking for explanations and metaphors. Experts speculated on what might have happened had most of the Bay Area not skipped work early to go and watch the game. Ballplayers were reported roaming the streets of Oakland and San Francisco doing good deeds or witnessing the heroism of others. To celebrate the resumption of the World Series, the fans in Candlestick Park sang the Jeanette MacDonald song from the 1936 movie, *San Francisco.* That film celebrated the redemption of gambler, Clark Gable and the resurrection of the city itself from the 1906 earthquake. Gable, distraught that the earthquake may have killed MacDonald, is shown that his fears are unfounded by his friend and priest Spencer Tracy. Gable gets down on his knees to thank God for saving both his love and his soul while MacDonald leads what is left of the city in the rousing chorus.

This pattern of response to extra-baseball events is an interesting one. The earthquake provided perspective, baseball offered salvation, and a faith in the resilience of the game and the human spirit helped to see us through. What's interesting about this pattern is its consistency. In the face of failure or tragedy, we turn again and again to the conventions of perspective, salvation, and resiliency. When something happens, we look outside of conventions as our first response, turn back to the game for our metaphors, and offer up our faith in the game as a sign of our determination and worthiness.

My sister doesn't remember the earthquake exactly that way, but in her own responses to the event, a similar pattern emerges. When the earthquake hit, most fans initially thought that the crowd had somehow made the stadium sway. She recalls a hush followed by calls to "play ball." Police cars drove onto the field and advised everyone to go home while there was still light. Donna and Scott took eight hours to make a drive that normally takes three. It took some time to coax her back into the ballpark—Scott took our brother Steven to the resumed game three—but even in her talk about the crowd, she made much of the calmness, concern, and community that this group of fans exhibited. For the short term anyway, a large group of people looked out for one another, as we might hope that fans at their best would anywhere. Later, when they returned to the ballpark, the celebrations of determination and will overwhelmed any anxiety about the outcome of the games.

Still, their experience with the earthquake at the ballgame became a metaphor for their experiences with the rest of life. Donna and Scott faced the earthquake directly, before meaning could be attached, while the rest of the family watched from the safer and fuzzier distance of phone calls, letters, and best wishes. They also directly faced the earthquake of cancer some six months later, while family viewed it from the outside. Our understanding of the struggle with, say, cancer, or for that matter with a baseball game or an earthquake, is a vicarious one. We aren't in the ballpark, we aren't near the center of the earthquake or, later, the hospital bed. Our only access is through interpretation and metaphor. Cancer is like an earthquake, we might say; life is like a baseball game; God is an old manager.

The year 1989 was a busy one for baseball. In August, Dave Dravecky made his miraculous comeback, Pete Rose was banned from the game for life, and, a week later, the commissioner who banned Rose, Bart Giamatti, was dead. A month after that, the earthquake struck. The year was also a busy one for my family. We began meeting at baseball games that May, collecting at Candlestick Park to visit, watch the game, and enjoy the sun and wind. These games were family reunions, a chance to say to ourselves, "This is who we are." We shared a common purpose with the other fans in coming together to discover what would happen with the game and with the family we were with at that game. We were there to watch the negotiation between desire and chance that makes up any human event. The die-hards of the group might keep score, hanging on every pitch, while the visitors would take advantage of the slow pace to catch up with the out-of-towners. Away from the park we often identified our understanding of family relative to baseball, wearing Giants hats to do the yard work, writing letters with baseball themes.

On August 10, 1989, my brother Steven and I snuck up to Candlestick Park to watch Dravecky's comeback game. We went, as did a lot of fans, to try to be part of the event, to yell loud enough to affect the outcome of the game, to see the experience before it was fetishized and explained to us by Sports Center or the newspapers. The game did not disappoint. If fans can will events to happen on the field, then the 34,810 of us willed Dravecky through eight innings, cheering nearly every pitch, and standing for each return to the mound. The Giants won 4-3 over the Reds, moving a game closer to winning the National League West.

Dravecky described his presence on the mound as a "miracle of God." His courage in putting on the uniform and throwing the first pitch was seen as transcending the game. Here again we bump into familiar patterns of response to the intersection of baseball and life. Dravecky was a hero for his efforts outside of the game to combat and defeat cancer. In addition, each of us who followed his story took away some new perspective on the importance of our own actions and families. On a second viewing of Dravecky's comeback, we returned to our celebrations of baseball. His pitching was a valentine to our sense of baseball's better nature. Ira Berkow of *The New York Times* described Dravecky's efforts this way:

> At its best, sports can fill an important, if not even soulful, role in our lives. It can demonstrate legitimate triumph over adversity; it can spotlight the notion that sweat can produce results; it can underline the belief that dreams can be realized. (D19)

The game offered both Dravecky and us a reason to struggle, a goal to strive toward, and a kind of salvation in seasons full of greedy owners and loutish players. Baseball was good, we told ourselves, and we were good to watch it.

In watching a game we practice a particular form of narcissism, a narcissism of control. The season, like life, is largely a process of accumulation. Any team or player can get hot or slump for a week or two, but only in the tempering of day-to-day action do we see the patterns of hard work and commitment. Our disappointment with today's game and its strained pitching and countless home runs may stem from our desire for metaphors of control and purpose. George Vecsey's comments on Rose's suspension centered on the idea of control: "The evidence suggests that Pete Rose never knows when to quit" (A19). Waiting for the lucky break of a three-run homer, while smart managing, is to admit to some of the pointless chance of human existence. The attraction of Dravecky's comeback was one of control. Here we had a control pitcher taking command not just of the game or of cancer but of life itself. Dravecky upped the ante when he "expressed confidence than everything would be all right. 'The Lord is in control,' he said" (Thomas D21). A lazy game in August became a metaphor not just for the importance of life, the nobility of baseball, and the resiliency of the human spirit, but a metaphor for God's actions on earth.

Six months after the Loma Prieta earthquake, my sister's husband Scott was diagnosed with cancer. After a pause for each of us to reflect on our own places in the world, our responses to this smaller, family earthquake centered around baseball metaphors. The season had just started, and talk of comebacks, playing day to day, perspective, salvation, and resiliency filled up the phone lines and the mailboxes. Here is an excerpt from a letter I wrote the day after I heard:

Dear Scott and Donna:

I talked with Dad and Mom last night, talked about you folks, about family, about hope and baseball. There are some connections there, I think, at least as far as baseball and hope go. The season's starting has given us a place to look, a place to gather, a focus if you will. Parts of us that sit around in the Winter get called into play now.

This was true. Family that had come together largely to enjoy a trip to the ball park marshaled their small efforts and hopes to help Scott and Donna.

Another form of narcissism that we practice at the ballpark is a narcissism of effort. It is easier to see ourselves in struggle than in success. A Mark McGwire or Juan Gonzales home run is only to be marveled at. The strikeout, the injury, and the error provide opportunities for identification. At the game, we celebrate those moments of effort over talent, the impossible catch, the gutsy steal, the pitcher pitching late in the game and without his best stuff. There is some comfort in these metaphors. If baseball was as resilient as W. P. Kinsella, Giamatti, George Will, and others said that it was, how could we expect anything less from Scott and his determined struggle? In addition to metaphors of control and effort, baseball provided metaphors of purpose. When we watch or listen to a game, we practice also a narcissism of purpose.

Our metaphoric efforts on Scott's behalf seemed to work, at least by coincidence. When he received a bone marrow transplant a year to the day after his diagnosis, we saw it as a second birthday, a comeback. On trips to the Stanford Medical Center, Donna and Scott would often take in a game at Candlestick. When the Braves and Twins both went from worst to first to play the exciting World Series of 1991, baseball seemed to provide its own blessing on Scott's hard work.

Through much of that work, Scott and Donna looked to Dave Dravecky and his claims about baseball, cancer, and God. Dravecky is a compelling figure in the game, a hard-working, God-loving, family man, and one of the many born-again players who turned up in the game in the 1980s. He seemed just the tonic as Scott worked through his own, less public struggle with cancer. Dravecky's claims about God's will are comforting, familiar, and simplistic. When the doctor tells him that he'll never pitch again "short of a miracle," Dravecky responds in hackneyed movie phrases:

> If I never play again, I know that God has someplace else he wants me. But I'll tell you something else, Doc. I believe in a God who can do miracles. If you remove half of my deltoid muscle, that doesn't mean I'll never pitch again. If God wants me to pitch, it doesn't matter whether you remove all of the deltoid muscle. If he wants me to pitch, I'll be out there. (25)

When Dravecky breaks his arm during the second game of his comeback, he sees even this as a new mission: "As odd as it sounds, I wasn't discouraged as I lay there, because with the excruciating pain came a strange sense of exhilaration, a sense that God wasn't finished with the story he was trying to tell with my life" (27-28).

It is this persistent effort to find God and purpose in events that both attracts and puts off readers of Dravecky and other born-again ballplayers. We cannot but be impressed with their earnestness, but neither can we shy away from critique and inquiry. Dravecky's reading of God in the details of baseball offers an opportunity to examine the conventions of control, effort, and purpose in our metaphors of the game and in the responses to Scott's illness. A critique of Dravecky's rhetoric is not meant to demean his good works. Still, no matter how earnest his thinking, Dravecky's discourse on God and baseball is ultimately formulaic and tautological, and although it can sustain him and his wife in their many efforts, it cannot sustain the heroic and redemptive image of the game that he puts forth. The deterministic result of these kinds of metaphors is not redemption but disappointment.

Dravecky's God is a big father to us all, someone we might play catch with, someone in control. When we stumble, he rights us. When we lack, he sustains us. When we lose something, he gives it back. For Dravecky, he is the father in the story of the prodigal in both the Bible and the movie *Field of Dreams*. When we come home, he'll be waiting. The attraction is one of control. Throughout *When You Can't Come Back,* Dravecky argues that control does exist and that God is exercising it. Life can be a "series of wild pitches" (47). He and his wife argue about whether it is Christian to seek psychological counseling. He argues that athletes are taught to "suck it up" but that they should realize God's workings in the world. As Dravecky puts it:

> Grace is a gift. The smell of hot roasted peanuts at the ballpark is grace. The passing cloud that shades you in the center field bleachers is grace. The ability Babe Ruth had to hit home runs came to him by grace. (181)

We live in a world of purpose, of meaning, of control, according to Dravecky, and baseball becomes a metaphor for that world. Peanuts, shade, sluggers, all of them are gifts from God, and the game itself is our small glimpse of the level playing fields of heaven.

God and baseball figure prominently in Dravecky's work as they did in Scott's struggle. Dravecky finds purpose and God in everything that happens to him. On page 35 of *When You Can't Come Back,* we read that "God put it in my heart"; on page 44, "My life was in God's hands"; page 158, "God has allowed me to be a vehicle to help young kids like these." We read that his first word was "ball," that he would have played for nothing, and that we would be happier "if only life could be more like baseball" (149). At one point, after Donna and Scott's car was broken into at a game they were attending to celebrate Scott's progress, I wrote saying, "Sometimes, maybe, things happen to folks strong enough to overcome them." It was easier to say that about theft than about cancer. We can sympathize with what we understand. At one point, Dravecky says that he can give up his arm knowing that God gave up his son. Near the end of the book he runs analogy into meaninglessness when he tells us that "Babe Ruth is to baseball what John 3:16 is to the Bible" (189). It might be easier for Dravecky to talk about God and purpose in baseball than in the more complicated areas of our lives.

When we get to those more complicated areas, the metaphors break down. One limitation of Dravecky's compelling story is the place for women in it. They are the spectators and fellow sufferers, but they are not the players or the sons hoping for a redemptive catch with dad. Dravecky's wife Jan is a steadfast helpmate. Her comeback from depression is played out in the more complicated world off the field and outside the hospital. As painful as they are, baseball and cancer provide purpose, something to fight for or against. Depression and feelings of lost control are more difficult to fix and combat. Jan Dravecky does not get to give an impassioned speech on baseball and God's will. Instead she prays to God to soften her husband's heart so that he might consent to her seeing a therapist (91). Brett Butler's wife Eveline, quoted in his born-again book on cancer and baseball, gets stuck having to claim that God helped her find a new apartment (Butler 96). Donna spent much of her energy waiting, challenging doctors, and keeping family together.

Scott's progress was good. Some combination of the bone marrow transplant, chemotherapy, baseball metaphors, his own faith, and Donna's confidence saw him through. From what we could tell, the cancer was gone in 1992 and 1993. In an odd echo to his and his family's seeming good fortune, the Giants of 1993 played inspired baseball, winning 103 games in what was perhaps the last great pennant race, losing the National League West to the Braves on the last day of the season.

Metaphor, though, can only take us so far. With Dravecky, as with most Christian commentators on American culture, we have to confront the deterministic argument that this is a fallen world. That's the first principle that he cannot abandon. When his career is baseball and his life is threatened by cancer, Dravecky turns firstly to perspective, to the idea that we live in a fallen world, secondly to baseball for metaphors of a purposeful and loving God, and finally to the themes of resiliency and understanding. "Wait 'til next year" becomes "in the sweet bye and bye." As he baldly puts it, "The truth is we live in a fallen world, and suffering is an undeniable reality in that world" (75). The second part of that statement is indeed undeniable. The first part is an attempt to come to terms with disappointment. If we live in a meaningless world or a world of chance, then anything can happen to us. Cancer becomes nothing more than bad luck. But if the world is fallen, then suffering comes with explanation and purpose, and if individuals cannot see that explanation and purpose then the fault lies with them. If baseball is a noble game, a "forum for divine intervention" (Berkow D19), then any stain on the game is the fault of the viewer and not the pastime.

To his credit, Dravecky struggles to set out a consistent version of this argument, but that struggle forces him to dismiss other explanations for the world. On page 80 of *When You Can't Come Back,* he suggests that if a positive attitude "stems from faith in ourselves, it's just another form of denial." On page 150, he says, "I am careful not to confuse life with God. Life is unfair, sometimes brutally so; God isn't." He does not confuse the two, but when something positive happens, it is a "miracle of God," and when something negative happens, it is evidence of the fallen world we inhabit. His explanations are as glib and false as a losing manager's claim that the other team "wanted it more."

The same problem occurs in our conflation of baseball and life. Despite his sympathy and intelligence, despite an earnest struggle with the idea of suffering and the reality of depression, Dravecky's argument becomes this: if you cannot connect to God, you either will or you should. It is an argument echoed in discussions of baseball. If you cannot connect to the game, you either will or you should. When we don't, when the metaphors of seasons and comebacks, of control and purpose and effort break down, we leave the game. The problem with analogy is an obvious one. When one side of the analogy gets doubted or damaged, the other side suffers as well. Suggesting that life could be more like baseball or that sports offers a window on the enactment of the divine belittles both life and sports. When life hurts, our affection for the game we paired with life suffers. When games as the enactment of divine intervention stop, our faith in the divine and our metaphors for the divine come into question.

Scott died on August 8, 1995. When his cancer returned in February 1994, about the same time that pitchers and catchers reported to a spring training full of talk of a strike, we stopped talking in metaphors of baseball. His hopes for a long season were disappointed. Family got busy with the rest of life. Baseball had no metaphors to explain his suffering and faith or the strong will of his wife, Donna. We did not talk in terms of rounding third, extra innings, or of how the game might "ease his pain." There was no baseball at his funeral. Donna still follows the Giants, attending a game now and then, but she doesn't talk about baseball as a metaphor for life. Her son, Andy, plays baseball now after a couple of seasons on a tee-ball farm club. He bats right and throws left and is getting over a healthy fear of the ball. The inclination might be to see his playing as a homage to Scott, a celebration of his spirit in the ever-renewing fields of the game, but baseball for Andy is just the sport that follows soccer in the schedule of a busy twelve-year old. Sarah, Scott and Donna's daughter, is more likely following in her father's footsteps. She is tall like he was, and like him she plays the trumpet.

Sometimes, life is nothing like baseball despite our metaphors and the baseballs that roll around on our desks. In fact, when our baseball metaphors no longer fit the more challenging and ineffable events in our lives, our response is often to disdain the game and its commentators for proffering those metaphors in the first place. We and they may have asked for it. Rather than not saying enough nice things about the game, we may have said too many. In our use of metaphors of the game, we are guilty of not knowing when to stop. As Roger Angell put it, "We seem to want to go on sweetening it up, frosting the flakes, because we want it [baseball] to say things about ourselves that probably aren't true" (345). Baseball has become a metaphor for resilience, control, effort, purpose, urban renewal, the desire of a lost child for reconnection with a loving parent, America, our struggles to lead a good life, the fight against cancer, and God's loving actions in a fallen world. That's a lot for even a workhorse National Pastime to carry.

Jesus might save, but baseball doesn't. It is an amazing game, fluid, graceful, complicated, and important, but all of our metaphors of control and purpose did nothing to save Scott in this world. His life and death played out outside of the fields of dreams and hope. Scott's death did not provide perspective. Baseball did not provide salvation. Our family follows the Giants still. Remnants of the group that signed the ball go to see games now in Pac Bell Park. And Donna is nothing if not resilient. Living her own life while raising two children in a world not fallen but where purpose is unclear, control is unobtainable, and effort is often unrewarded, suggests a determination stronger than anything found on the diamond. We cannot protect life by reducing it to a game. We cannot protect the game of baseball by taking it to church with us. Nostalgia for some sort of pastoral or heavenly game of catch with Dad is going to continue to limit our appreciation of the contemporary game. Complaint about the fallen state of that game and our world will limit our actions and exacerbate that disappointment.

BIBLIOGRAPHY

Angell, Roger. *Once More Around the Park: A Baseball Reader.* New York: Ballantine. 1991.

Berkow, Ira. "Dravecky's Taste of Honey." *The New York Times* 17 August 1989: D19.

Butler, Brett. *Field of Hope.* With Jerry B. Jenkins. Nashville: Thomas Nelson, 1997.

Dravecky, David, and Jan Dravecky. *When You Can't Come Back.* Grand Rapids, MI: Zondervan, 1992.

Thomas, Robert McG. Jr. "Dravecky Was Told He Risked Fracture." *The New York Times* 18 August 1989: D21.

Vecsey, George. "Pete Rose Got What He Deserved." *The New York Times* 25 August 1989: A19.

23

Boys of Summer, Suicides of Winter:
An Introduction to Baseball Suicides

Loren Coleman

Baseball researchers have an incredible affection for both statistics and stories. In a similar fashion, within the research field of suicidology, suicidologists know the value of stats and case studies in research surveys and the ultimate objective, suicide prevention. The metaphor and lessons from baseball suicides may prove useful to suicidology, and the awareness gained from suicide prevention among a population of vulnerable athletes could save future lives.

In 1987-1988, I undertook a study of baseball player suicides, which produced some intriguing results leading to a statistical prediction. At the time, I was a project director/principal investigator of a three-year federal project on rural adolescent suicides at the University of Southern Maine. As a personal parallel project, in 1987, I wrote the book *Suicide Clusters,* the first examination of the historical effects of behavior contagion and the contemporary Werther Effect (the copycat phenomenon resulting from graphic media reporting of methods) on suicides. Having had a passionate interest in baseball all my life, I wondered if the databases that existed for ballplayers could give any clues in terms of stories or statistics that might

I would like to acknowledge the support and data given by various members of the Society of American Baseball Research—namely Frank Russo, David Lester, Bill Deane, Dick Topp, Glenn Stout, Frank Phelps, Rick Wolf, Jim Barbour, Bill Weiss, Bob Sproule, Steve Ferenchick, Bill Kirwin, F. X. Flinn, Mark Pattison, Rex Hamann, Bob Bailey, Paul Wendt, Tim Herlich, Jim Sandoval, Neal Traven, Mark Kanter, John Matthew IV, Jason Goodman, Gaylon Moore, and the late Art Lewis.

inform trends and patterns in baseball players' suicides and suicide clustering.

Through the assistance of members of the Society for American Baseball Research (SABR), I was able to track the sixty-eight known suicides among baseball players, as of 1988. Let me share what I found through my survey up through that time.

Looking at the Data

Of the major league players active between 1871 and 1988, 13,160 players and ninety-five nonplaying managers had been identified. Of these, 6,374 were deceased (as of 1988) with 578 dead but with cause of death being listed as unknown. Of the sixty-eight known baseball suicides as of 1988, the percentage of suicides (a little over 1 percent) was lower than the then current percentage of deaths in males due to suicide (1.9 for 1,980 deaths in the United States). Of course, the baseball individuals who killed themselves stretch over many age cohorts. Furthermore, by the time individuals get to the major leagues, they have been largely pescreened for suicidal and psychiatric behavior by the minor leagues' or college days' grueling schedule, bus rides, dingy hotels, and overall high stress level. The numbers of suicides among major league alumni thus was rather surprising.

These 1871-1988 major league suicides, by method, grouped thusly, following normal patterns among the general population: 50 percent used guns; 22 percent poisons/overdoses; 8 percent unknown causes; 5 percent jumping; 3 percent hanging; and 2 percent drowning.

Doing an analysis of these players by age, the range of ages was between twenty-six and eighty-three with 53.2 percent of the players being in their late twenties through their forties.

Analyzing the players by position, I found 45.3 percent of the players committing suicides were pitchers or had done some pitching. Intriguingly, even though the number of pitchers who are left-handed outnumbers the percentage of left-handers found in the general population by a factor times three, not one baseball player that committed suicide who was a pitcher between 1900 and the time of my initial survey in 1988 was left-handed. I will speak about this further later.

Suicides of Winter

The reality and metaphor of the "winter" has a special meaning in the results that rapidly became apparent in my study of ballplayers' suicides.

Players rarely commit suicide during the regular baseball season. That baseball players kill themselves off-season if they are active players—during the actual winter—or in the winter of their years— seems to clearly be a pattern:

Suicides sorted by age break down into youthful suicides happening soon after the end of the playing years, and older males committing suicides in their declining years. Searching through the archives, only one active player, Willard Hershberger, a Cincinnati Reds catcher, completed his suicide during the actual season in which he was an active player. He used a razor in a scenario that in many ways mirrored his father's suicide. On August 3, 1940, in a Boston hotel, Hershberger spread towels on the floor so others would not have to clean up a bloody mess, as he had to do after his father killed himself. Hershberger, thirty years old, held himself responsible for a bad call on a pitch he felt lost an important near-end of the season game.

Psychology professor David Lester and SABR member Richard Topp published a small baseball player suicide paper in 1988, discussing how they found that seven players "killed themselves within one year of the last season they played, three within two years of that date, and six within three years" (p. 934). Besides Hershberger, they mentioned four suicides that were directly baseball-related:

> Marty Bergen had broken [his] hip in a close play at home plate which ended his career, Tony Brottem was depressed after his release from a minor league club, Pea Ridge Day was depressed after an operation failed to restore his pitching arm, and Benny Frey had just retired rather than face being sent to the minor leagues. (Day's mother had also died by suicide.) (p. 934)

These were all dramatic early era suicides. Marty Bergen, twenty-eight, a Red Sox catcher up through the 1899 season, took an axe to his two children and his wife on the morning of January 19, 1900, then cut his own throat with a razor. Tony Brottem, thirty-seven, saw the end of the road and used a gun on August 5, 1929. Pea Ridge Day, thirty-four, on March 21, 1934, slit his throat with a hunting knife. Benny Frey, thirty-one, died on November 1, 1937, when he ran a hose from the exhaust into his car.

There are other recent demonstrations of the phenomenon of young baseball players taking their lives soon after their playing time has ended. Don Wilson, twenty-nine, is an example from 1975. A Houston Astros pitcher, Wilson enjoyed a no-hitter on May 2, 1969, and then he experienced a rapid decline (15-10 in 1972, 11-16 in 1973, and 11-13 in 1974). Tragically, when he decided to kill himself on January 5, 1975, the carbon monoxide from his car seeped into his home and took the life of his five-year-old son. Danny Thomas, twenty-nine, who killed himself by hanging on June 12, 1980, was an outfielder for the Brewers. He had refused to play on Sundays because of his religious beliefs and lasted only one season in the majors. He seemed to have never recovered from his rejection.

Another pattern in these suicides is death in late March and early April—right before or near Opening Day. For the general population, the month of May is the one with the largest number of suicides, a trend not found among baseball players. One of the more memorable "near Opening Day" suicides is that of Boston Red Sox manager-player Chick Stahl's March 28, 1907, suicide and the strange death of his young bride soon afterward. Stahl killed himself by drinking carbolic acid. He was having an affair, and the stress was too much. His wife was found mysteriously dead in a doorway shortly after Stahl's death.

The "end" can be very symbolic, in terms of the temporal clues.

Some old records, such as Ed Delahanty disappearing over Niagara Falls, do not make this suicide study because of the gray area they occupy. Some single car accidents may also be hidden suicides.

Clustering?

As a side note on the impact of behavior contagion, celebrity models, and imitation, some clustering of these individual baseball players' suicides have occurred—1927, 1934, 1945, and 1962. The year 1950 is a special case. During a time of an overall low suicide rate nationally, six individuals either actively or formerly connected to major or minor league baseball committed suicide during the season between March 11 and September 3. I will discuss 1989 at the end of this examination.

Due to the lack of reliable data, I could not examine the suicidal deaths at the college or minor leagues too closely; but some of the well-publicized baseball suicides in recent years have been of college or former college students. One of these individuals is Bruce Clark Gardner, who shot himself near the pitching mound at the University of Southern California's diamond on June 7, 1971. Gardner's mother would not allow her son to sign out of high school into the majors. When Gardner graduated in 1960, the Dodgers signed him, but for a bonus smaller than his earlier offer. He went directly to AAA Montreal (International) where he was 0-1, 3.97 in sixteen games. After the 1961 season, he went into the Army for six months under the reserve training plan and while at Fort Ord he suffered an injury to his pitching arm. Gardner was never the same pitcher again.

An interesting research study would be to examine if the Werther Effect has an impact within the levels of baseball—do the suicide deaths of major leaguers result in an increase in suicides among minor league and college baseball players?

1989: A Suicidal Year?

Certainly, the goal of investigating all of this in 1987-1988 was to attempt to predict and prevent future suicides and to increase awareness within a vulnerable population. The data appeared to exhibit that a bubble was about to burst, as statistics over the long term do not lie.

At the end of the baseball season in 1988, based upon past patterns I predicted that as the decade ended there would be a significant suicide of a baseball player that would get media attention. I wrote a letter dated October 4, 1988, to then commissioner Peter Ueberroth and every team owner noting that a baseball player suicide was statistically likely in 1989 or 1990, and asking that a study be undertaken to see if a retirement counseling program would be justified.

As *Sports Illustrated* detailed in the July 31, 1989, issue (p. 7):

> Sadly, Coleman's prediction came true last week. On July 18, at his home in Anaheim, California, former All-Star relief pitcher Donnie Moore drew a gun, shot and critically wounded his wife, Tonya, with whom police say he had been arguing, and then shot and killed himself. Moore, thirty-five, had been released on June 12 by the Kansas City Royals' minor league affiliate in

Omaha. Friends say that Moore was haunted by memories of the two-strike, two-out, ninth-inning home run he gave up to Dave Henderson of the Boston Red Sox while pitching for the Angels in Game 5 of the 1986 American League Championship Series. If Moore had retired Henderson, California would have won the series four games to one. Instead, Boston won Game 5 in extra innings and then triumphed in Games 6 and 7 to advance to the World Series against the Mets.

My earlier findings showed Moore's death fit the typical pattern for baseball player suicides. Moore, as did half the players who took their lives, used a gun to kill himself. Furthermore, as with all pitchers before him in the twentieth century who had killed themselves, Moore was a right-handed pitcher. (Curiously, teammates had given Moore the nickname "Lefty" because he seemed perhaps a little unpredictable as the mythic left-handed pitcher is said to be. Amazingly, of course, among left-handed pitchers, one wonders if it is their flexible styles that have produced acceptable coping mechanisms for their stresses that have served as a protective factor against suicides.) Also, Moore followed the pattern: more than half the other victims who committed suicide did so between their late twenties and late forties, and 15 percent did so within two years after their major league careers had ended. Moore's final big league season was 1988.

From *The New York Times*' Ira Berkow in 1989, to a special ESPN Classic program in October 2001, the Donnie Moore tragedy is today seen as the baseball suicide to discuss. Unfortunately, in 1989, the Moore suicide was only one of many. On April 6, 1989, two days after the Pittsburgh Pirates' opening day, Carlos Bernier, an outfielder for the Pittsburgh Pirates in 1953, hanged himself in Puerto Rico. Mike Reinbach, thirty-nine, a Baltimore Orioles outfielder for one year in 1974, drove his car off a San Diego cliff, in a suicide on May 20, 1989. On May 2, 1989, Virgil Stallcup, a shortstop with the Cincinnati Reds in the late 1940s and early 1950s, shot himself. On May 31, 1990, Charlie Shoemaker, a Kansas City second baseman in 1961-1962 and 1964, also shot himself. A year later, on May 30, 1991, Jim Magnuson, the first left-handed pitcher (White Sox and Yankees in the 1970s) of the twentieth century to commit suicide, did so through alcohol poisoning.

An Enduring Mystery

Suicide, by its very nature, is a mystery. In 2002, over eighty baseball players exist in the database that denotes all big leaguers who have committed suicides. But these people lost to suicide are more than numbers; they are fellow human beings whose absence affects us all.

Today, Major League Baseball is extremely aware of the need for professional counseling and other supports for those who leave the field, off-season and in the winter of their years. Nevertheless, more study of this sad subject is necessary, and a safety net needs to continue to be constructed. The boys of summer grow into men who face all the stressors and risk factors as the rest of us, and have the added burden of perceived failure that is magnified by the celebrity of being a major league baseball player. While the mere achievement seems remarkable to most of us, the loss of such a status can be crushing to these gentlemen—beyond anything most of us can ever imagine.

BIBLIOGRAPHY

Coleman, Loren. *Suicide Clusters*. Boston: Faber and Faber, 1987.

_____, and David Lester. "Boys of Summer, Suicides of Winter." Presented at the 22nd Annual Conference of the American Association of Suicidology, San Diego, 14 April 1989.

Lester, David, and Richard Topp. "Suicide in the Major Leagues." *Perceptual and Motor Skills,* 67 (1988): 934.

Russo, Frank. The Deadball Era. 2002. <http://thedeadballera.crosswinds.net/suicides.html>.

Sports Illustrated. 31 July 1989: 7.

Wolf, Rick, and David Lester. "A Theoretical Basis for Counseling the Retired Professional Athlete." Unpublished paper. 1989.

Index